Working in the Silence

An analysis of a short period of human rights witness in the Palestinian West Bank

Based on the Palestinian Field Journal

of

Maurice Hopper *Maurice Hopper*

8th November 2003 to 7th February 2004

*To Harold and Sheila
in friendship*

ISBN 978-1-85072-371-4

This book is printed on paper from managed forests.

Printed in Palatino Typeface
from Author's Disc
by Sessions of York
The Ebor Press
York, England

Working in the Silence

Meditating in the full awareness of the situation around me...

of developing the silence,

the still centre,

while focusing on the people, the farmers,

the Gates and the waiting.

Recognising the importance of silence to give space for things to come to me...

Dedication

John Aves

For his friendship of just sixteen weeks, died Bethlehem 25th January 2004.

The Terror

Chorus
Burn down their houses!
Beat in their heads!
Break them in pieces on the wheel!
Bass
Men were ashamed of what was done.
There was bitterness and horror.

A Spiritual of Anger

Bass and Chorus
When Israel was in Egypt's land,
Let my people go,
Oppressed so hard they could not stand,
Let my people go.

Michael Tippett
~ "A Child of Our Time" ~

~

This work arose out of the situation in Europe
before the 1939-1945 World War

Acknowledgements

My thanks go to Gladys Russell, Ann Rochester, Mike Golby, Mary Jannaway, Nicola Hopper, Jack Priestley, Ann Hopper and Wendy Eames, whose reading and commenting on all or parts of the text has been greatly appreciated. I also thank Tracie de Angelis Salim, Martin Anthony Hill and Donald Maclauchlan for help in checking matters of detail and the staff and volunteers at Sheldon for providing the context for my final editing.

I remain responsible for any errors in the text.

I should also like to thank my fellow Ecumenical Accompaniers and other 'internationals' for their support and tolerance during my time in Palestine.

I thank all those who expressed their faith in and support for this work. I would also like to record the support offered to accompaniers working on the Gates by the staff of 'Hamoked', the Center for the Defence of the Individual.

The positions stated and views expressed are personal and independent of either the Ecumenical Accompaniment Programme in Israel/Palestine or the World Council of Churches. Much of this work is based on my perceptions, which may be at odds with what some people consider to be facts.

My very special thanks go to Abdul-Latif and the people of Jayyous, who unwittingly have become the subject of this work.

In many ways, this is their book.

Contents

Part Four - Reflections on Accompaniment

(The weeks in the chapter headings refer to the weeks spent in Jayyous.)

Notes

The Text.

The text of this work is in two parts. There is the text of the Journal written at the time of my visit. This is supplemented by the sections in italics, being reflections on the main journal text, some contemporary to the journal and others which have been added or extended later. In these reflections, I have referred to my preparation reading and follow-up research. The notes and references numbered in each chapter are to be found at the end of the book. Being a modern world issue and one where printed communication is sometimes difficult, there are many references to the websites of relevant organisations. In the way of much ethnographic research, the names of most of the participants in the story have been changed, partly as I was unable to contact many of the people in Jayyous for their permission to identify them.

Place names.

In disputes over territory, the spelling of place names is important. I have chosen to use the English spelling from Israeli maps for places in Israel. I have settled on the Arabic-English spelling for places in the West Bank. For clarity, I have used the internationally recognised Jerusalem, rather than the Hebrew (Yerushaláyim) and Arabic (al-Quds). It is interesting to note, Dr Shukri Arraf of the Institute of Palestinian Studies has researched the cultural shift in which over 7000 Palestinian names have been 'Hebraized' over the last 125 years.[1] The Jewish Agency, established in 1922, had a committee for approving these name changes.

Ilan Pappe says, "Here, dispossession was accompanied by the renaming of the places seized, destroyed and now recreated. This mission was accomplished with the help of archaeologist and biblical experts… whose job it was to Hebraize Palestine's geography."[2]

List of Maps and Diagrams

With the exception of Figures 8, 9 and 10 the author asserts his copyright on these diagrams.

List of Illustrations

With the exception of the cover illustrations, all these pictures are from the author's collection of digital pictures made to record his period of accompaniment. The copyright on these photographs is held by Quaker Peace and Social Witness and the World Council of Churches.

Preface

"And the Walls Come Tumbling Down"

The *Oxford English Dictionary* defines the purpose of a *Preface* as being that of, "stating a book's subject, scope and aims." In the case of Maurice Hopper's story, this might seem, at first sight, a relatively easy task. This book takes the form of a diary, noting events which took place in one specific location, namely the crossing point at the village of Jayyous in Palestine, over a short twelve-week period, from 16th November 2003 to 3rd February 2004, with the intent of demonstrating what life was like then and there.

Yet, at the same time, it is akin to the account given by a medical scientist who can describe a patient's condition from the observation of a few molecules in a test tube. There is an inestimably greater story contained within this microscopic sample and, although the author here begins to draw out something of the greater story in the final pages, the reader remains free to draw on his or her own knowledge of the epic.

The central image around which the events of this particular account take place is a fence. It is a fence made of coils of barbed wire with crossing points which can be closed or opened at will by the strong, responding (or not, as the case may be) to the requests of the weak. In some places, the fence is a wall and the symbolism of that should not be missed. For this is an old story and walls have played a part in it from the known beginning. In the account given by the Biblical Book of Joshua the very first obstacle that the Israelites faced when they crossed the River Jordan to invade this land, already occupied by others, was the wall that surrounded the city of Jericho. That story is well known and there is no need to repeat it but in the ensuing narrative, time and time again walls are built, destroyed and built again. One of those ancient walls, known by many today as the Wailing Wall, has itself become a sacred place to the Jewish people.

The fence with which Maurice Hopper is concerned separates a significant village from the fields, which its farmers tend as their forefathers had done for generations. It also separates children from their school and communities from one another. Much has already been destroyed, especially hundreds of olive trees, some planted as long as five centuries ago, to say nothing of the wells on which all-living things depend.

There is a certain monotony in these accounts. But it is a monotony totally in keeping with the plot and Maurice Hopper's account catches this "waiting for Godot" mood brilliantly as his subjects turn up too late or too early, pass through, wait or go home. Occasionally there are explosions, predominantly from the young who express more quickly than their elders the frustrations which will inevitably lead to further conflict.

This land, at the eastern end of the Mediterranean Sea, has a long, long history of conflict and the desire for domination. It is not only very narrow, sandwiched between desert and sea, but it is the meeting place of three continents – a corridor linking Asia, Africa and Europe. That is why it has for so long been an arena of conflict, while at the same time having the capacity to be the great meeting place of all the major cultures and religions of the world.

Maurice Hopper draws no firm conclusions. "All I can do", he suggests, "is report". But he can ask questions of us and leave his readers to think about their own answers. What might have been the position if Jerusalem had been declared an international city after the Second World War and made the centre for the United Nations rather than New York? How many of the 'pilgrims' who visit this land are aware of the situation? Why do we hear so much from the Israeli side and so little from the Palestinian? To which I would add: Are there justifiable parallels between the situation of the "people of the land" in Israel/Palestine and the original peoples of the land in North American and sub-Saharan Africa?

There are greater tomes on the subject than this but Maurice Hopper has not just been and observed: he has entered into the day-to-day mundane life of Palestine's most deprived inhabitants whose voice is rarely heard in the West. He deserves to be listened to.

Dr Jack Priestley,

Former Principal,
Westhill College of Higher Education, Birmingham.

Introduction

"To say anything worth saying about peace we have to try to say something about life."

Adam Curle[1]

"Why are you watching that sort of film?" It is about two-thirty on the afternoon of the 11th of September 2001. We are visiting my mother in her residential home and find her watching the television, not her normal habit in the afternoon, a rest on the bed being more usual for this 94 year old. I suddenly realise this is not some American 'blockbuster' that she has uncharacteristically strayed upon. It is the news, and there is Channel 4's Jon Snow to prove it. In the twenty minutes we are in the room, the rolling news pictures run repeatedly, so we see the image of the World Trade Center being hit by the aircraft about fifteen times. The total destruction is yet to happen.

We go, as planned, to the garden centre with our friend Laurel who is waiting in the car outside. We drink tea and wonder if the world will ever be the same again. The plant pots and things to put in them can wait. We return home to watch the endless news trying to adjust to what is going on.

The hope for a response from the hand of forgiveness, of some understanding of the hurt that must be behind such actions, slowly dies. When the President finally speaks it is about hunting people down, about "wanted" notices, about "international gun law", of "smoking people out of their holes". Too many westerns: too little understanding of the rest of the world. My country, right or wrong.

How will I react to this terrible act against so many people, who on the face of it seem unrelated to the cause of this aggression? Where are the voices of calm, the voices of the peacemakers, the voices of understanding? A war has been declared, so as with any war, it is increasingly impossible to speak out against it.[2] These people have died in the rich world so their deaths are noticed. I ask myself about the deaths of thousands of people who die every day, unseen

1

deaths for want of clean water or health care, because they do not live in this rich world. People in the rich world have many expectations, but often have little hope, while those in the poor world have few expectations, but they do have hope for the future.

It takes time for the irony to be noticed that this date in 1906 is the day that Gandhi began his nonviolent movement in the Johannesburg, South Africa. Gandhi launched the modern nonviolence movement, so touching the world forever.

Jayyous stands some two hundred metres above sea level overlooking the low-lying coastal land of Israel. Here the sun rises over the hills of Samaria with their olive-covered slopes stretching east to the Jordan Valley and it sets beyond the Plain of Sharon, its light dancing on the sparkling Mediterranean Sea. From Jayyous its three thousand inhabitants may go, with difficulty, through checkpoints to the city of Nablus set in the hills twenty-five kilometres to the east, but they cannot go to the Mediterranean Sea as the Israeli Separation Barrier, or Security Fence, now cuts it off.[3]

The Israeli Separation Barrier has cut a swathe the size of a motorway through the village lands, uprooting 2,500 olive trees in Jayyous alone. It has separated the Jayyous farmers from their land, land handed down over many generations and for which they hold deeds from the Ottoman Empire, the British Mandate and the period of Jordanian rule. This is the best land in the village. It is farmed intensively with trickle irrigation, poly-tunnels and much human investment of time and energy, producing a wide range of fruit and vegetables for both the village and the wider market.

The farmers' access to this land is restricted and controlled. Only a limited number of farmers have a 'tasreeh' (permit) to go to their land, and for those who have them the Gate in the fence is only open for short periods. This interferes with their work patterns and delays the movement of produce. On occasion, the Gate has remained unopened by the Israeli Defence Force (IDF) for days or weeks at a time, causing

2

young plants to wither and the harvest to fall to the ground, un-gathered. The Separation Barrier has also cut off six of the seven wells to be found in Jayyous. Water is important to all life but it is especially important in this arid environment, with its limited winter rains.

The four year-old son of one of the villagers often asked, "Why can we not go to the sea?" He can see the Mediterranean from his house in Jayyous. His father who is a highly educated and peace-loving man does not have a permit to go to Israel. He says, "I am sad to answer him, but after the Separation Barrier I think he knows why we cannot go, because he does not ask anymore." The father is one of the forty percent of Jayyous people who have a 'tasreeh' to go to his family land, so his son can go to help pick the clementinas (sic), guavas and olives. How do you tell a four year old why he cannot go to the sea? How would we react if we were in this boy's place? Will he get a permit to go to his family land when he is old enough to have his own 'howada' (identity card)? Will his family land still be there or will it be subsumed into Israel?

The Separation Barrier has been constructed by the Israelis on the grounds that it will bring peace to Israel by protecting them from suicide bombers. Construction was started by the Israeli army, and their private contractors, in 2002. It continues to this day (September 2007), with Israeli spokespersons saying the route is determined by the requirements of security. While it is not directly related to 11th September 2001, the construction of the Separation Barrier has taken place under the cloak of the "War on Terrorism". It stands in contravention of any normal reading of international law.

It has been one of the greatest privileges of my life to be able to live in the village of Jayyous for a short while and to meet its people. It allowed me to penetrate the public world of international politics and the often-poor media coverage of the situation, to gain insights into what it is like to live under the thirty-seventh year of the ever tightening, post-1967, Israeli occupation of the Palestinian West Bank. This opportunity came to me when I was allowed to join the World Council of Churches (WCC) Ecumenical Accompaniment Programme in Palestine/Israel (EAPPI). I was an accompanier based in Jayyous for twelve weeks between November 2003 and February 2004.[4] The term "Ecumenical Accompanier" is derived from the programme name, and perhaps shows a rather detached perception of how this title would work in the field, especially when printed on the back of one's jacket. "International Friend" might have been easier to translate into both Arabic and Hebrew. As 'ecumenical' has even less currency in Palestinian and Israeli society than its limited circulation in the Christian world, in the field it often becomes "Economical Accompanier".

Part of accompaniment, at least in my experience of it, is that there are long periods of seemingly "doing nothing", periods of watching, waiting and listening. This leaves a great deal of time for reflection. Much of this work is based on my daily journal kept during my time in Palestine. Some of the reflections were recorded at the time while others have developed over the intervening three years. The work is therefore a snap shot of a short period. The situation and conditions have changed since my visit. Some things have improved and some things are worse. I have only written about what I have seen, with just a few verifiable exceptions to bring some information up to date.[5]

The process of reflection as part of a research methodology has its origins for me in my professional development and education work, critical reflection having had a considerable impact on my own career. This enhanced, formalised and made more positive what had always been my rather negative and critically analytical approach to life and situations.

How did I come to the experience of accompaniment?

"I know now... that one is never ready for the next step in life's journey. We learn what we need to know on the road itself." Elise Boulding.[6]

This is an interesting notion for a former teacher. If taken literally it may seem to question the value of formal education, or is it suggesting that learning can only come from experience, wherever that may be found? The two-week "training programme" that UK Ecumenical Accompaniers (EAs) attend before going to Israel/Palestine perhaps illustrates this dilemma. This training attempted to prepare us for this next step in our lives, introducing us to a range of different experiences. In reality, these were impossible to predict, as we did not even know where we were to be working. With EAs based in West Jerusalem (in Israel), Bethlehem (in Palestinian Refugee Camps), Hebron (close to urban Israeli settlers), Yanoun (close to rural Israeli settlers) and Jayyous (on the Separation Barrier) the training requirements are all very different. It is therefore impossible for this formal training to cover all aspects of accompaniment in a short induction programme.

Once in the field EAs become reliant on the experience and understanding they carry with them. Here I begin to agree with the notion above. Life has brought us to where we are and made us who we are through an accumulation of experience, situations worked through, changes accommodated and skills acquired. Perhaps more importantly life has brought us to hold values that support and guide us through life's continuing journey. Once in the 'field', we are in charge of our own modus operandi or indeed a modus vivendi.

What was it in my life that prepared me to work in this situation? A number of experiences contributed; perhaps most obvious of these was my professional life in classrooms. Indeed much of my accompaniment activity may be seen as being rather like a teacher's break duty, being in the playground to stop trouble by just being there. The time spent at the Gates in the Separation Barrier during my 12 weeks in Jayyous added up to about the equivalent of a quarter of the time I had spent on break duties in 27 years of teaching. Much of my time at the Gates was spent watching, slightly from a distance, allowing the farmers their space but being obvious enough to let them know they were being accompanied and to let the patrols of the Israeli Defence Force (IDF) know they were being watched. One confirmation of the effectiveness of this was a general statement about 'international accompaniment' from one of the Jayyous farmers. "The soldiers have done less bad things since you have come to Jayyous."[7]

Another life experience that came into play was my association with the farming community. This came from regular childhood holidays on my Uncle's farm in deepest North Devon in the 1950-60s. These formative visits from Surrey to the West Country gently introduced me to a culture not found in the leafy avenues of the outer London suburbs. It was characterised by isolation, contact with the land, weather and the seasons, long working days, and the sharing of resources. This was especially the case with sharing of water from the streams that marked the boundary between two farms. Furthermore, the role of religion in the community was still strong in 1950's rural England. All these chimed with this new experience in Palestine of living in a strongly agricultural community with the ever present requirement to follow the seasons, to care for the environment, set in a strongly religious culture and an evolving pattern that accommodates changes slowly.

This experience was especially sharp when, as a boy, my Uncle Miles asked me to paint a map of the Holy Land on his office wall, the North Devon weather being too wet to go out with him to feed the animals. It was copied in pencil from the large family Bible; a line for the coast, and a line for the River Jordan and some places in between. The background was the wall colour of duck egg blue, turning to a pale brown caused by wood smoke from the open fire towards the high ceiling.

Dark blue watercolour for both lines set the framework, and green and red dots with the names carefully copied in black labelled the towns and cities. That was all; there were no modern borders, no "Green Lines", no arguments about water resources. This was the Bible map of the Holy land for a Methodist lay-preacher, whom I would now consider rather fundamentalist, a man whose simple faith and peaceful life had been challenged by the horror of the 1930/40s in Europe and the resultant formation of Israel, but who could only see this as the Bible land. Strange also that one of my first 'A' level geography lessons taught in 1973 was about the growing water crisis in the Jordan Valley, using a similar map. How different these maps were to the present maps of the Holy Land issued by such groups as B'Tselem, an Israeli human rights group, showing the break-up, or 'cantonisation',[8] of Palestine, the spread of Israeli settlements across this land and the reduction in the size of the Dead Sea due to water extraction from the River Jordan. How strange that my original map on the wall should be coloured light blue, between two dark blue lines (almost like the white and blue of the Israeli flag), and that I selected red, green and black as the other colours for the map (the colours of the Palestinian flag).

Part of the North Devon experience involved travelling on the "Atlantic Coast Express", which allowed the close observation of railway operation from London's largest terminus to the smallest of country stations. This interest came from my father, a lifelong railwayman, who was totally engaged with his work and very keen to pass on his knowledge. This, together with my education as a geographer and its demand to observe both the landscape and human activity within the landscape, relates to my wish to record situations. This previous experience was formative in devising a system of records of the Gate openings on the Separation Barrier. However, regular observation become a serious endeavour, going beyond recording for its own sake to eventually providing evidence about the Gate opening times to the International Court of Justice,[9] as part of the Palestinian case questioning the legality of the Separation Barrier. The Court found in favour of the Palestinians.

The ideals of internationalism had always been there in the background during my youth. On a family holiday in The Netherlands in 1961, we went to see the Peace Palace, home of the International Court of Justice in The Hague, not one of the city's usual tourist attractions. How was I to know that 43 years later I, with the help of my colleagues in Palestine, would be providing some evidence for this International Court of Justice? Part of the view of my world came from my father who was perhaps rather more prepared to listen to and to accept the "foreigner's" point of view than the average Englishman. He also worked for the United Nations' International Labour Office for two short periods in the early nineteen sixties, experiences which made a great impression upon me. He went to work with railwaymen in Egypt and Thailand on staff training programmes - places which seemed a very long way away in those days.

It took years for the Apartheid[10] regime in South Africa to collapse, but for me the awareness of this injustice started in the late 1950s when the groceries delivered to our non-car-owning household were returned to the shop. The box was seen to contain a tin of South African fruit, despite a request not to send items of that origin. Future orders came from the 'International Stores' under the heading "No South African goods". This event clearly made a deep impression on me. There were principles that were more important than food!

Later in life, I visited Berlin shortly after the collapse of the DDR (East Germany) in late 1989. I was able to stand at The Wall by the Brandenburg Gate and pass through the checkpoints at the Friedrich Strasse Station and Checkpoint Charlie in the early weeks of 1990 - places that had fascinated me as a teenager. I used to wonder if the East could keep out capitalism. Why was communism so bad it had to be kept out of the West? It had overthrown the terrible Tsarist Russian regime that kept millions in poverty. Russia had a major, if ruthless, hand in bringing down the Third Reich, suffering countless human losses in the process of the fight for freedom. So, "why the need to control freedom?", "what were the threats?" were among my many, often naive and unresolved questions at that time.

As a geographer, I was always interested in how the divided city of Berlin functioned as two cities on the 'skeleton' of one city. Some western lines of the U Bahn (the underground railway) ran through closed and closely guarded underground stations in the East. There were tram routes that ended at The Wall, the concrete blocks laid across the tracks being indicative of the suddenness of the divide. There were houses rendered useless by bricking up the windows facing the border. There were divided families and a divided culture, a divide that became increasingly breached by modern communications, especially television, before the eventual demonstrations starting in Leipzig and Dresden in the early autumn of 1989. These demonstrations led to the breaking down of The Wall in Berlin and the 'Iron Curtain' fence that had been constructed across half of Europe. Over the following years, it has been fascinating to see the rebuilding of the East, especially the reconstruction of Dresden, bombed almost five years to the day before my birth. When 'The Wall' came down there was talk of Peace Dividends now that the Cold War was over. There was a feeling that this was "the wall to end all walls", rather as in 1919 it was felt that the 1914-18 War was "the war to end all wars". How wrong people were in 1919, and how wrong we were again in 1990.

In simple terms, the nature of the settlement of the 1914-18 War set the grounds for the 1939-45 War.[11] This has always been a feature on my "landscape". My parents, born before the first war, were married the day before the second war started. Like many of their generation, although not in the usual way, it was clearly a defining period in their lives. While my father did not see active service, being in a protected occupation, he was seconded from the Southern Railway to work at the War Office and eventually went to Ceylon (Sri Lanka) in military uniform where he helped to run the railways. My closest contact with this war was to come later when visiting the English Channel Islands. My former wife came from Jersey, her mother and grandmother both having been there during the German occupation of those Islands from 1940-45.

9

According to Hitler, the Islands were going to be part of Germany for all time and they consumed huge amounts of steel, concrete and labour building defences to make it so. The war ended with the Islands being by-passed during the invasion of Europe in 1944, with Churchill saying of the German garrisons, "Let 'em rot". His attitude meant the Islanders were not freed until the very end of the war in Europe, being reliant for another year on Red Cross ships to bring basic supplies of food and medicine. The Islands are, today, littered with the remains of the occupation that prove, like the fragments of the Berlin Wall, to be an attraction for tourists.

One of the "remains" of the 1939-45 War was my English teacher when I was aged 15 and 16 years. Helmut Mirauer was a German who left Germany in the late nineteen thirties to come to England with his family. They were interned during the 1939-45 war, their anti-Hilter stance not counteracting their German origins. He became a modern language teacher but also taught some English. I will always be indebted to him for his tutelage in my native tongue, which, due to my cyclical sense of failure, had not blossomed under other teachers. After I had qualified as a teacher, he wrote the following, "...you are young enough still to cherish ideals which I hope you will continue to fight for even if you know that we can not ever attain them". This testimonial, said as much about him as it did about me. It projected onto me the ideas that had already been so important in his classroom, the ideas of justice, freedom of thought and of questioning the position held by authority. I wonder if I ever made this sort of impact on my own students. As Helmut said, "It is a real joy, rarely achieved, for teachers to hear of the progress of former students."

Underlying all this previous experience was the early foundation formed by attending Quaker Meeting and Sunday school classes up to about the age of 14. This, supplemented by the influence of my mother's stories about her work supporting conscientious objectors at their tribunals during the 1939-45 war (while my father worked at the War Office), had brought me to a pacifist stance, albeit untested. My generation did not have to say "No!" to National Service. As a pacifist, I only had to try and answer questions like, "What would you do if a (German) soldier was going to kill your daughter?" I could find no answer to this question, as I thought we should be in the same European Community as the Germans and not at that time having a daughter. (Why is this question always about daughters? Are sons any less important?) To say you would do the right thing at the time is rather less than convincing, especially when there are so many layers in any answer to this question, ranging from the practical, like possession of weapons and the ability to use a common language, to the deeply moral questions about killing or allowing someone else to be killed.

So it seems that experience, wherever it comes from, be it educational or from life, supports new activities, the new leadings in life. While not being fully ready for accompaniment, one soon learns or creates a role or life in accompaniment. The way one approaches the task reflects all those things that bring one to this new situation. Perhaps a facet of accompaniment not talked about a great deal is the impact on the accompanier, growing out of the deeply affecting experience of living with oppressed people, and to some extent becoming one of them, if only by identification.

For me one of the most important aspects of this was the strength of this experience, which could not be diminished. This had not been the case in my career in education where, during the period from the early 1970s to the year 2000, successive governments had removed much of the professional autonomy of teachers. Becoming involved in curriculum development made me vulnerable to the realisation that my experience could be disregarded. The arrival of the National Curriculum and a 'pupils to be taught' model of education meant much of my professional satisfaction quickly disappeared. This transition also saw the end of the cherished goal of a 'student-centred' approach to learning. This eventually made me decide there was no longer a place for me in the classroom. The more flexible lifestyle of a self-employed artisan, chair-maker and woodworker allowed me to take up a role as an accompanier.

The accompanier experience also took me from the position of the armchair pacifist wishing to see a better world to one where at least I had done something, however small, to (as my mother would say) "try and make a difference". I suspect the resultant impact may have been more on me than on the Middle East. For the first time life both offered and required a validation of my pacifism. I know a number of people who do not start something because they are not ready. It was a tendency in my father and I often feel it in myself, especially at times of uncertainty. Readiness seems to be a luxury when one's "next step" is to become involved in being an accompanier. However, the experience of being an accompanier makes one more ready, ready for life, all of life.

Why "Working in the Silence"?

Much is silent about my experience of accompaniment; the silence of waiting; the silence of expression, of body language; the silence of no-common language (at least for deep things). There is the silence of keeping one's own counsel, appreciation and interpretation: the silence of reflection. There is the silence of truth, the silence of power, and for a Quaker there is also speaking from the silence. There is also the need to act in accordance with one's beliefs, however insignificant and unnoticed, which may be the silence of witness.

What is the position of silence in the modern world, or indeed in the situation of accompaniment? Bernhard Dauenhauer's work suggests silence is a conscious, communicative activity that 'makes sense'. It is, in other words, appropriate action within the world we inhabit, and it is part of how we make the world intelligible. If we understand why it makes sense to keep silence, we will understand something more, not just about silence, but about persons and the world they inhabit. (12)

The title of this work came from a comment made by an aged Greek Orthodox Monk at the end of a meeting in Jerusalem outlining the work of Ecumenical Accompaniers. He came to me with an outstretched hand and, not knowing I was a Quaker, said "You are doing something in the silence, without coercion, working with the spiritual, the practical and the suffering of humanity." What else is there to do?

Part One
Finding an Approach to Accompaniment

Chapter 1

In Jerusalem.

Introductory Week

If you are ready to leave father and mother, and
brother and child and friends, and never see them
again – If you have paid your debts, and made
your will and settled all your affairs, and are a free
man – then you are ready for a walk.

Henry David Thoreau (Walking, 1861)

Saturday 8th November, 2003

*After returning late on Friday from the second training week
in Birmingham, Saturday passes in great haste and before I
know it, I am on the late afternoon train to London. The train
is almost empty and the driver seems set on establishing some
sort of record. We are over fifteen minutes early into Reading
and several minutes early at Paddington. The train responds
to my feelings that it is time to get on with the task, after
weeks of waiting, whether I am ready or not.*

Sunday 9th November

An early start sees me leaving central London for the airport at
04.30. The taxi driver, a former PhD student of International
Affairs, expresses strong opinions on the Middle East. After
arrival at Tel Aviv, and meeting some of the other people in
our team, we travel by shared minibus to Jerusalem. As we
drive in the gathering gloom, the smells of this land drift in the
open windows bringing back memories of past visits to the
Mediterranean. Smells are one of the most noticeable
sensations of travelling in a new country; these are mostly new

Middle Eastern smells.

It is dark by the time we arrive in Jerusalem at the Jaffa Gate. There is a very friendly, and very Arab, welcome at the New Imperial Hotel, set in a side alley just inside the Old City. The room is basic and clean. We walk to the Jerusalem Hotel, through the Christian Quarter and via the New Gate. We dine with all the other members of the team that have arrived yesterday and today; the company includes Norwegians, Swedes, Danes, Britons, Americans, a Canadian, a New Zealander and a Swiss.

When I arrived at the passport control desk at Ben-Gurion Airport, the women passport officer could not hear me, as my ears had not "popped" and I could not adjust my volume and did not wish to shout. I pointed to my ears and said sorry, at which she smiled. "I would like to be here for Christmas, so may I have a three month visa?" "You have a three month visa!" "Where are you staying?" Before I could stop her, she had stamped a visa in my passport as well as on the separate visa paper. This action renders my passport useless in many Arab countries, as they do not permit entry to people who have been to Israel. It seemed strange to be into Israel so quickly after hearing stories about how difficult it was going to be. Do we just have to smile? However, one of our party took an hour and a half to get through.

Today has been the "International Day Against the Wall", with 72 demonstrations in 27 countries. There are no demonstrations for me today. How lucky and privileged I am to be able to do something different. It is good to feel we have started, despite being very tired after the journey and a day of new experiences.

Monday 10th November

Some "ding-dong" bells accompany the first light. Lying on my back, I realise the room has only one square corner, but then this is old Jerusalem. There is a simple breakfast with local tea, which is rather weak and just fine for one who does not like his tea stewed. The hotel is decorated with embroidered galliabias.[1] I think I might get one later to take home.

We walk via the Suq Khan Ez-zeit to the Damascus Gate and on to the Herod Gate. Here we take a 'sharut' (Hebrew for shared taxi) to the Augusta Victoria Hospital, where the EAPPI office is situated. The day is spent in meetings despite five of the UK team not yet having arrived. The afternoon includes a visit to the Watch Tower of the Lutheran Church of the Ascension, next to the hospital. This allows the comparison of the land to the east and west. The east is light brown, dry, and cut through by new 'bypass roads' to the exclusive and intrusive Israeli West Bank settlements, with the desert hills of Judah beyond. The west is green, with the modern city of West Jerusalem on the horizon. To the south is the Mount of Olives, including the Church of the Ascension. To the north are French Hill and the University. "There has been a policy, pursed by all Israeli governments since 1967, of surrounding greater Jerusalem with two rings of settlements, access roads and military positions. This is designed to cut off Arab East Jerusalem from its West Bank hinterland".[2]

In the church it is interesting to note the black and white tiles in the floor of the nave formed a pattern made up of negative and positive Swastikas. This ancient design, with its "good to be" meaning, has its origins in Sanskrit and can be found in many buildings in both the east and the west. In the west it was also adopted in the early twentieth century by the Boy Scout Movement and was a popular motive in architecture and print design. Symbols are so unpredictable in how they are used and their meanings changed.

Several of us walk back to the old city across the Valley of Kidron, along the North Wall to the Damascus Gate and on through the Suq, to the Jaffa Gate via the Church of the Redemption. An international group of us eat together in the Armenian Quarter, and return to the hotel through wet streets with groups of orthodox Jews and Palestinians. The former are hastily making their way home from the Western Wall (the Wailing Wall) while the latter are out for their post-fasting meal, it being Ramadan. On completing the text of an e-mail to Ann in the Imperial Hotel Internet Café, the power goes down for ten minutes. My e-mail is lost so I write a shorter one instead. Such is life: it rains and the power goes down. It is all part of learning to live in a new environment with different expectations.

The Augusta Victoria Hospital (AVH) is one of four medical and social support programmes run by the Lutheran World Federation in Jerusalem and the West Bank. The hospital is located on the Mount of Olives. In 1898 The German Emperor Wilhelm the second and his wife Empress Augusta Victoria visited Palestine and agreed to the request of the German congregation to build a hospice on the Mount of Olives to treat pilgrims visiting Jerusalem and those suffering from malaria. It fulfilled its intended purpose for only four years; with the outbreak of 1914-18 War, the building was taken-over as the headquarters for the Turkish army. In 1917 the British Army occupied AVH under General Allenby and again during the 1939-45 War, when it was used as a 1400 bed hospital and rehabilitation centre. With the creation of the State of Israel in 1948, the International Committee of the Red Cross established the Augusta Victoria as a hospital for displaced Palestinians. In 1950, the United Nations Relief and Works Administration (UNRWA) took over responsibility for the Palestinian Refugees.[3] To this day, UNRWA makes 75% of the hospital's referrals. It is a major cancer treatment centre, which requires repeated visits by patients. However, West Bank Palestinians have increasing difficulty gaining access to these facilities due to Israeli checkpoints and pass restrictions. So here we have a potted history of the 20th Century Holy Land in one building.

Tuesday 11th November

Eight of us walk through the Suq to the Damascus Gate, which seems very busy this morning. The Israeli Police are questioning some young Palestinian men just inside the Damascus Gate. We quickly negotiate a "service" (Arab word for shared taxi, pronounced ser-vees) to the AVH. After further meetings, we begin to work out the organisation of the Jayyous team. This team of four men from the U.K. had been selected from the 21 members of the international group of EAs by the manager in Jerusalem, a selection based on 'paper' information. We were told our locations and therefore our team partners just three days before leaving for the Middle East.

Returning to the hotel the area around the Damascus Gate is crowded with traders and people out after fasting all day. There are women Israeli Police hanging around inside the Gate. It seems to be a favourite place. Most of the shops are still open. They range from smart clothes and shoe shops, to women sitting at the side of the street with bundles of herbs or trays of vegetables.

Picture 1 A side street in the Old City, Jerusalem.

Wednesday 12th November

After a morning of meetings, the afternoon sees Yossi (Joseph), an environmental studies teacher from the Israeli Committee Against House Demolition (ICHAD), taking us on a "field trip" starting in the housing area of Giv'at Shapira.

Field Notes:

Palestinian housing is characterised by different styles, no landscaping, low rise, lower taxes, lower income, minimal services, rough, poor, illegal, water tanks on roofs, disorganised, steep slopes, little vegetation.

Israeli housing is characterised by design, organised, roads/pavements, bus stops, a unified modern style, solar panels, roads – the No. 60 By-pass road, high rise, legal, good infrastructure, high tax, high income, subsidy through development grants and infrastructure grants, more gently sloping green open space. Yossi points out that to keep the spaces green the 400,000 Israelis living outside Israel's formal borders, 200,000 around Jerusalem and 200,000 in the West Bank use 9 times more water than nearly 3 million Palestinians.[4]

We move onto the Qalandia Checkpoint to the north, between Jerusalem and Ramallah. This is a dusty, noisy place full of congested traffic accompanied by much tooting of horns. There are minibuses and taxis arriving, dropping people in the road. At the checkpoint for Ramallah, people stand in lines under tin roofs. The whole scene is under the eye of the soldiers both on the ground around the barriers and on the rocky mound above. There are many minibuses and taxis waiting on both sides of the checkpoint. Others pass by on the unchecked road that turns towards the West Bank. There are people selling food and drink to this 'captive market'. In the background is the southern edge of Ramallah behind the separation fence, running away to the northwest. Beyond the fence are settlements for Israelis. These settlements are on Palestinian land, but they have West Jerusalem bus services, which suggests they are considered part of Israeli West Jerusalem. These Israeli settlements are high-rise for pre-Oslo building and low-rise for post-Oslo developments.[5]

Picture 2. The Qalandia checkpoint from the Jerusalem side. The checking areas are under the tin roof in the foreground while the long narrow roof is for the queue of Palestinians waiting to show their passes. The vehicles in the front of the picture are on the road to the West Bank. Note the soldier sitting below the camouflaged watch tower and the Israeli settlement buildings on the horizon in the distance.

This place was to become a familiar stop on my journeys to and from Jayyous, part of the "normality" of life under occupation. The help offered by those standing around, with directions for buses and taxis, always surprised me; the welcome to a stranger in the land [6]

We also visit the checkpoint at Abu Dis in the southeast of Jerusalem. Here a rough tarmac road ends abruptly in a row of low concrete wall slabs, covered with graffiti: "Where is the peace in the wall?"   "Peace comes from agreement not separation." "Walls don't solve problems." "God leads us to peace."

There is a gap in the corner through which people clamber. Two Palestinians approach, an elderly woman and possibly her grandson, and the woman starts to climb over the rough concrete blocks. The grandson goes to help. An Israeli soldier looks down. He moves to help and the woman recoils. Eventually the soldier jumps down and helps regardless. We are asked to leave by some Palestinians as our presence is slowing down the rate people are being allowed through this checkpoint. As we turn to go we see a row of young Palestinian men lined up against the wall while their papers are checked. It looks as if the men have been there a long time. They look tired, angry, depressed and do not respond to my attempts to make eye contact. Humiliation for both young and old seems to be the order of the day.

> *This place was visited just once. It was small and intimate. It confronted me with the day-to-day situation. It also confronted me with the evidence that the presence of accompaniers can be negative as well as positive. This five-minute visit made more impact on me than all of the preparation weeks. Here I was at a "wall" again. How does one turn this experience into an appropriate response and subsequent behaviour?*

Thursday 13th November

> *The visit to Abu Dis the previous day caused a lot of discussion about photographing people in humiliating situations. The picture in question depicts the men lined up at the checkpoint. No permission, however informal, had been requested of, or given by, the subjects to have their picture taken. Some of the group, including myself, stand on the side of caution while another said this was the only picture worth taking all afternoon. The photographer seemed hurt by the criticism. Perhaps these sorts of ethical questions should have been discussed during the induction programme. Does this begin to highlight the difference between an observational and*

a journalistic approach to our work of accompaniment?

The morning sees a very interesting visit to the Israeli human rights group, B'Tselem, which means "in the image of human dignity". B'Tselem was established in 1989 to collect and provide information about the occupation. The authorities respect B'Tselem, and their reports on issues, topics or incidents, all carry a comment by the Israeli Government. All their field workers are Palestinian. The main issues monitored are movement, security, documentation, water, employment (36% of Palestinians have no work, 70% in Gaza live on less than 2$ a day), human rights, the Separation Barrier, new Israeli settlements and blocking of growth in Palestinian housing development. It is good to sit and listen after a very bad night. Returning to Jerusalem the minibus drops us at the American Colony Hotel, but I am not sure why. However, it provides a stark contrast with discussion ranging from two dollars a day to piped music. When I go to the gents (the bathroom) in the hotel the "military band" is playing the Blue Danube Waltz!

We walk on to our next visit at Sabeel, the Christian Theological Center. Here we attend a Swedish service. I am glad Elisabet points out that some of the group would not take communion; there seem to be too many assumptions made and lack of flexibility about personal preferences. Questions posed and comments made at Sabeel include, "What is the church saying about the situation from a theological point of view? Should the church do more about justice and mercy? Is there a need for a new 'Liberation Theology'? Thank you for your coming. Thank you for listening and being with us. This is our home and we can live together."

One of the most important aspects of this visit was the purchase of a booklet entitled "Suicide Bombers - What is theologically and morally wrong with suicide bombings? - A Palestinian Christian Perspective".[7] After thirty pages of evidence and argument, this little book draws the following conclusions. "We cannot condone suicide bombings in anyway or, for that matter, any use of violence and terror whether perpetrated by the state or militant groups... We

*must not allow ourselves to succumb to hate or walk the road
of vengeance and malice... This cycle of terror perpetuated
today is simply shutting the door on the future for both
people. It is killing not only the present but also the future.
We must guard against murdering the future. That will only
shut the door to healing and reconciliation." "Ending the
occupation will certainly end the suicide bombings." I find
this expresses exactly my convictions on this important
matter.*

After this session Maria, Julia and I visit the Garden Tomb on
our way back to the Old City. The garden has its origins with
General Gordon who, it is said, found the tomb. The gardens
are very green, indeed a little piece of England in Jerusalem,
which has a spiritually restorative effect, but leaves me feeling
physically very tired.

*I wonder how do the olive wood cribs and olive wood covered
testaments, in the tourist shop relate to the removal of olive
trees along the Separation Barrier? Knowing about the
sourcing of materials takes on a new dimension in this land;
how morally sustainable is this wood?*

*This was not a good day, so it was good to have the support of
being in a group. However, I am rather concerned about the
relationships in the Jayyous team. Quote of the day
"Militarism runs through Israeli society. Israel does not have
an army; the army has Israel".*

Friday 14th November

I walk to Augusta Victoria Hospital. Having seen a flying
checkpoint, operating outside the hotel on Thursday morning,
I now run into several more. The Damascus Gate is all fenced
off with only small entry/exit points. At the crossroads on the
northeast corner of the City Walls, close to the entrance to
Qubbat As-Sakhrah, the Dome of the Rock Mosque, a
checkpoint is slowing the traffic and one road is closed. A
helicopter flies overhead. At the bottom of the Kidron Valley
another checkpoint is passed and I walk on up the hill to the

Augusta Victoria Hospital, where the World Lutheran Federation's minibus is being checked. We have further nonviolence training, which is almost the same as the sessions we had in Birmingham. At lunchtime there is a flying checkpoint outside the Augusta Victoria Hospital with a truck pulled over. These 'flying' or temporary checkpoints are one or two jeeps used to block the road, each with their complement of four Israeli police or soldiers, stopping vehicles and pedestrians to check the Palestinians' passes and permissions. At the end of the day I return to town by 'service' to the Herod Gate. It is very crowded around the Damascus Gate so I decide to walk to the New Gate and avoid the Suq. It is Friday. Just as the Jewish community is going home for the Sabbath, the Arab community is celebrating the feast at the end of its holy day. We go out for a meal to celebrate Maria's birthday. I send a short report on nonviolence training to the London office as requested. We have a day off tomorrow.

> Human Rights Legal note: - During the nonviolence training it came to light that, as visitors to Israel, Ecumenical Accompaniers come under Israeli Civil Law, even when we are in the West Bank. The Palestinians come under military law, which allows six months administrative detention that can be repeated without a break. This sounds like possible life imprisonment without trail. It is comforting at a personal level to know we are under civil law, but disturbing to have the Palestinians' position confirmed.

Saturday 15th November

I walk through the Suq to the Herod Gate with Julia to meet Maria and John. We call at the Educational Book Shop on Salah Eddin Street and go on to St George's Anglican Cathedral. We return via the New Gate to the Church of the Holy Sepulchre with the Omar Mosque standing next door. We go on to the Church of the Redeemer (Lutheran). There is a story that the various Christian denominations using the Church of the Holy Sepulchre cannot agree on who should hold the key, so it is held by a Muslim caretaker.[8] There seems to be a parable in there somewhere. Julia and I finish the day by trying to find a way onto the rampart walk around the old city. Clearly, this is now a security risk as it is variously locked, has turnstiles only for coming down from the wall or guarded by Israeli soldiers. I have a light meal in the evening and take a walk around the Armenian Quarter with Charles.

There is the Muslim call to midday prayer as we walk along the Nablus Road, with the dust, sun and traffic. We go through the archway into a courtyard, with shrubs and flowers and the well-swept stones. A yellow stone doorway takes us into the nave of St. George's Cathedral. There are rows of cane-seated chairs with hymnbook racks, each with a kneeler. The kneelers are stitched with Eastbourne, Lincoln or some other English town or city. With slightly darker limestone, you could be in "Stow on the Wold" or "Bourton on the Water". Tea and coffee are offered, and taken, in the garden. This could be in England, until you notice the grapefruit and the pomegranate trees. Is this how we adjust, by noticing more carefully the things we will not be seeing for a while as we get deeper into this culture? The presence of this Englishness seduces me into hanging onto my own culture in a way I have not experienced when travelling abroad for shorter periods before.

Perhaps the ability to retreat into their little bits of home is part of the reason for the division of the Christian Church in Jerusalem. Do we first identify with Rome, Greece, Armenia or England to name a few, before identifying with the Christian God? Does this equally apply to the three religions of this city? Does each group, Jew, Muslim and Christian, only identify with their God and, in this city, their piece of land, rather than identifying one overarching and universal God?

Chapter 2
Going to Jayyous
Week 1

"Ships in harbour are safe, but that's not what
ships are built for."   Anon

Sunday 16th November

While talking to Mr Dajani over an early breakfast, he says the
New Imperial is running at 10% of the pre-intifada (year 2000)
bookings.[1] Presently it is on 4% occupancy, which used to
average 45% and with just four workers compared to the
previous fifty. This seems to be a reasonable initial indicator
of the state of the Palestinian economy.

We set out for Jayyous at 09.00 from the Jaffa Gate in
Jerusalem, with Abdul-Aziz the taxi driver.   He gives a
detailed commentary on the settlements and movement
problems along the way. He picks out the contrast between
Arab and Israeli areas and the different standards for
Palestinian areas A, B and C.[2] We come to a checkpoint to the
south of Nablus. I put my hand in my pocket to find my
passport as we approach, but our minibus has Israeli number
plates so we can drive through without stopping. Later there
is a flying checkpoint near Funduq. My hand does not go to
my pocket. We drive through. One quickly learns the way of
things.

We arrive in Jayyous at 10.45.   Tom and Steiner, our
predecessors on the Accompaniment Programme in Jayyous,
are waiting for us, and we are greeted with welcoming
handshakes from our new neighbours. I am asked by a
villager if I am British and told, "It was not so bad under the
Mandate". I suspect a rose coloured and polite view of the
past. In the afternoon we walk to the village of Kafr Sir, with
Steiner, to meet the village elders. In the evening we have a
meal with the Danish Medical Students.[3] It is good to have
got started at last. This has been a good day.

This day marked a transition not just in location but also in experience. In the morning, we were still being 'told' about the situation, at the hotel and by the taxi driver. During the journey and the afternoon, we were beginning to be 'in' the situation and gaining direct experience and being able to make our observations and responses without direction from others. If this accompaniment is going to work, it will need all the resources we have available as individuals to make the most of this opportunity.

Picture 3 The Separation Barrier and the Jayyous North Gate, from the village side. The western end of the Jayyous ridge is in the background. Much of this slope has been 'landscaped' to make a way for the Separation Barrier and covered in razor wire. The Barrier may be seen in the background cutting through the end of the ridge on the right-hand side of the picture.

Monday 17th November

In the morning I go to the North Gate with Charles, at midday with Rex and in the evening with Sam. We are welcomed by the farmers and truck drivers. I meet many people around the village, and attend Tom and Steiner's farewell party in the evening. This has been a busy day, including a meeting with the International Solidarity Movement (ISM), and a group of

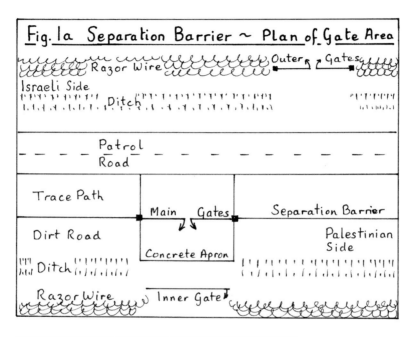

Fig. 1a Separation Barrier ~ Plan of Gate Area

Razor Wire ▸ Outer ▸ Gates

Israeli Side

Ditch

Patrol Road

Trace Path

Main Gates

Separation Barrier

Dirt Road

Concrete Apron

Palestinian Side

Ditch

Razor Wire

Inner Gate

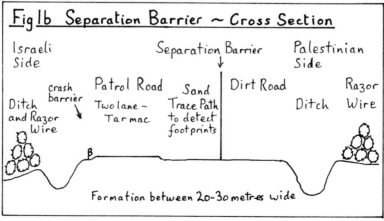

Fig 1b Separation Barrier ~ Cross Section

Israeli Side

Separation Barrier

Palestinian Side

crash barrier

Patrol Road
Two lane –
Tar mac

Sand
Trace Path
to detect
foot prints

Dirt Road

Razor Wire

Ditch and Razor Wire

Ditch

Formation between 20-30 metres wide

local people, one of whom is the hydrologist Abdul-Latif, of the Palestinian Hydrology Group.

The following extract shows how we picked up the recording of events at the Gates. It is the first of many such reports, hand written into a notebook kept at the house. Initially this is rather haphazard, with some Gate openings not being entered in the record. A list of the basic observations to record is soon devised to bring a degree of consistency to the information.

An extract from the North Gate Log Book, 17th November 2003.

"Charles and Maurice (the new EAs). Jeep 611056Y arrived and opened the Gate at 07.05. Twenty-six farmers went through the Gate before it was closed at 07.30. A truck was turned back, for not having the correct permit. Da'ud arrived at 07.35 but not soon enough to get through despite the soldiers being asked to keep the Gate open to 07.45, the time on the sign, saying, "We have to open the Falamyeh Gate". They drove off in the wrong direction! At 07.58, a truck arrives having been held up at the Nablus checkpoint. HaMoked [4] was called at 08.10. They cannot help as driver is out of time. Da'ud left at 07.53 and the truck went at 08.35 taking us back to the village."

Tuesday 18th November

After morning Gate duty, Steiner and Tom leave for Jerusalem. We rearrange our rooms, now we have one each, in between going to observe at the Gates. There are two gates in the Separation Barrier in Jayyous. The North Gate (referred to as the West Gate in Israeli documentation) is to the northwest of the village in a location where several tracks to the farmland have been blocked by the fence. This is the main gate for the farmers and is a good fifteen minutes walk from the centre of the village. However, as the Gate is below the village, it takes about twenty minutes to walk back up the hill. The South Gate is on a rise to the south of the main village ridge and only five minutes walk away across a shallow valley. This gate is for the children going to school from a family who live 'outside' the fence. Only a few farmers seem to have permits to use this gate.

Picture 4. Jayyous from the south. The Separation Barrier twists through the landscape in the foreground. The South Gate is over the ridge behind the olive trees between the minaret of the Mosque (centre) and the water tank (to the left).

It is 13.10 at the South Gate and the sun is high in the sky on a still day. The bleached landscape shimmers in the heat. All seems peaceful as we approach the Gate through the olive grove at the edge of the village. One farmer, Abu Hassan, waits beyond the fence to come into Jayyous, sitting beside the road in his grey jacket, with his head covered in a black and white shamagh complete with a rather worn-out akel holding it in place. Three Bedouin children, just out of school, wait to go through to their house on the other side of the fence. Some other children from Jayyous watch as Charles plays his chanter, the recorder-like part of the bagpipes, while sitting on the edge of the concrete block that holds the inner gate latch. Three Israeli Apache Helicopters fly north towards Natanya. A Japanese journalist, Chizu, arrives and starts interviewing the children.

At 13.30 some fence workers arrive in a pickup truck. They casually look at the sensing wires on the Gate, moving the cables around. After ten minutes they go and the Bedouin woman, Dharifah Shareb, arrives with another child. She is dressed from head to toe in black and carrying a cardboard vegetable tray containing a black plastic sack, on her head. She walks past the inner gate to the edge of the concrete apron and puts down her load in the sun, not expecting to wait too long. Her phone rings and she pulls it out of the tray and answers. She is sorting out a supply of water for her house.

Jeep 611014Y goes south at 13.55, slowing down but not stopping. One of the village lads asks Charles "Why Britain makes such a problem for Palestine in 1948?" The statement, "I love Hitler as he killed the Jews," from this youth is the beginning of a further history lesson from Charles, whose Arabic is listened to with great respect and attention. Another Apache flies over. Dharifah picks up her box and brings it back beside the base of the Gate, which offers a little shade. She clearly thinks the wait is going to be longer than expected. She is laughing and smiling. It is 14.10 and the Jeep with the key has still not come. Some of the kids are getting restless and throwing stones around, using broken pieces of the Gate, which have been thrown into the ditch, as targets. The older kids tell the younger ones to stop this as the call to prayer sounds in the village.

At 14.25 jeep 611014Y comes from the south and heads north non-stop, only to return in few minutes to stop and watch. Nobody moves. At 14.30 it goes away. The older lads, including the one who asked such demanding questions of Charles, drift away for lack of action, but soon return. A fellow arrives at 14.40 with a tractor towing a tanker trailer of drinking water for the Bedouin house, stopping beside the open inner gate. He has 4,500 litres of water for the house that has run dry and arrives with plenty of time to cross at 14.45, the time he has been given for the Gate to be opened.

Jeep 611014Y pulls up again. The soldiers watch, and shortly get out to unlock the Gate. The lock is turned and the bolts pulled. The padlock falls off the Gate rail into the dust where some birds had been having a dust bath. The Gate is opened. The old man tells the village boys to get out of the way. Three more Apaches fly over. The Japanese camera runs. The

Bedouin family are through. The soldier looks at the driver's papers. As the Gate is shut, we ask what is the problem. He does not have the right papers as he has come from another village with the water and, while having his identity card, he does not have a 'tasreef', the folding permit to cross the Separation Barrier and travel to a house just 500m the other side of the fence. The jeep drives off. We phone HaMoked, having been given the number but not knowing much about them other than they can help get the Gate open.

We wait for a response from HaMoked. A little boy is sitting in the sun on the bright yellow gate latch, looking like a kid on a piece of playground equipment. At 15.10 a car with blackened windows goes south, some 'bigwig' inspecting the fence. At 15.14 a truck goes north. At 15.17 three cars head south, while at 15.25 the truck returns full of soldiers who shout abuse at those of us waiting at the Gate as they pass. At half past three, the tractor driver is still waiting. With a caring attention to detail, he notices some pieces of barbed wire sticking out of the ground next to the concrete blocks where the children play and fetches a pair of snippers from the tractor to cut them off and make things safe. At 15.45, with sun shining on the Mediterranean behind Tel Aviv, we still wait. At 15.59 two shots are heard from the hill west of Jayyous, then three; and then one more. The driver says he will wait another three minutes and then go. At 16.08, he says his good-byes and turns the tractor and trailer in the limited space between the Gate and the track. He will come back tomorrow.

Wednesday 19th November

We are back at the South Gate by 05.55 with the jeep 611056Y arriving at 06.10 on the inside of the fence. It passes without stopping. It is interesting how quickly nothing seems so important as getting this water tanker through the Gate, a different sort of 'back to basics'. Water is so basic to human life that it is hard to conceive of people who can stop others having access to this basic need. At 06.25 the farmer shows-up to arrange for the water to be here at 15.00. The jeep comes back from the north at 06.30. At 06.35 611014Y arrives from the south, stops and goes on north. At 06.45, the woman and her children arrive from the house on the far side of the fence and a fellow arrives from Jayyous with a donkey. He ties it to the inner gate.

At 07.25 the jeep, 611014Y arrives from the North Gate and the soldiers get out quickly to let the family through after the man with the donkey has gone out. The old man speaks to them, but by 07.30 they are gone despite having closed the inner gate as well as locking the main gate. Why all this hurry? At 07.35 the water tanker arrives having been told to be there at 07.40. The woman says she has no water in the house. There is heavy smog over Tel Aviv as 611014Y goes north without stopping at 07.48. Is this just a way of blocking the water again today?

A white jeep, number 65, turns up and soldiers stay in their vehicle. Dharifah goes to talk to them, calling through the Gate, while the old farmer watches, the tractor driver sits in the shade. We phone HaMoked at 08.00 and the driver talks to them. At 08.07 611056Y arrives from the south, stops for a while then goes down to the new outer gate and stops. It then backs up and stops above the Gate. The soldiers get out and the old man is told to open the inner gate. The tractor moves back to allow this. The tractor is driven up to the soldiers slowly while the old man follows. The tractor and tanker go through. The old man goes through. By 08.17 all is done, the Gate locked. The jeep stops to close the outer gate on the track to the Bedouin's house. The water will last about three weeks, when this procedure will start all over again.

Should we have made greater attempts to mediate in this situation? Asserting power by withholding water clearly needs questioning. The mother and the tractor driver seemed, in a rather slow and dignified way, to be able to manage the situation, where a solution seems impossible to us as outsiders. We are also not aware of all the other 'moves' we cannot see. Clearly, something or someone has caused the white Jeep to appear. I doubt if it was just due to the presence of a bunch of 'internationals'.

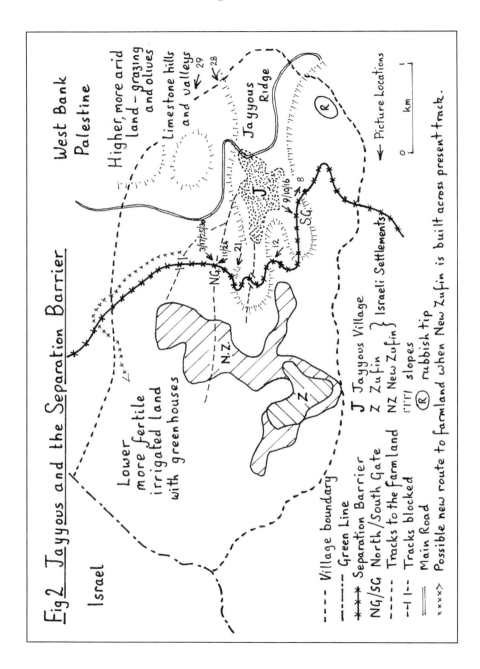

Fig 2 Jayyous and the Separation Barrier

West Bank
Palestine

Higher, more arid land – grazing and olives

Limestone hills and valleys

Jayyous Ridge

Lower more fertile irrigated land with greenhouses

Israel

- – – Village boundary
- *** Separation Barrier
- NG/SG North/South Gate
- – – Tracks to the farmland
- –|– Tracks blocked
- ═══ Main Road
- xxxx> Possible new route to farmland when New Zufin is built across present track.

- ─·─·─ Green Line
- J Jayyous Village
- Z Zufin
- NZ New Zufin } Israeli Settlements
- ''''' slopes
- ℞ rubbish tip

← Picture Locations

0   km

There have been several mentions of 'ringing HaMoked' in the last few pages. Tom had given me the phone number, saying if you have trouble at the Gates, ring these people. "They are good at getting the Gate open." It is only as I work through the coming weeks that I realise the importance of this small Israeli organisation that initially is a friendly voice on the end of the phone, but has the skill to convert a good many of our periods of frustration into a Gate opening. They are able to contact the 'DCO': the District Co-ordination Office. Formerly a joint Israeli Palestinian institution for the administration of civilian affairs in the occupied Palestinian Territories, the Palestinian Authority was removed from this joint administration at the start of the second Intifada. The DCO is effectively the civil administration wing of the Israeli military. I learn later that by early 2004, Hamoked had 30,000 files on cases ranging from freedom of movement to violence committed by the security forces, from house demolition to issues over Jerusalem residency. The 8751 new cases notified in 2002 exceed the number for the six-year period 1996-2001. We will add to their stock of files on denied access over the coming weeks. Even at phone's-length there is a feeling of true partnership with this Israeli group.

In the afternoon, after another visit to the South Gate, I go to have a hair cut and the electric power goes down when the barber is half way through using the clippers set at the local fashion of number 4. He finishes the other side and my beard with his scissors. In the evening we have a meeting with Society Jayyous to discuss ideas for working with the community in addition to Gate watching.

I have still not got used to the power going off at 14.00 for about four hours each day. This is in addition to there being no power between 02.00 and about 08.00 in the morning. This is taking me back to rural North Devon before mains water and electricity was installed in the early 1960s, when there was no electricity in the hours of daylight. Mains power could have been installed here. The French Government paid for a heap of pylons, to be found at the west end of the village, but the Israelis would not allow Jayyous to be connected to the grid. *This is not as bad as denying access to water, as we can live without electricity. However, the two are connected in that electricity is used to pump the water.*

I feel rather diffident about most of the suggestions for additional activities during the evening meeting, as they mostly seem to involve teaching something. What can I usefully teach in twelve weeks? I also realise most of what I would wish to teach like basket making or other craftwork would involve resources that are not available here. How good it would be to have skills in music, singing or dancing, skills contained within and exercised without the need of supporting equipment and resources.

Chapter 3
Irrigation and Ghettos
Weeks 1 - 2

Thursday 20th November

At the North Gate the farmers wait early in the morning. The inner gate is open. The first in the queue is a farmer with a donkey cart. He is talking to other farmers and the donkey, eager to do its day's work, moves unnoticed up the ramp towards the Gate. A jeep is heard approaching, the farmer stands by the inner gate and calls the donkey, which immediately turns and comes back down the slope. The man is still first in the queue but is told to wait as the soldier calls others forward to have their passes checked at the open Gate. Now the last to move forward, the farmer is refused passage, as "He cannot control his donkey". He turns to go as the inner gate is closed. I ask the soldier, "Does he have the right papers?" He says he does not speak English. However, he spoke it very well yesterday. We ring HaMoked and the farmer talks with them and sadly goes home. He says his donkey understands more than the soldiers do. (There seems to be a minor debate in the village about the use of the word donkey as a term of abuse about soldiers, or as in "Sharon is a donkey", with some, like this farmer, saying the donkeys are our friends.)

We meet the Mayor of Jayyous, Fayiz Hussein Mohammed Salim, before Abdul Latif takes us to see the damage to an irrigation project in Habla to the south west of Jayyous. This involves a journey that takes us first east and than south from Jayyous to Azzoun, where we cross the main number 55 Road from Tel Aviv to the Israeli settlement of Kdumim (built on land near the Palestinian village of Qedumin) and the Palestinian city of Nablus. We continue south in our minibus taxi to the village of Kafr Thult, where we turn westwards on a single-track road. Approaching Habla from the south we pass along an 'isthmus' of land, with the Separation Barrier fence on both sides, to reach the town. Habla is surrounded by the Separation Barrier. This is a journey of about 25km around the various walls and fences for a direct distance of just over 10km.

It reminds me of Steinstucken, a small, isolated part of suburban Potsdam that was surround by the Berlin Wall and attached to West Berlin by a narrow corridor.

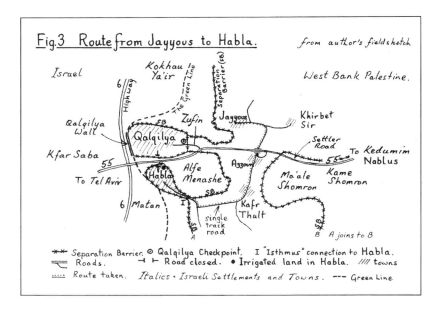

We walk from the centre of Habla into the citrus groves, full of oranges, clementinas and lemons, hanging from small trees with shiny dark green leaves. Large metal pipes run between the fields, bringing water pumped from the well to a system of small black plastic pipes that irrigate the individual trees. This excellent example of fruit tree irrigation brings a good harvest.

Suddenly, as we walk through the grove, there is a scar across the land, an earth bank capped in razor wire. There are red warning notices saying "mortal danger - military zone" in Arabic, Hebrew and English. The main 150mm iron distribution pipe is fractured and thrown to one side. The small plastic field pipes bend up from the ground. A marrow plant is growing on the rolls of razor wire in front of the fence.

How does one harvest a marrow from the razor wire? When the bulldozers cleared the citrus trees, they clearly had little regard for the investment made by the farmers in the planting or irrigation of their fields. This land is farmed co-operatively by a group of about twenty Palestinian farmers, with the irrigation system being funded, through the Palestinian Hydrology Group, by the Spanish government through the European Union.[1] This information is carried on a large and relatively new sign at the entrance to the irrigated area. Who was checking on how the money was spent, and more importantly if the project survives? Is this a different sort of aid corruption?

Picture 5. The Separation Barrier and broken irrigation pipes (small and black in the foreground and large and straight to the right). Notice the marrow growing on the razor wire in the background.

How well this scene illustrates the comment by the French

economist Jean-Baptiste Say, which is quoted in that rather dated work, 'Common Security – Programme for Disarmament'. "Adam Smith calls the soldier an unproductive worker; would this was true, for he is much more a destructive worker: not only does he fail to enrich society with any product, and consumes those things needed for his upkeep, but only too often he is called upon to destroy, uselessly for himself, the arduous product of others' work."[(2)]

We walk across a field of cabbages, each of which has its own water feed from the system of trickle irrigation pipes. This method is probably the most efficient form of irrigation, in that it only waters the location around the plants, so reducing the amount of water that is wasted by evaporation. It can also be used to deliver liquid fertiliser to the plants. The water comes from the Western Aquifer, being brought to the surface by a pump, which stands in the corner of the field. Some of these pumps date back to the time of the British Mandate[(3)] but the amount of water they can pump dates back to 1967, and the start of the Israeli occupation. While the Israelis continue to increase the amount of water they extract from the Western Aquifer for their use, they restrict the Palestinians to the levels of 1967, when the population was much smaller and the consumption was therefore lower. Figures for 1997 show 360 million cubic metres of water available per year from the Western Aquifer, with 94% going to Israel and 6% going to the Palestinians.[(4)] The water in the Western Aquifer is collected underground from the winter rains over the hills of the West Bank and is therefore a resource of the West Bank. Under international law, it is not permitted to remove resources from an occupied area.[(5)] Research suggests that the level of the Aquifer is falling: it is not being recharged naturally at a rate that can keep pace with the volume extracted.

Perhaps it is time for a geography lesson. Irrigation is a compelling topic, as I know from my geography teaching. It is one of the few activities that has fundamentally changed the human condition over thousands of years.

It has the attractive qualities of improvement, of the duty to make use of resources provided by the environment, to provide food where production was limited and increasingly during the twentieth century to provide engineers with the canvas for increasingly controversial grand projects. A topic that captures the imagination, it allows the creativity of the human species to make a mark for the benefit of others, both neighbours and later generations. However, irrigation is not without its problems. It does of course change the natural balance and so changes the processes in operation. One of the biggest problems is the salinization of soils in irrigated areas, where soluble salts are precipitated in the topsoil as the result of the evaporation of water drawn to the surface. This can eventually cause the soil to become useless for agriculture. Irrigation is something of a balancing act, with many large-scale projects now running into long-term problems. The perception of irrigation as an improvement may indeed be something of a paradox, unless it is carefully managed.

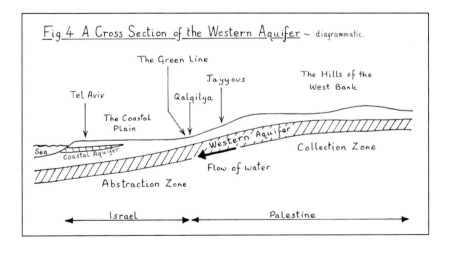

Fig. 4 A Cross Section of the Western Aquifer ~ diagrammatic.

One of the areas where problems are developing with irrigation is not far away from the disruption in Habla. The use of water from the River Jordan has already removed the northern lakes from the map of Israel and the Dead Sea is being reduced in size as water is increasingly taken from the Jordan by the Israelis for irrigation. Will it eventually suffer in the same way as the Aral Sea in Central Asia, where the volume of water was been reduce by 75% between 1961 and 1995? This was due to the implementation of the former Soviet Union's policy of growing cotton on the surrounding arid lands. The Aral Sea was mostly a crime against nature and a disaster for a small number of fishing communities left high and dry as the Sea got smaller. The control of water in the West Bank by Israel is more directly a crime against millions of people. The level of extraction and use of water by Israel is well beyond that which is sustainable, and its use of water is wasteful in the extreme. Israel uses trickle irrigation to water roses on the roundabouts in West Jerusalem, while Palestinians are restricted to 25 litres of water a day in the dry season.

In his 'Obstacles to Peace' Jeff Halper an Israeli, who is a leading challenger of the Israeli Government's policy of military occupation and all its accompanying instruments of control, points out that 80% of the water coming from the West Bank goes to Israel and its settlements; only 20% going to the area's 2.5 million Palestinians. This is part of the 'Matrix of Control'[6] (I am aware these figures do not match those quoted above. Both are from respected sources.)

Israel's proud boast that it is "greening the desert" comes at a huge cost, both human and environmental. Indeed it is the Palestinians who are using the resources in the most responsible way, focusing the use of water in small projects for maximum benefit to produce fruit and vegetables, while using most of the West Bank for extensive farming of olive trees and grazing sheep and goats. This extensive farming, which has a low environmental impact, contrasts with the intensive farming methods used by the Israelis on the Plain of Sharon, based on high levels of water consumption. When will it dawn on the Israelis that this lack of environmental security is as important as, or even more important than, the military or political security? Its use of water resources in this way is increasingly unsustainable.

On our return to Jayyous, I go to North Gate at 16.00. After a long wait for gate-repairs to be completed, during which some donkeys have stood for an hour and three quarters, with the men lying on the ground next to the road, it takes fifteen minutes to check about 20 people. The jeep's searchlight swings from the queue to the pass-checker and sometimes towards me standing well back where the fellows wait for a ride up to the village. Sometimes there will be as many as six on a single tractor. As the last truck comes through, a voice from the dark says "You are welcome" and a gesture signals me to come and wait with them. "You are welcome." At the edge of the village, a door opens and a dish of juicy sweet cakes is passed into the van so the men may break their fast. Due to the delays, this is nearly an hour later than it need be. However, I am offered the dish before the men. I say and gesture "After you". They will not have it; I must eat first. I feel bad about having taken food at midday as we are not keeping the Ramadan fast. Another hand offers me four freshly picked 'clementinas'. "I am honoured." I walk back to the house with watering eyes stopping only to buy some bananas, small, local and very fresh.

During the evening, it was assumed in conversation with my colleagues that I would be coming to Palestine again. I am puzzled by this assumption, which seems to be founded on poor perceptions and little evidence. It makes me think about why I have given this impression. How well do we 'read' each other? How well do I 'read' the Palestinians? Am I just projecting my perceptions onto the various characters we work with? Are my perceptions grounded in evidence? If only I had more Arabic, so I could understand more. Are they just providing us with what they want us to see or what they think we want to see? All these questions add together to make questions about what is the evidence. What is the truth in this situation? I have always held concerns about the nature of evidence and the nature of witness. We only 'see' the evidence with 'our eyes'. Others may see completely different evidence. So, what is the true nature of bearing witness?

Friday 21st November

I attend the South Gate in the morning. An old man and a boy wait to come into Jayyous.

Freedom

Here I sit, free to go,
They sit behind the Gate,
I can go if I please,
But I will wait for the jeep with the keys.

This machine issues little freedoms,
All in the name of security.
Will it return for this man and boy's freedom,
to be valued, to be granted today?

Who's freedom? Freedom to move;
Freedom to be secure; freedom to live,
Freedom to go. How can I be free to go,
when these people may not cross?

We wait.

At eight, I call HaMoked,
But it's too late,
The man turns from his grief, and,
Walks away, his only freedom being not to stay.

He has gone and so given me my freedom to go.
In this unsatisfactory freedom we leave
the prisoner's fence behind.

We have a planning meeting with the ISM team, discussing how we can cooperate in our work in Jayyous. I am affirmed in my desire and ability to carry on with the Gate work; this, for me, being the deep and simple purpose of being here, to be with, to accompany those whose freedom of movement is restricted, and to record the situation in words and pictures. I cook for the house this evening; pasta, vegetables and some minced meat found in the fridge to make a meaty sauce for my colleagues.

Saturday 22nd November

We make a visit to Qalqilya, to the south west of Jayyous, with Abdul-Latif. To reach this important centre we travel by taxi to Azzoun and join the main number 55 Road travelling west towards Israel. Just before the checkpoint into Israel, we turn right and soon come to the checkpoint for entry into Qalqilya. This is the only point of access to this city of 40,000 people that has been completely encircled by the Separation Barrier. We see the checkpoint, walls and fence. We also visit the mayor and Deputy Governor, attending a meeting with the Swedish Consular General and the new "UNRWA man", a Swede. These meetings are a very interesting experience, displaying a mixture of Political, social and power interactions. Although it is completely walled and fenced around, Qalqilya is not much like "Walled West Berlin". The wall is higher. The Berlin Wall, even by the Brandenburg Gate, was little more than four metres high, the top could easily be reached with a stepladder as indeed it was by those removing souvenirs in 1989-90, including myself.

The Separation Wall is at least eight metres high, the Palestinian graffiti hardly reaching a quarter of the way up. It is made in the same way as the later generations of Berlin Wall, being 'L' shaped concrete sections, which 'stand on their own feet', once the ground is levelled. Here the graffiti is on the 'other side'. In Berlin those being 'kept in' could see a white wall painted by the Eastern authorities to more easily detect and shoot escapees, while the those in the West were able to approach the wall and spray pictures and slogans on the concrete. Here, those being corralled are the ones who apply the graffiti and those in 'freedom' attempt to hide the wall by landscaping it behind earth mounds. Much of it is hidden from the Israeli side where it runs parallel to the new north-south highway that has moved the focus of Israeli communications eastwards towards the West Bank. This piece of Separation Wall to the west of Qalqilya has one merit. It is built on the 'Green Line', the recognised boundary between Israel and the West Bank. Elsewhere the path of the Separation Barrier seems arbitrary, its location being under the catch-all expression, 'the requirements of security'.

Picture 6.   The Separation Wall west of Qalqilya.   The eight metre (28ft) high concrete wall, found on the Israeli side of Qalqilya.   The other side of this wall is landscaped with earth mounds to hide it from the Israeli motorway.

The day leaves a terrible question hanging in my mind: are the Israelis doing to the Palestinians what was done to the previous generations of Jews across much of Europe, culminating in the history of the 1930s and the Holocaust? Are the Israelis building a ghetto for the Palestinians? Can it help? Does it help?

As a geographer, I look at the maps and see the patterns of separation.   The map from B'Tselem's report "The Land Grab" tells a great deal about separation and removal: of allotting areas to different religious or national groups. This map is like a piece of Swiss Cheese with two 'countries'[7] on the same land, with one, Palestine, being reduced to the 'holes in the cheese', the enclaves, the cantons, the reservations or the 'ghettos'. To fence people in is perhaps part of the some basic animal territorial instinct still found in human kind. It is based on segregation, discrimination and difference, which may be forced upon people or be desired from within.

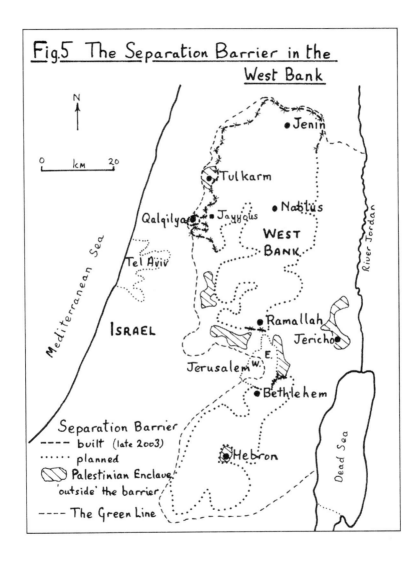

Fig.5 The Separation Barrier in the West Bank

We have seen this separation in South Africa, where

communities were legally separated by racial origins and power and wealth structures maintained by that separation. We have seen it in the DDR (The German Democratic Republic – East Germany) where the builders of the Berlin Wall erected it in the name of security to protect the workers of the East from the threat of the Western capitalist. We have seen it in Belfast to keep the nationalist and the unionist, the catholic and protestant apart. We even see it in modern societies, where there is the tendency among those who have the greatest wealth to fence themselves into secure communities for protection from those they perceive as a threat.

This brings me back to the "What would you have done about Hitler?" question of my youth, the question that was used to test my pacifism. It also poses a new, more pointed, question about what can individuals do about regimes that do not respect International Law and oppress others in the name of their own freedom and security. My father continued his friendship with a number of Germans, especially Hans Shocke from Kemp-en-Rhine, during the 1930s, visiting Germany and seeing what was going on.[8] There are others, like Hermann Field, who took practical steps to help Jewish and other oppressed people to escape from Eastern Europe during 1939.[9] There were Germans who, being anti-Nazi, became oppressed by the regime and had to leave, despite their desire to resist. These included Sebastian Haffner[10] and the family of my former teacher Helmut Mirauer.[11]

Some oppressed people left Europe in the 1930s for the US, Palestine and other places. Great Britain maintained entry restrictions on those from Eastern Europe.[12] However, to leave is not an option for many Palestinians. While the Christian community was about ten percent of the population fifty years ago, it has now been reduced to just over one percent. This is because the Palestinian Christians tend to have smaller families but also because it is easier for them to migrate. Palestinian Muslims are increasingly not welcomed in the rest of the world, not even in neighbouring Jordan, which is burdened down with Palestinian Refugees from the

1948 and '67 wars, and now with millions of Iraqi refugees. Indeed to stay in Palestine is part of resisting the Israeli Occupation, as extremist Israelis just want the Palestinians to go, so there will no longer be a people to occupy, and the land will become empty. This will finally resolve the paradox of having to build a wall around "a land with no people."[13]

It takes a Palestinian to remind me that the most important role of the European Union in its evolving history since 1956 has been to bring lasting peace across much of Europe.[14] *Indeed co-operation in Europe really started in 1951, with the Treaty of Paris, setting up the 'European Coal and Steel Community' to allow the free movement of resources between France, Belgium, the Netherlands, Luxembourg, Italy and Germany. While this may not offer any solution to the historical problem of the 1930s and 40s, it might provide an insight into the future for this divided land. Perhaps a 'Middle Eastern Water Community' should be set up to manage a greater equitability in the sourcing, supply and use of water in the region. If peace and equality were to be worked at as hard as war, we might prevent further conflict, as the European Union has done over the last fifty years.*

The question remains. What can individuals do in the circumstance where International Law is disregarded and little or no effort is made to enforce it by those who established its tenets after the 1939-45 War?

As soon as we are back in Jayyous, we are called to a meal at our landlord, Sharif Omar's, new house. He tells us about recent demonstrations in France during his visit to the European Social Fund. He also tells the story of promising his new wife a house when they returned from Jordan just after the 1967 Israeli Six Day War, walking back to Jayyous from the Allenby Bridge. There was never enough money for a new house while their children needed to go to school and university on the income of a citrus, vegetable and olive farmer. He recently built his new house when his children had finished at university. Shortly after the house was completed, the Separation Barrier was built, and he went to live in the shed on his land. His wife did not like being in the new house on her own so wished to live in the shed as well. Now the "Israelians" (Israelis) do not let them stay on their land over night. Indeed, they do not give Sharif Omar a pass to allow him to go to his land.

He tells us about the twenty-day closure of the Gate in September (2003), and how this destroyed the guava harvest and the young cauliflower plants. He takes us through the pattern of harvesting, with guavas in September, olives in October, clemantinas in November, and oranges in December. These are just two of the twenty-one types of citrus fruit that are grown. There always seems to be something to harvest from this carefully worked land. The wheat crop is harvested in April, but about 95% of the farmers' income comes from fruit and vegetables. He does not tell us about the way some of his land has been taken by the Israelis for a quarry to provide materials for building settlements, roads and the Separation Barrier.

Sunday 23rd to Tuesday 25th November

Sunday morning finds us returning to Jerusalem for a series of meetings. After a journey with just two checkpoints, we are back to the New Imperial at 12.00, with a "Welcome home!" from Mr Dajani. This time I am in a room on the front of the house, referred to as the "Kaiser's Room". It was the room used when Kaiser Wilhelm II visited the Holy Land in 1898 with his wife, the Empress Augusta Victoria. This room has a view of the new David Museum and, if you go onto the balcony, the Jaffa Gate, and is somewhat more spacious than the room over the side street at the back of the house in which I previously slept.

I go for a walk on my own to the southwest of the Jaffa Gate to investigate the railway station as marked on the map. It is closed, and altogether a sorry sight. The ripped up rails have been left lying on the ground, while two rather drunken lower quadrant starter signals stand over the end of platform. These signals are reminiscent of the London and South Western Railway and certainly of UK origin. In the period after the

British capture of Palestine in 1917, this station would have felt even-more British, with locomotives and carriages, including hospital trains, requisitioned by the War Office from homeland railways. I return through the German Quarter, finding a pair of British Mandate post boxes with blank spaces where one would expect to see the crown and monarch's initials. However, I have to attend to modern communications and send some e-mails including the weekly report to London, before going to the AVH for a meal. An e-mail from ISM member Susan, in Jayyous, brings the news that the South Gate has been closed.

What are we doing here in Jerusalem when we should be in Jayyous? There are two interesting moments in the two days of meetings. There is a valuable session with a representative of the Israeli 'left', i.e. those who oppose the occupation. This provides a good analysis of the relationship between opposition groups in Israel. At a service at St George's, I sit in the choir seat dedicated to the Dioceses of Bath and Wells. The service is followed by a talk from the vicar, who says some interesting, if concerning, things about Christian Zionism.

The most relaxing moments in this weekend were the few minutes spent investigating the old railway station. This is an old habit when abroad. Even when not travelling by train I always seem to end up at the station. Is this why I do not need to search for Englishness abroad as I can just find a railway station, even one that is closed, to contact my 'cultural roots'? It is strange how evident the influences of the two great powers, Britain and Germany, are in this place. It is more than just the tangible, physical evidence. They are there in the facilitation and the cause of the State of Israel. Indeed it was the re-mapping of the Middle East, along conventional imperialist lines, and with the British Government anxious for international Jewish financial support during the 1914-18 war, that caused it to make the incautious and ambiguous promise, the Balfour Declaration, to establish 'a national home' for the Jews. The declaration, a terse letter to Lord Rothschild, has just two significant sentences.

51

"I have much pleasure in conveying to you, on behalf of His Majesty's Government, the following declaration of sympathy with Jewish Zionist aspirations which has been submitted to, and approved by, the Cabinet. His Majesty's Government view with favour the establishment in Palestine of a national home for the Jewish people, and will use their best endeavours to facilitate the achievement of this object, it being clearly understood that nothing shall be done which may prejudice the civil and religious rights of existing non-Jewish communities in Palestine, or the right and political status enjoyed by Jews in any other country."[15]

It is interesting to note that Edwin Montagu, the Secretary for India, the only Jew in the cabinet and a man against the Zionist Project, had warned that this policy would prove disastrous. It was at his insistence that the last clause of this declaration be inserted. This small piece of paper stirred the first sigh of the whirlwind to follow. *Hobsbawn says, "this was to be a problematic and unforgotten relic of the 1914-18 War."*[16]

Picture 7. Israeli Post Boxes in Jerusalem. This is evidence of previous 'occupation'; they seem to be the standard British model but without a crest.

Chapter 4
Return to Jayyous - Focusing on the Issues
Weeks 2-3

Wednesday 26th November

On returning to the village, I make a quick visit to the South Gate. A week after the tractor driver so carefully cut off the pieces of barbed wire sticking out of the ground, the area is now covered with coils of razor wire fixed to stakes in the road-way. On Sunday 23rd November this Gate was closed to all vehicle traffic, but it is still available for the children coming to school in the village. They have to walk round the end of the inner gate, where the ground is falling into the ditch, making the surface of the path unstable. *Is this the IDF's response to the water tanker going through last week?*

When Charles and I go to pay the rent at the 'Baladiya' (Town Hall) we find the "Brits" are in town, complete with a Range Rover 'flying the flag', having driven up from Tel Aviv and Jerusalem. The party includes some old military colleagues and diplomatic contacts of Charles and we go with them to view the situation from the top of the Baladiya's tower. As we were only going to pay the rent, I left my camera at the house so I missed the opportunity of recording this event and the landscape from this vantage point. The first event, the presence of the "Brits", was unrepeatable, the second, an opportunity to take pictures from the top of the tower, never offers itself again. After this, I am never to be without my camera.

A village meeting addressed by Dr Mustafa Barghouti follows this 'excitement'.[1] He is establishing a new political party that is attempting to bring all the various fragments together. With some 250 men at the meeting, there is standing room only. The only woman is a German journalist. Dr Barghouti starts to talk, competing with the call to prayer, of which nobody seems to take notice. There are a great many interruptions (as is the local custom), but eventually the meeting falls quieter than normal as the audience becomes more engaged. Amongst the Arabic I hear mention of Nelson Mandela and Mr Bush (the latter with a dismissive hand gesture) before I leave for the Gate. "Clearly a good speaker", Charles tells me later, after I return from the North Gate, "it was all rather predictable to start with, but moved on to the need for one plan, policy, and a new party". There was considerable support from the floor. However, after this attempt to pull things together the first question was about the Separation Barrier and "my fields". This brought the overarching and positive crashing back down to earth into the realm of individual problems and demands.

Is this situation going to be resolved with broad policies or small solutions, from the top down or from the bottom up?

This evening I am challenged about my food by today's cook. While at Sharif Omar's on Saturday night I was seen to eat a little of the various meat dishes that were pressed upon me. I responded by saying, "When I am "at home" I would like to eat my preferred food, which is vegetarian. However when I am a guest in someone's house I will eat 'diplomatically', accepting what is offered." It is not difficult to live here without meat as so many fresh fruits and vegetables are available. I am able to prepare meals that include meat for my colleagues. It surprises me how important this matter suddenly seems. Is it about maintaining something of oneself in the group, or just being awkward? I am not a vegetarian for moral reasons, although that is a factor. I do not eat meat because it is so wasteful of farming resources and inefficient as part of the food chain. This seems to re-settle an issue discussed when the house management plan was agreed. This episode illustrates the importance of conforming to things that do not matter so as to be able to be different in the things that do matter, and when to know the difference. It is also interesting to see how I used the words "at home". This place has become, at least for the next few months, 'home'.

I go to bed thinking about Abdul-Latif's comments, during our evening talk, about the sustainability of the Separation Barrier as a solution. He says, "The solutions have to come from here and here", indicating the heart and the head. He also says, "You are now part of the village and you don't need an invitation to be part of village life." I also ponder the off-the-cuff, unofficial comments from the "Brits", "This (the Separation Barrier) has never happened before, so we have to use new approaches". A more worrying comment was "we can't tell them (the Israelis) anything". I drift into sleep thinking about the other wall (Berlin), the so-called 'Peace Walls' in Belfast and apartheid in South Africa; "... they happened before", so why is this such a challenge to the Foreign Office?[2] I also wonder about this counsel of despair which suggests that we are unable to see any way of putting pressure on the Israelis, through either direct contact or through international channels like the UN, to reflect on the impact of their illegal actions.

A challenging day, full of different experiences and responses; will they all be like this?

Thursday 27th November

I am early to the North Gate. Seventy people go through in two openings. The first is long (20 minutes), slow and uneventful, with many women and children arriving during the opening. One fellow arrives after the Gate is shut but within the "advertised" times so when the jeep returns on the inner road we try to get the Gate open. More people turn up. A quick call by one of the farmers to the Mayor at the Baladiya, which is passed on to the Captain in the District Co-ordination Office, and back to the patrol, and the soldiers open the Gate again. However, they get an 'ear full' when another patrol turns up during the opening with 'Mr Nasty' in Jeep 611014Y. Even over this short time, one of the regular Israeli soldiers has attracted our attention enough to gain a descriptive nickname. The children go through the South Gate at lunchtime on their way home from school without incident. How quickly the abnormal situation of children going through this military gate on their way home from school can become normal, 'without incident'.

Picture 8. A sunrise over the South Gate.

Picture 9. Waiting at the Jayyous South Gate. Dharifah sits on the foundations of the inner gate waiting for the South gate to be opened. Her son sleeps on the concrete by the gate latch

Friday 28th November

Twice I go to the South Gate on my own and later I cook dinner. An easy day compared to some with no one going out this morning so I am able to enjoy the sunrise reading about discernment.[3] How many more good mornings will we have? At lunchtime, after a delayed opening, Dharifah, the Bedouin women, and her sons return home. As I leave the Gate, the soldiers call me back asking what I am writing down. I tell them, "Just some times". "Is it about our behaviour?" "No, just some times." I ask them when they think the rain will come. I do not go past the inner gate so they have to come towards me across the dusty road. I am glad I have not been using my camera. Later I talk with Lionel, a young American member of the ISM, about him being held by the Israelis in one of the jeeps. He was taken to the Qalqilya checkpoint, having to find his own way back to Jayyous at night. We also talk about me taking over the reporting of the Gate observations to the Mayor of Jayyous. I sort out many pictures and make a CD of both pictures and writing.

Saturday 29th November

In the morning we sit on the front porch, eating a late breakfast and talking about the five objectives for our work set out by the Ecumenical Accompaniment Programme:

1 Monitoring and reporting violations of human rights and international humanitarian law.

2 Supporting acts of nonviolent resistance alongside local Christian and Muslim Palestinians and Israeli peace activists.

3 Offering protection through nonviolent presence.

4 Engaging in public policy advocacy.

5 Standing in solidarity with the churches and all those struggling nonviolently against the occupation.

The first three of these objectives, especially one and three,

58

seem very much to describe our day-to-day activities. Opportunities for work connected with the fourth and fifth objectives would offer themselves when away from Jayyous, in Jerusalem and when we return home.

Having spent much of the morning in discussion of our objectives, the evening is spent listening to Abdul-Latif. He has visited us on several evenings to discuss our welfare and possible additional activities. Three days ago, after Dr Barghouti had addressed the village meeting, he spoke about the need for, "… a change in both hearts and heads" to solve the problems of Palestine. This evening he develops several themes coming from this idea.

He says Palestine is a well-educated community. It has one of the highest rates of further and university education anywhere, with few young people leaving education before the age of 18 years and many going on to university, a large proportion on vocational courses. The Israelis disrupt the education process, by interfering with student and teacher access to campuses with checkpoints and general closures of the West Bank.[4] Many teaching and learning hours are lost and work is being done to increase the role of the Internet to overcome these problems. He says much could be done in education to pursue the cause of nonviolence and reconciliation to give rise to a new generation with a different view of the future.

He says there is a need for economic, social and cultural links with Israel. He points out that Qalqilya used to be a market centre for both Palestinians and Israelis before the Separation Barrier was built. This is supported by the shop fronts seen in the town, with Hebrew, Arabic and often English signs. The Separation Barrier has destroyed the few remaining opportunities for contact between Israelis and Palestinians.

He turns to the prisoner issue, saying this is a real block to reconciliation. As we have been, told Palestinians can be held for up to six months without charge, and this can be repeated. In addition, there is a strong correlation between young men held (it is mostly young men) and families that do not get permits to go to their land. A son who makes remarks about the occupation is arrested and imprisoned, while his family suffers, in a form of double punishment. This is just part of the draconian implementation of the occupation, using *'collective punishment'* which is illegal under international law.

He again points out that Europe has reduced the significance of its borders, at least in the area covered by the Schengan Agreement, where there is un-controlled movement between countries such as Germany and France. (The U.K. is not a member of this Agreement, so we still have border controls when travelling to mainland Europe.) These countries were at war with each other: Germany occupied France but now they live together in peace. He refers to the "One State Solution", one state for all, which raises interesting questions about democracy. Israel is a democracy. Palestine (the West Bank and Gaza) is occupied by this democracy and there is no real democracy, as any party elected can only govern under the control of the Israelis. If there were one state, the Arabs would be in a majority and Israel-Palestine would no longer be a Jewish state. If an independent Palestine was a full democracy, it may elect a government that Israel (and the USA) will not talk to and will not control.[5]

As early as 1937 the Zionist Congress decided the creation of an independent Jewish state would take precedence over a Jewish-Arab agreement, following the guiding principle set out by Ben-Gurion.[6] In simple terms, he suggested that only two of three objectives were possible: to have a Jewish state, to have a democratic state and to have Eretz (Greater) Israel. Today in Israel we have the first two, a Jewish democratic state. However, Israel is still hankering after an expansionist policy at the expense of its neighbour Palestine, not only in terms of land but also in terms of Palestine's ability to function as an independent democratic country with fixed borders. Israel is trying to have all three objectives. This results in conflict with the Arab community. These communities in some Israelis' eyes should remove themselves to the 'empty' Arab spaces around the Greater Israel. The myth of 'an empty land for a people without a land' continues as a major element in the Zionist vision.

Be there one state or two, the issue of the Palestinian refugees must be resolved. For fifty-six years, since 1947, Palestinians displaced by Israel have lived in camps in Jordan, Lebanon and the cities of the West Bank and Gaza. These 'camps' are towns with houses, shops and services funded by UNRWA, which of course means being funded by the international community. Many of the families in them still hold the key to their houses in what is now Israel. This is a huge problem in terms of physical and psychological re-settlement of refugees.

Abdul-Latif talks about Israel as being, "… a badly behaved child, which has been given life by the West, but is now out of control as it breaks all the rules". "When will the 'western parents' take their responsibilities to enforce the international rules?" As we have seen above there seems to be no will to put pressure on the Israelis. He says the openness of the Palestinians and the tradition of "welcoming the stranger in the land" may have been the Palestinians' greatest weakness.[7]

He also comments that the Palestinians blame the Israelis for everything; but they cannot be blamed for the rubbish in the streets and many other minor problems of the occupation. However, it is part of the psychology of an occupation that it saps responsibility for one's own actions; someone else is always in control. He finishes by saying Israel is like a bus, "the Israelis are on the bus with the driver telling them not to look, to hold on tight, it will be all right: I must be right, I am a good driver, my name is Sharon.

> *Thinking back to the discussion of our objectives, it is clear to me that this conversation needs to become a central part of my advocacy. Even in the short time I have been here I have seen or heard from others evidence that supports and triangulates Abdul-Latif's witness.[8]*

As so often happens we are working at very different levels simultaneously. At a more mundane level, the communication saga runs on. By the end of the day, we have a basic Internet connection provided with the help from Abdul-Latif. Sharif Omar arrives to talk about his proposed hunger strike and to discuss some improvements to the kitchen. He walks around the house to see how we have settled in and finds I have no bed. I have been sleeping on two foam mats on the floor, which is fine for me. He says it will soon be too cold for this and gets on his mobile phone. Within fifteen minutes a bed has arrived, on the back of a tractor. He tells us about the 'tent demonstration' starting the following day. He also says it is time to renew the kitchen and that someone will come round tomorrow to make a start.

This has been another day of great contrasts ranging from the practicalities of communication, kitchens and beds to the engagement of Gate duty and the discussion of our philosophy. It has focused on the real issues, both of the programme and the situation. I feel we need to follow the objectives set out by the programme and interpret these as best we can for use in the situation in the field, but also to take our leadings from the Palestinian perspective. The best way out of having too many 'masters' is to develop a degree of autonomy with appropriate responses to the day-to-day situation with the resources at hand. These resources are the Palestinians, the EAPPI team and other 'internationals' in Jayyous.

Abdul-Latif's words have high-lighted the Palestinian position and provided another dimension to the situation, compared with the programme objectives. I hope to develop these issues with Abdul-Latif and find ways of bringing them to a wider audience. We also need to be at peace with ourselves, before we tell others what and how to do things. I see Abdul-Latif as a man remarkably at peace, considering the environment in which he lives.

Sunday 30th November

Sharif Omar is allowed through to his land at 13.00, after putting up his tent by the Gate at 08.00. He is told he can give the "officer" a list of the farmers that require permits when he returns. In the evening the recently arrived Ben Pike and his friend Jamilla walk down to the North Gate with me. He has come to Jayyous as part of making a video about the

Separation Barrier. Jamilla (his interpreter) talks about her identity problems of being born in the Galilee, having Israeli papers, being a Christian who speaks Arabic, but the locals can tell she is not Palestinian. Add to all this that she is a liberal, liberated (western) woman and one can see the difficulty. Standing at the Gate, I say to her, "I wonder what I am doing here?"

Ben and I discuss the hydrology of the West Bank and construct a cross-section diagram which confirms my assumptions about the Western Aquifer and introduces me to the Coastal Aquifer, of which I was not aware (See Chapter 3 above). The Coastal Aquifer appears to be polluted by sewage from above and by the penetration of salt water (seawater), which extends inland as the water pressure is reduced by pumping the fresh water from the rock.

Monday 1st December

Charles is in Jerusalem, Rex has gone to Ramallah this morning, Lionel has gone south to meet a friend and Susan is off in Azzoun. Sam reports the tent is still at the North Gate. I start to gather the information and rough out ideas for my Journal Letter on the water situation for EAPPI to distribute in the U.K. Sam and I decide not to cook tonight, the state of the kitchen making it rather problematic. Despite the builders working in the kitchen and grazing through our tea and biscuits, fruit (mostly gifts), nuts and pitta breads, and the inability to advance the communications situation due to the dust, this has been a useful day, responding to the situation if not achieving any of our objectives. I air my sleeping bag in the sun, which also dries my washing quickly.

It has not taken many weeks to settle into a new pattern of life here in Jayyous. I am up between 05.30 and 06.00 most days ready to go to the Gate. There is usually light in the sky as I leave the house. The sun rises after arriving at the Gates, the shorter journey to the South Gate is completed as the sun shines on the south side of the Jayyous ridge, while the longer journey to the North Gate is also completed before the direct sun light arrives, being on the north side of the hill. I return to the house for a morning of washing or writing or transferring pictures to the computer and editing them.

At midday it is time to go to gate duty again, returning to the house for lunch if not taken earlier, further writing, reading and possibly a nap. By 15.30 it is time to go to the afternoon gate watch. Every third day I cook the evening meal which is sometimes delayed by one of the team being late back form the North Gate if the farmers have been kept waiting. With the sun setting about 18.00 the evenings are mostly spent in the house, often with visitors from the villages coming to talk to us.

It is a quiet and rather simple life, strangely and surprisingly detached from many cares of the world. I am living out of a rucksack and some hand luggage. The food I eat is purchased fresh each day. The clothes I wear do not need washing so often as at home. There is no radio or television for us to hear and see. Despite being at the centre of the storm, it seems relatively calm.

Chapter 5
The Rain Comes
Week 3

Tuesday 2nd December

sabaaH al-khayr - Good Morning

The flap of tin, the squeak of nail,
The whip of cable, the bend of post,
The crack of plastic sheet, the tear of rope,
Attempt to silence the cockerel's, sabaaH al-khayr.

Winter's wind is here,
Joy of late summer soon gone,
Rain is welcomed, with kissed fingers to the sky,
and the cockerel sings sabaaH al-khayr.

Things are breaking up around here,
Discussion has now joined the deaf,
A spreading arbitrariness, "I'll do this",
Just like the cockerel's sabaaH al-khayr,

So, they go to the fields today, un-discussed,
The weather could be better,
The time will always be good for watching,
Will I hear the cockerel's sabaaH al-khayr?

The fields will still be there,
There are plenty more days,
The choice is mine to make for the best,
It's always early with the cockerel's sabaaH al-khayr.

"To pass without let or hindrance",
Her Majesty's injunction is ignored,
These fields are closed; they are a military zone,
I will just listen to the cockerel's sabaaH al-Khayr.

For the first time, the cockerel's daily greeting is nearly overwhelmed, as is the call to prayer. Lightening, thunder and rain have arrived, along with the self-righteousness of a man who did his washing yesterday. Well timed or did I realise from the sky that rain would soon be here? The annual rainfall is about 700mm. The rain is restricted to the winter months although its arrival this year has been rather late, as it normally comes in November and continues until early February. The seasons change rapidly. With the rain comes a sudden drop in temperature. While it still seems hot (25°C) in the direct sun, the shade temperature can be as low as 5°C.

Sam insists on doing the North Gate this morning so I can even have another slow start waiting for the builders to arrive. I hope the rain eases for midday duty; it feels as if it is here to stay, Dartmoor style! The builders continue to make chaos and walk in a lot of wet, cemented dirt.

Picture 10. The Bedouin Family wait to come through the South Gate on the way to school in Jayyous. The mother will spend the morning in the village to be on the same side of the Barrier as her children all day.

Charles returns with some Church of Scotland people bearing gifts for the Jayyous nursery school, including a large Thomas the Tank Engine, a well meant, but rather inappropriate gift from a different culture. The work on the kitchen is going well. I feel better for an easy day and doing some sorting and working my way out of the doldrums with a few simple (office) systems. Work is in progress on Journal letter and I need to think about something for the Devon Religious Education website, possibly about children going to school.

Wednesday 3rd December

At the South Gate, the jeep arrives late and the Bedouin girl is late to school. I go to the North Gate for the midday duty, but the Gate is not opened, as there are no 'customers'. Work on kitchen is going well. At the North Gate in the afternoon, the soldier is concerned about photographs being taken, but he does not confiscate the camera. Despite this incident, it has been an uneventful day.

Abdul-Latif came to talk in the evening. "If you have $100 and someone takes $30 will you accept $70 back? Later you are offered $50 and even later $25 with a $5 administrative charge to sort it out. Is that acceptable? He relates these figures to the way Israel has been cutting down the land area of Palestine in 1948, and by building settlements since 1967 (See Fig 6 over). He asks, "How can we overcome the difficulties of rebuilding the society after the end of the occupation, being aware of the social damage it has caused?" Unlike France in the 1939-45 War, Palestine has been occupied for nearly two generations.

Abdul-Latif's concern focuses on social changes. For example, due to unemployment, many young men do not have enough money to marry and so a growing number of women between 19-25 are unmarried. In Jayyous, there have been only fifty weddings in three years, instead of the usual one hundred and fifty. Therefore, there is the potential for 'intifada spinsters', as when men marry, even though they are older, their brides will be selected from the youngest women.

There is possibly some confusion here over what would be the changes in society caused by the passage of time. All societies

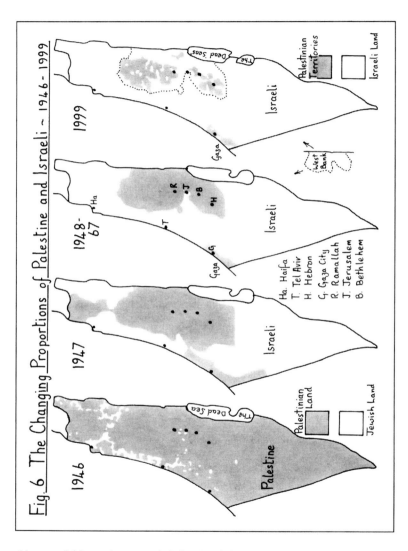

Fig. 6 The Changing Proportions of Palestine and Israeli ~ 1946 - 1999

Maps compiled from various sources including Qumsiyeh, M Sharing the Land of Canaan p 33.

change, but possibly Muslim societies have not changed as much as many in the twentieth century. Societies cannot be protected from change. Changes of attitude have occurred; socialist Israel has become just another capitalist state, part of globalisation, with the de-mutualisation of the Kibbutz, decline in co-operation, just like the rest of the world with the growth of the free market and even the privatisation of torture. It is hard to balance the world of the bottom line with the overriding issues of human rights that are being threatened by the above: no one must get in the way, the certainty of the right way, the only way, the chosen people, world capitalism: and that is not to mention the social impact of these changes.

Jayyous is not detached from the world. Ours is one of the few houses that does not have a satellite dish for receiving global television and some are able to connect to the Internet. These people are aware of what is happening elsewhere. It is rather like the influence of the western media in Eastern Europe before the fall of the Iron Curtain. The role of the media in shaping and changing society and culture has never been more significant.

Abdul-Latif adds, "How can we make agreements for tomorrow, with Sharif Omar thinking he had agreement about list of the names of those needing passes to give to the officer? As so often seems to happen, the arrangement made on the Gate several days ago has collapsed. On a larger scale, how can Palestinian and Israeli leaders make agreement? If you are going in the wrong direction you stop and go back to find the right road and check the map and sort out the right road." *Perhaps the intended destinations are not the same. What does the phrase, "We want peace," actually mean?*

Any attempt to bring a settlement (an agreement, not a housing development)[1] or make peace seems to be predicated on the two communities following very different roads. I believe the Palestinians have tried to get the best out of the situation, arguing that Israel must observe international law with regard to its borders and the occupation. However, the Israelis seem to have two motives and desires, one for peace and security today and another for the Greater (Eretz) Israel tomorrow. (Eretz Israel is the concept of an Israeli state stretching from the Mediterranean to the Euphrates in Iraq as depicted in the blue lines on the Israeli flag and the maps on the back of some small value coins.) Evidence for this dates back to the beginning of the State, when it appeared there were two agendas, one to create the State of Israel and another to enlarge it as soon as possible in contravention of UN Resolution 181 setting out the basis for the establishment of that State. The Partition plan contained in the resolution was agreed by most Israelis, but was rejected by extreme groups and individuals. The Israeli Declaration of Independence, proclaimed on 14th May 1948, pledged the state would be based on the principles of liberty, justice and peace with full social and political equality, and that it would loyally uphold the principles of the UN Charter. The Declaration specifically promised equal rights to the Arab inhabitants of the State of Israel, and extended the hand of peace to all the neighbouring Arab states. However, Ben-Gurion, one of the 'founding fathers' of Israel, "… strongly expressed [a] preference, not to indicate the boundaries of the new state in the independence declaration, in order to leave open the possibility of expansion beyond the UN designated borders." Menachem Begin, of Irgun[2] advocated the historic borders of Eretz Israel should be followed. Ben-Gurion said, "The Choice was between a democratic state of Israel in part of the land and a Jewish state over the whole land and the expulsion of its Arab inhabitants".[3] This tension between these two concepts of Israel has left us with the situation today with neither Israel in her UN borders or Eretz Israel; and there are still Israelis, and other powerful groups especially in the U.S., pulling in both directions.

It is pertinent to note the U.S. Declaration of Independence does not say anything about the country's borders, which has allowed it to grow unhindered from the original thirteen states. It may be interesting to note the Declaration of Human Rights, which came into being on the 10th December 1948, is not as old as the State of Israel. Also that the State of Israel was admitted to the United Nations in 1949 with the *clear proviso that Palestinian refugees would be allowed to return to their homeland or be fully compensated for their lost property.*[4] *This has not come about.*

Thursday 4th December

Having been to the South Gate, I go to Azzoun to pay the phone bill. I am offered tea in two shops but only take it in one. I find fresh feta type cheese, floating in brine, so I buy some along with some packets of soup not found in Jayyous. I travel to Azzoun by 'service', paying 1.5 New Israeli Shekels (NIS) about £0.20 with several other people in a minibus. I pay five Shekels on the return journey, passing the money forward in the old yellow German 8 seater taxi. On arrival in Jayyous the driver realises I paid too much and refunds 3.5 NIS. There is honour all round; I did not ask and he made a refund. However this honourable transaction is carried out in the Occupier's currency. One has to be careful not to use the small value Israeli coins, which carry a map of Eretz (Greater) Israel on them and are often rejected by Palestinians. This effectively makes the lowest value coin a much higher value than in most currencies.

I return to the house to clean the bathroom, removing the walked-in cement and the worst of the dust. If there is one thing of which to be certain, builders are the same the world over; they always take longer than expected.

Friday 5th December

In the morning, a young man returns home to the village from an Israeli prison with lots of people on the streets giving him a very noisy greeting. There is a wedding in the village and a quiet duty at the South Gate. The building work is becoming an annoying distraction, partly as it is limiting the availability of the computers due to the level of dust. It also means someone is tied to the house while the builders are working. Charles kindly agrees that I can gain access to e-mail using his computer. He also agrees to the Gate Reports being compiled on his machine. I devise tables for the collection and presentation of this information, which will come from the observations made by the four of us and the two members of the ISM team in Jayyous. The news of an impending return to Jerusalem for further meetings is not good, but I get good support from my colleagues to use the visit to take time off and have a rest. They say I have been working too hard, so this is good advice. I plan to spend some time in Israel proper. Not a bad day.

> *The information technology problems seem to have taken an inordinate amount of time and energy over the last few weeks. It is rather ironic that my colleague's computer problems were solved by Abdul-Latif. He has spent many hours establishing the Internet connection and as a tutor on how to make best use of Microsoft machines. So much for western aid! The Apple seems to be a better tool, especially for handling digital pictures, and it has the charming benefit that it is warm when running which is comforting for my hands in the cold room. I believe it also keeps me sane at times, especially as I selected eight pieces of music to listen to, which is as near as I shall ever get to selecting my 'Desert Island Discs'.*[5]

Chapter 6
Israeli Visitors
Weeks 3-4

"We have to ask searching questions about the meaning of peace, the realities of human nature, the essence of justice [and] the right ordering of society."   Adam Curle[1]

Saturday 6th December

This is a day of mixtures - sunny, raining, cold, warm, high spots and drudgery, the interesting and the tedious. I have no early Gate duty, which makes for a slow start. I spend time writing up a backlog of gate reports from last week when the computers were hidden away from the dust. We talk more over breakfast about plans for Jerusalem next weekend.

At 09.35, Sharif Omar calls to say the meeting at the Baladiya, the town hall, will start at 10.00. This is to welcome a party of Israeli students on tour, organised by the Peres Peace Group in Israel to learn about the Separation Barrier around Jayyous. We know these will be secular or reformed Jews by the day of their visit. Charles and I quickly go to the Town Hall to help make posters. We listen to the information provided by Mr Casper from United Nations Office for the Co-ordination of Humanitarian Aid, and join the party in the bus down to the Gate. There is a tricky bit of driving over the rough track, with a very smart new minibus. We arrive at the North Gate in time for the midday opening, which is much delayed by an invasion of Israeli students and a camera crew going right up to the Gate.

The soldiers are rather confused to see Israelis coming from the Palestinian side of the Separation Barrier and call up a second jeep, so there are soon four men on the ground. Eventually they clear the apron of everybody including those wishing to cross. I encourage the visiting Israelis to move away from the Gate as they are delaying the people who wish to go to work and say that the soldiers need their show of power. They respond that so many people will have frighten the soldiers. *(I wonder if I am accompanying the clearly jumpy soldiers at this time.)* I talk with Israeli students and some agree the wall is in the wrong place. Others are interested in our work, wanting to know about the WCC/EAPPI website,[2] and are clear on the need for peace, but worried about how it might be achieved. Others are rather more defensive. Some will be going on national service during the next weeks, patrolling the Separation Barrier around Jerusalem. It is good to talk and to listen. More importantly, there is a lot of talking between the Palestinians and the Israelis. Sharif Omar is on very good form, not missing the opportunity to make many excellent points. We return to the village in the bus, before the visitors go on to Qalqilya.

Picture 11. Israeli visitors, Palestinians, a film crew and soldiers at the North Gate.

During the afternoon, I check over Rex's article for the Journal Letters. I sort the pictures from lunchtime and make a new CD ready for going to Jerusalem. In the afternoon, I attend at the North Gate with Charles, which is the wettest yet. I am glad to have my red waterproof jacket, and once again thank "Moorland Rambler" in Exeter for being able to supply my colour choice in the right size: apparently red is not in fashion this year, so much for free market choice. The Gate opens late and one man is held for a long time, so I contact HaMoked, the human rights group, who are able to help. I walk up the hill in the rain having declined a lift on a rather dodgy looking tractor.

A good day all round; a little interest and some excitement does one good.

Information from the meeting to welcome Israeli Students

This morning's presentation included the following information from Mr Casper of the United Nations Office for the Co-ordination of Humanitarian Aid (UNOCHA).[3] The information comes from the UNOCHA's Monitoring and Assessment of the human consequences of the wall. It has reported to the UN General Assembly and the Security Council.

The main instruments of the occupation are Israeli policies of closures, curfews, house demolitions[4] and the Separation Barrier.[5] The closures stop movement in and out of the West Bank and make it difficult to move around within the Palestinian Territories, as the Israelis often call the West Bank. The Israelis enforce curfews on the Palestinian population especially in cities like Nablus whenever they feel there is a threat to their ability to control the situation. The Israelis also persist in their policy of removing houses which have no planning permission or are seen as a security risk, including those in the way of the Separation Barrier and too close to Israeli settlements. A thousand homes have been demolished since 2000 at over 30 per month, but since January 2003, this has gone up to 74 per month. This is a major issue in a society which not only has a growing population but also the tradition that a husband must build a house for his bride. The Separation Barrier in late 2003 extended from Jenin in the north to just south of Qalqilya, with other relatively small sections around Jerusalem and Bethlehem. The map in Figure 5, on page 47, shows the route of the Barrier around the West Bank.

There are 73 checkpoints, 34 road gates, 58 ditches, 33 wall gates (like those in Jayyous), 95 concrete block barriers and 464 earth mounds mostly blocking minor roads. In the period March to June 2003, there were 1400 access incidents (Palestinians being held at checkpoints for extended periods) and 300 cases of access denied at checkpoints. This does not include those who do not have the correct papers to allow them access. When permits are issued for access to the land owned by Palestinians, it is made clear that this does not indicate a right to the property. People in the villages trapped between the Separation Barrier and the UN Green Line need a permit to live in their own homes.

The UN recognises the Israeli right to defend itself, and says it has the right to build the Separation Barrier, but that it should be built on Israeli land, i.e. on the Israeli side of the UN Green Line, the pre-1967 border. The present Separation Barrier becomes a violation of international law simply by following the wrong route. In an attempt to ameliorate the situation the UN also says the Gates in Jayyous should be open for a minimum of three, one-hour periods per day.

The Israeli Occupation has done much to increase poverty in the Palestinian West Bank. The index of impoverishment has increased from 21% in September 2000 to 60% in the same month in 2003, when unemployment stood at 40%. In the same period the number of children passing grade four mathematics has dropped from 72% to 51%. Much of this has been the result of Israeli reaction to the second Intifada. If closures were lifted, it is suggested poverty would be reduced by 15 percent. Nine million kg of produce from Jayyous and 650,000 work opportunities (working hours) are lost per year due to the restrictions on access to the land in Jayyous and the inability to get produce to the markets in cities like Nablus.

At the end of the meeting, the comment was made on the effect of the occupation continuing from generation to generation. "You cannot get peace out of a gun." A man, whose child was killed asks, "What can I do for peace?" and Sharif Omar, who does not have a permit to go to his land says, "... but most of all we need the fellowship of the Israelis".

Sometime after returning home to the UK, I made contact with one of the Israeli students who visited the Jayyous Gate on this day. He said, when asked about how he felt about the day, "My thoughts were mixed, as I am against the wall

(Separation Barrier) for several reasons. I can't seem to believe the (Israeli) Government's "excuse" that it is an anti-terror wall. In Israel there are mixed feelings towards the wall, the left and the right are against it: the left for human rights reasons and the right since it fears it will detach the occupied territories from the 'full' (Eretz) Israel. I believe Israel should have a united front to fight the terror; though I believe that the wall would not fight it. I believe that the wall is illegal under international law, and think it should be dismantled, although from Israel there is a great belief that this helps to reduce terror acts."

At least these Israeli visitors cannot use the defence that 'they did not know' which arises in some Israelis, as they do not believe their country has put the Separation Barrier in Palestine. They think it is on the Green Line. Nuremberg established that ignorance was not a defence. However, even intellectuals like Günter Grass used the 'denial defence' of not knowing what had happened in the concentration camps when shown pictures of the death camps in 1945. "'You mean Germans did that?' We kept asking. 'Germans could never have done that.' 'Germans don't do that.'"[6]

Sunday 7th December

It is strange to arrive at the North Gate at 06.45 to find no one waiting. There is an eerie feeling. A jeep, seen from the lane, went by at 06.42 going south. The skies are grey after the over night storm. Coughing behind me tells me that someone is coming. A man arrives and tells me that fifteen years ago he spoke excellent English working in a Jordanian hotel after completing an accountancy course at university. He is on his way to pick oranges on land that may have no future for him. He is a nephew of Sharif Omar's. A donkey cart arrives with a sheet of plastic over the donkey as protection from the rain. The donkeys generally look well cared for even if they are hit with sticks to get them going. Sometimes they are prodded in places which should not be prodded, a reminder of the scene in the film of 'Lawrence of Arabia', when Jenkins's camel is suddenly made to run. The donkeys are in much better shape than the sheep (locally expressed as 'sheeps'). The sheep in the pen at the top of the hill are in a bad way, providing evidence of the comment that many are living on a very much-reduced diet due to the lack of fodder or freedom to move to grazing land the other side of the wall. *I wonder if the RSPCA would be interested in news about this, but it is rather a long way to send an inspector.*[7] At 07.15, a jeep arrives inside the fence, checking the culverts, and goes on its way. Many men have morning coughs, a combination of smoking and colds brought on by the rain and cold in recent days. Few of them have waterproofs. Some just wear heavy jackets that absorb the rain. This is fine if you have another jacket to change into. A tractor arrives at 07.30, and there is still no sign of the jeep.

The Gate is opened quickly at 07.40, but the processing is slow. The Gate is shut at 08.05. The yellow van is searched for 10 minutes by soldiers with their weapons cocked and aimed along the floor of the van. This happens while another soldier works through the stack of folded plastic trays and cardboard boxes. I ask one of the soldiers if they could find some wire to hold the inner gate shut, as the catch does not seem to work anymore. The design and functioning of the catch is a mystery that has been addressed a number of times in idle moments at the Gate. The solving of this problem is not helped by the fact that the gate has travelled about 300mm to the right, so leaving the latch post out of reach. The soldiers are getting worried about this as there is a good chance that the whole inner gate will go base over apex into the ditch, at the end of a long swing. I suspect the farmers are giving the gate an extra push each time it is opened so it meets the end of its travel with greater force. This act of resistance moves the hinge post and the concrete block in which it is set a little more each time.

At last the kitchen is finished and the house returns to a degree of normality. I assist Charles in a long morning's work cleaning and replacing kitchen equipment and furniture. This work is broken by a conversation with Peter, an environmentalist from the University of Southern California, who is especially critical of the way the Israelis do not care for their fragile environment. It is good to get a second opinion on my own growing perceptions on this matter.

The afternoon duty at the North Gate is busy. A Belgian TV crew and another from Abu Dhabi are filming. In the evening there is great excitement as first Abdul-Latif and then Sharif Omar, his wife and grandson arrive to inspect the new kitchen. They bring carpets and extra blankets for the bedroom floors. I show Sharif Omar's wife pictures in my album of my family and some of my traditional wooden chairs. She says how pretty Ann is. I wonder what she thinks about the new kitchen, having spent many years in this house bringing up her family using the old one.

> *The distractions of the kitchen, computer and communication problems have been getting me down more than I realised over the last week or so. I have even felt a little bored by the lack of involvement and progress. 'What am I doing here?' is a question I have asked myself on a number of occasions. However, this busy day made me feel things were back 'on the rails' again.*

Monday 8th December

This morning the sky is clear and the temperature low for the walk down to the Gate, setting out at 06.20. For the first time I warm two of the small round pitta breads on the gas ring and put them in my pockets, which keeps my hands warm until I have finished this 'breakfast on the move' walking down the lane. Going to the North Gate I begin to catch up with a man riding down on a donkey. Beyond this man is the state of Israel. How many Israelis will be going to work on a donkey this morning? In some ways Israel is a developing or third world country, especially in areas such as environmental management, but in others it is a highly developed, first world, country. Palestine, being occupied, does not truly fit any of the criteria for defining its place in the scale of development. Any economic indicators are distorted by the occupation, be it trade in agricultural products or access to health care.

At the Gate, the man riding the donkey joins a fellow with a donkey cart. This man wears a traditional, grey galliabia, a woolly hat and Wellington boots. His donkey cart is the standard variety for this part of the world, but has a reflective red triangle from some smart European car on the back. In all there are five farmers waiting when the Israeli army jeep, number 611056Y, arrives and the process of opening the Gate starts with the soldiers carefully looking around. This is not a 'good' number as this jeep often carries a group of 'hard guys'.

There are more people coming down the lane. Five minutes after opening seven farmers arrive on a trailer and, unusually, three more in a car, which is parked up the lane. There is another donkey cart, which carries one of my colleagues down the hill. He hoped to cross to the fields, but the farmer he was going to work with has not made contact, so he will not cross today. Just seven minutes after the opening begins he asks, "Do we protest about the early closure?" I say, "Let's see how things develop" and continue to see yet more traffic coming down the lane. They come in dribs and drabs. A pedestrian, who was most likely too late for a ride on a tractor, is followed by a donkey cart with several people on it and another donkey with a rider. Each arrives at the Gate and joins the queue, which is never more than about five or six people long, another tractor appears coming down to join those waiting.

Slowly the soldiers check the people going to their land. The passes say that they only allow access and are not an indication of ownership of the land which these people and earlier generations of their families have worked for many years. A regular fellow (I call him Big Boy) who has a large coat and fruit picking bag is, as always, searched by the soldier while he is watched by his colleagues, one by the Gate and another beside the jeep. All three soldiers have guns at the ready. There is a fourth soldier, the driver, in the jeep on the radio.

It is just after seven o'clock and nearly forty people have gone to the land, and we are still 'seeing how things develop'. The latest arrival is a tractor with eight people, including a woman and child in the trailer. Another donkey cart comes.

Momentarily, I catch sight of the sun on the fence, and the rock and earth moved to build it, as it goes over the hill to the north. It is strange how with light and colour this oppressive form can almost be transformed into a thing of beauty.

The jeep is being revved. It sounds as if it is has a problem idling, its engine being left running through each opening. At 07.10, another walker arrives. The last tractor in the queue starts-up and moves forward. The soldiers move down the apron in front of the Gate to close the inner gate. I move forward to say it is not yet time to close the Gate and there are more people coming, as I was told by the last man down the hill. My little lie (for I do not really know), that is repeated three times, becomes the truth as I hear a tractor and trailer roaring down the hill. As it gets closer, I see the driver is carrying a cardboard box in one hand, rather like a waiter with a tray. I wonder is it full of cream cakes. This is unlikely, but I have no chance to ask as he drives straight up to the Gate.

Another person comes running, this fellow shaking hands with the soldier and taking as much time as possible to keep the Gate open. Next comes a donkey cart with a woman driving. She is wearing a long velvet skirt with a mixture of rich brown, russet and yellow strips. She and her husband slow things down with some very poor "donkey driving" as the sound of another tractor speeding down the hill is heard. It takes the corner too fast and there is a roar as the trailer rolls over to about sixty degrees and stops against the stone wall. Will we be able to keep the Gate open for this one? Amazingly, the trailer, full of concrete blocks, is righted, watched by the smiling Israeli soldiers, the distraction allowing the tractor to reach the Gate at the limit of their patience and so get through.

One of the last men to arrive is turned back as he does not have the right papers with him. We can do little, as both accompaniers and Palestinians we have pushed our luck already. He was late and with the wrong papers. We exchange 'Shaloms' and 'Have a good days' with the soldiers, and as a thank you, I offer to close the inner gate rather than adding this task to the humiliation of the man who has been turned back. My pleasure of success is tainted by the knowledge that keeping the North Gate open for an exciting extra eight minutes, allowing over fifty people through has caused the South Gate to be opened late and the children of the Bedouin family to be late to school. The North Gate was shut at 07.28 so the South Gate will not be opened before 07.38 and school starts at 07.45.

I walk back up the hill into the rising sun, realising it is going to be another very hot day. Later in the day, the North Gate is closed, with people only being allowed back to the village at lunchtime. There has been a bomb. We are told that all gates, border crossing and checkpoints are closed. Will anybody get through tomorrow? Is the West Bank "closed", as we sometimes hear on the news at home? The evening Gate opening is much delayed. Supper is made for 10 New Israeli Shekels (£1.40). This is supplemented by other caterer's left over purchasing.

For me this morning was a good watch. However, what do I mean by this? It was good, from a journalistic standpoint, in that it had plenty of action to describe. However, it had some difficult parts to it. The Bedouin boys would probably be whacked with the teacher's cane for being late, something I held with total abhorrence when I was a teacher. By 'enjoying' ourselves 'seeing how things develop', we made the situation at the South Gate more difficult. There is always in the back of one's mind that the real issue here is not around the fifty plus people we have seen go to work today, but about the other 60% of the farmers that have no permit to go to their land. These people are invisible to us. What are they doing this cold and damp morning after the storm? Which of the men seen in the village during the day could be at work on his land if he had a pass? If the West Bank is closed, we may not be able to get out. I am free of the computer and house problems only to find I may be a prisoner in this land.

Was this a typical Gate Watch? There is no typical Gate Watch. There are many signs one can read about how it is going to be. I was just glad that I decided to record this one in detail, in both notes and pictures.

Tuesday 9th December

I start the day at the South Gate followed by a visit to the limestone pavement on the south ridge; the tulips are in good leaf, but no buds yet but there are lots of cyclamen leaves showing. I go back to the house for breakfast and then make a visit to the south side of the town ridge. There are excellent views of the Separation Barrier in the valley between the ridges. It is interesting to see how new houses are still being built on the western edge of the town ridge, close by the Barrier.

Picture 12 The Separation Barrier, the military road, the fence, the dirt road and the earthworks. This used to be an area covered in olive trees.

A planned meeting with a German Green Member of Parliament is cancelled, due to checkpoint and closure problems. I go back to the house for a quick lunch and straight to the North Gate. I record a long story from Abu Fareed, a teacher in Kafr Jamal, during the long wait. I give up waiting to walk to the Baladiya for a meeting. The Gate is eventually opened at 15.20, nearly three hours after the 12.30 advertised opening time, just as our meeting with the Mayor and the Save the Children Fund team is ending.

Abu Fareed's Story

He has 500 dunums of land. (There are four dunums to the acre. A modern metric dunum is 1000 square metres, but the unit is based on an old Ottoman measure, being forty paces in length and breadth. Paces were rather longer in those days. A football pitch would be about ten dunums in size.) His land is on the other side of the fence, which he used to visit every day after returning from school teaching in a neighbouring village and spending time with his family. Now he has to leave school early to get to the Gate in time to go through to his land at the midday opening. He cannot take his family, as his wife does not have a permit. His oldest son is 18 years old and going to University. He has four boys and two girls, the youngest being 1 year and 3 months.

He says the 'internationals' "Make something good for the Palestinians. In Europe, people understand the situation for the Palestinians. We have lost our paradise. They, the Israelis, have shut the door on our paradise. What is the effect on the young people who see their parents letting go of their land? What are they feeling? We don't know how many years they shut the door. It is killing our dream, our land, our trees and our 'stones'.[8] What can we say? What about the children? Life is OK in the sun, but what will they think of the 'Jewish'. Can we be surprised if he make a bomb on his body?"

He has crops of clementinas, guava, lemons and over 1000 olive trees, too many to harvest on his own. He was born on the land. His father died in 1994. He moved to Jayyous at the time of his marriage, just at the start of the building of the Israeli settlement of Zufin. He tells me the following story.

On the 18th of February 1984 his father's house was searched by the Israeli Police and he was asked to put his thumb to a piece of paper to say they had found nothing. He is suspicious that the piece of paper is to do with letting his land go so he refuses to sign. He has held this land under Ottoman, British, Jordanian and now Israeli law and he will not leave. He was handcuffed and the skin on his hands is torn. He had a gun put to his head. They kept trying to get the thumbprint for the piece of paper. When he put his thumb inside his fingers the policemen broke his fingers trying to get the thumb out. They took him out of the house into his land to kill him. They pushed his Kafia (scarf) into his mouth and again put a gun to his head. This is a man described by his son as being 'ill of the heart'.

A Bedouin dog started barking and chased off the policemen. Still with the handcuffs on, he got on his donkey, his clothes dirty with blood and rode to his son's house in Jayyous. When Abu Fareed opened the door of the house he 'lost his mind' with anger at what he saw. They took him to the doctor in Qalqilya and where his wounds were treated and to the police station to get the handcuffs removed. He was told to go home. They went to the police in Nablus and again were told to go away. They then went to the senior policeman for the West Bank, a Christian. He took pictures for a lawyer and removed the handcuffs. When he telephoned the other police stations, they knew nothing about the incident. After three months, the police sent a message to say the handcuffs had been lost from the police station and that the case was closed.

Abu Fareed's brother had lost his sight under British rule due to an incident with a piece of unexploded ordnance. I thank Abu Fareed for his story and feel bad about breaking my unwritten code of accompaniment that you stick with a situation to the end. He waits another 2 hours for the gate to open.

Zufin, which has been established on land expropriated from the village in 1993, became an Israeli settlement with about 1600 dwellings, mostly large family houses. It is attractive for people working in Tel Aviv being only 45 minutes drive away. There will soon be an option of travelling by train from Rana'ana, just 10 minutes away by car or bus and 20 minutes on the train to Tel Aviv. In 2004, the construction of a new settlement of "Nofei Zufim" ("North Zufin") started on the western part of Jayyous lands. It lies three kilometers to the north of Zufin settlement.

Why did the Israelis build this settlement on some of the best farmland in Israel-Palestine?

Just before the meeting with the visitors from the Save the Children Fund, we spoke with a group from Sweden. Charles had spoken with ICRC at the South Gate about the delivery of plastic sheet for the leaking roof on the Bedouin house and about the drinking water problems that will become an issue in about a week. We also heard today about the voting at the UN General Assembly where Great Britain and Germany side with Israel and the United States in voting over the presentation of the Palestinian Case on the legality of the Separation Barrier to the International Court of Justice in The Hague. I speak to my wife Ann in the U.K. to get more information on this.

A depressing day with the effects of the occupation, both now and in the past, close at hand. I do not attempt to defend the position of the British Government.

Wednesday 10th December

I go to the South Gate for early watch, sitting on my favourite stone, six rocks from the end of the wall.

I finish reading "Discernment".[9] I had found the early pages of this very illustrative of what has happened to me over recent years. It is a wonder to me how the Quaker spirit assimilated itself into my character as a youngster without truly understanding what was happening. This set up tensions, which I have always found it difficult to put a finger on, in both professional and private life. It is only now that I have allowed myself to get in touch with the things that are important to me and so begin to grow through the recognition of experience.

However, some of this feeling of clearness is in the balance as relationships within the Jayyous team are rather difficult. This especially relates to the degree of solemnity, of weight, of value given to each other's stories. There is little listening in depth to the experiences of each other. There is a sense of competition developing about telling the most terrible, the most worrying and, at times, the goriest story. This competition just makes me close down, to internalise a lot of what I see and hear. This may make me a less valuable member of the group in terms of collective evidence, but does make me feel less like a piece of 'blotting paper', just soaking up other people's anger. It seems to devalue the simple approach as set out in the five objectives (see 29th November), of offering protection by presence, which seems to be the most applicable to the situation in Jayyous. It also denies the value of silence.

I am still looking for the 'research question'. Is this part of what I should be doing here? On the other hand, should I be rushing off to other places to see a little of many things. It is my style to stay here, accompany these people, and do whatever emerges from being here. This internal dialogue, both personal and practical within the situation, seems to the only way forward at this point. Something will develop as a focus out of the experience. I think back to the research I did for my masters, where I collected the stories of the adult students I taught before the study formed itself around the information gathered. I need to affirm this is part of me and part of what I bring to this situation.[10]

Two watches at North Gate today, at lunchtime meeting Charles returning from the land, and a long, cold and dark watch, as the evening opening is delayed by over an hour. Farmers used to sleep on their land overnight but this is now prohibited, on the threat of arrest. Abdul-Latif visits to discuss his proposed research project on Jayyous. There is a strong temptation to get involved with this but my ability to help is most likely over-estimated. Although it is a very attractive idea, I doubt if it is for me. It should really be a task for a Palestinian and indeed a Palestinian woman, who would be truly able to get inside the situation and culture. I make my apologies and take an early night, as I am feeling very tired. I start reading "The Remains of the Day", which is about a man immersed in the life of an English country house.

Chapter 7
A Visit to Israel
Week 4

Thursday 11th December

We meet at the Church of the Domitation in Jerusalem, with about half the clergy who signed the original statement by the Heads of Churches in Jerusalem, which brought about the setting up of the Ecumenical Accompaniment Programme in Palestine/Israel. The Armenian Patriarch Torkom the 2nd, the Armenian Apostolic Orthodox Patriarch of Jerusalem; Patriarch Michel Sabbah the Latin Patriarch of Jerusalem; Michael Sellers, an Anglican; Anha Abraham, Coptic Orthodox Archbishop of Jerusalem and Archimandrita Mtanious Haddad, Greek Catholic Patriarchal Exarch, Jerusalem. There is also the Franciscan, the Reverend Alberto Prodomo, who supervises the Status Quo of the Church of the Holy Sepulchre

It is a very interesting meeting, in which we hear about the work of other teams. It is also interesting getting responses from the above delegates and watching the group dynamics. The good humoured, jovial Anglican politely softened the differences, while the Latin Patriarch seemed rather too justificatory. Best line of the session came from the Armenian who, commenting on the wall painting of the Last Supper at one end of the room, says, "We can agree it happened somewhere close to here". This is followed by his saying "There is a need to move towards reconciliation on the way to peace". John Aves, an Anglican EA from Norwich, serves the tea. Later we also attend a session with Bishop Yunoun, who says, "You have come to speak the truth to the rest of the world. You are the eyes, ears, and nose of the Palestinians."

I find I am not too happy about the first part of this statement, "the truth". What is the truth? I do not know the truth about the situation just because I am here. I can tell people what I have seen. This may be the truth at the level of sound

information. It may be the facts about what happened during a particular incident as seen and recorded by me. I am in the 'provisional wing' about truth. Evidence is the truth until we find something better. This may seem a rather scientific approach for someone conducting "fuzzy" research, but it comes from the need to question certainties. The Holy Land is full of 'contradictory certainties'; certainties of the right to the land, certainties of the right to security, certainties of faith. I am closer to the Gänseliesel (Goose girl) fountain in Gottingen that is inscribed, "They are here not to worship what is known, but to question it."[1]

I can sit more comfortably with the second part. To report what we see, hear and indeed smell; the role of the "rapporteur" seems to fit exactly with what I am doing. However, even such reports need to be covered by the caveat that this is only my interpretation of what I have seen and heard. This is especially so as I am working in a relatively narrow area and have little chance of using some of the traditional checks and balances, such as triangulation of cases, to confirm my findings in the single case. On returning home my talks will have to carry a warning to that effect, perhaps by just saying how long I spent in Jayyous compared to my time in Israel. There is a difference between being a 'rapporteur' and an advocate, as it is suggested we should be. The latter suggests the building of a case, possibly of being selective with, or selecting from the evidence to support a cause. The reader must decide which path I am following in this task of writing up my witness and adding a reflective commentary.

The comments go on; "You are speaking for those who are alone. (*I have no problem with that.*) We are not anti-Semitic (*...or that*). We are pro-peace and reconciliation. (... *Agreed.*) We need to liberate Israelis from the arrogance of the occupation. (...*Agreed.*) There is no hope in changing USA so we must change Israel. 'The Wall' is a symptom, the occupation the problem. It is an Insecurity Wall." (... *Agreed.*) It is interesting to hear the Palestinian Bishops have approached Sharon for a 'ceasefire'.

In my mind this is all set against the words of Abu Rashid ringing in my ears from the two days ago, "... demolishing the trees and stealing the water is terrorism... demolishing the 'stones'... history, culture and environment. There can be no peace with the wall."[2]

It is good to have the pattern of activities for the next seven weeks sorted out at last, in various administrative meetings. The major undertakings for me, away from Jayyous, are; A visit to Ramallah Friends Meeting with Julia on the 28th December and going on to Jerusalem for the 29th. There is a group Retreat in Galilee, which we are obliged to attend, on the 9th to 11th January and a debriefing on the 4th to 6th February. This means that the 91 days of our stay are effectively reduced to 69 days, which makes just 75% of our time actually accompanying. Add to this that some EAs seem to spend a lot of time away from their designated locations visiting other EAs in a form of "ecumenical tourism", and I wonder about our focus on the task in hand. There seems to be a tension between the needs of the EAs and the needs of those being accompanied.

Friday 12th December

We walk to the ultra-orthodox Jewish area of Mea Shearim. There is a very sudden change of atmosphere by crossing an intersection and passing a sign about dress and behaviour. These roads are closed on the Shabbat. The people wear dark clothes. The children are miniature adults in black hats and long coats; the women wear hats, wigs or scarves. Most of the men study, while the women work. Some live on grants from religious groups or individuals, mostly in the U.S.A. *(Does this work like a medieval penance, buying favours with God?)* These people often do not support the secular State of Israel as it is seen as unholy. Their banners across the street say, among other things, "Israel will only be possible when G-d/Messiah makes it so." For them Israel is not a secular creation determined by the political decisions since 1947.

Picture 13. An Ultra-Orthodox Banner in Mea Shearim.

We continue south to Jaffa Street and to Ben Yehuda Street and Zion Square. Ben Yehuda was the founder of Modern Hebrew. He devised new words, based on the old texts, to cover such things as electricity. This is much opposed by the ultra-orthodox as being unholy. There are many problems for the Israeli State with such a fragmented society, with the orthodox pulling strings of control in many aspects of this modern secular society, for example marriage.

We walk on to the Jewish Quarter of the Old City including the new Jewish part of the Suq, with the ruins of the Roman Cardo on view; and we become tourists again. This Suq, hung with Israeli flags, is almost empty compared with the busy alleyways to the north of David Street in the Arab Suq Khan Ez-zeit, where there is the essence of day-to-day needs with everything from beans to baby-wipes, among a great mixture of people. The Israeli Suq is for rich tourists interested in Jewish symbols and arts and crafts. There is also the large golden Menorah intended for the new temple when it is built, that is presently housed in a glass display case. We continue on our way walking through what was the Moroccan Quarter. This was an area of Palestinian Arab houses until they were destroyed in June 1967 to allow better access to the Western Wall after the Israeli Army had taken control of East Jerusalem.

The Wailing or Western Wall is closest to the Holy of Holies with stones that date back to 30BC and the time of Herod. The wall is against the Temple Mount with the Dome of the Rock mosque and Al Haram Al Sharif stretching back from the top of the Wall. The vertical, the Wall, is Jewish; the horizontal, the ground above, is Islamic. The Western Wall can only be approached after passing through that modern element of life, airport style security.

As I am now a 'tourist', I fulfil the role by walking back through the Arab Suq and purchasing a shawl for Ann. I also find a shop selling galliabias in David Street, just down from the Jaffa Gate. The charming shopkeeper says he has them in my size. Despite the Christmas music, from St Michael's Book Shop by the Jaffa Gate, and the decorations in the Hotel (which seem to serve severally for Eid, Christmas and Hanukkah), even with the proximity of the holy places, it feels strangely unlike Christmas, but then I am never one to start the celebrations too early.

Picture 14 David Street in Jerusalem, looking up form the Christian Quarter Road.

Saturday 13th December

The Norwegians use a song from their children's television in the collective worship at the start of our meeting. It includes references to standing up for people's rights, freedoms and global awareness.[3] This is followed by a presentation from Jamal Juma' of PENGON, The Palestinian Environmental Non-Governmental Organisations Network, which runs the Stop the Wall Campaign.[4] "Where are they building the wall? Why are they building the wall? Conquest and Annexation: conquest with confiscation orders hung on olive trees and a week later the Caterpillar[5] bulldozers moving in to clear the way to the Promised Land; annexation through settlements, and controlling agricultural land and water. Building the Wall to divide the people; Ghettoisation."

"Annexation of the land and water includes 16,000 dunums (4,000 acres) just for the 145 km of wall up to November 2003 since the military order to commence construction on the 2nd Oct 2002. Already 100,000 olive trees have been destroyed, some over 500 years old. UNESCO is concerned about the loss of cultural Heritage.[6] Thirty-six ground water wells have been isolated. There are limits on the water that may be pumped for the Palestinians, and wells in the route of the Separation Barrier are destroyed, including 1.2 million US$ invested by the French Government in a well near Falamyeh. In Qalqilya, half of the 1200 shops are closed due to the loss of the Israeli customers. There is a destroyed generation, a destroyed culture. Adults have to live on and not show their tears. There is huge social pressure of passing on the culture from generation to generation. This is just the sort of social characteristics that is often called for in the West, good communities, and social order, so why destroy it here? It grows with the trees."

"Most Israelis don't know and don't want to know. The Oslo agreement (1993) is ignored by Israel. The number of settlements has doubled in the ten years 1993-2003 compared to the 27-year period 1967-1993. There are nearly a quarter of a million illegal Israeli settlers in the West Bank. How do the Palestinians see it?"

This presentation has been quite the best that I have heard in setting out the Palestinian position.

Leaving the New Imperial at 10.45, I walk to Zion Square on Jaffa Street, in Israeli West Jerusalem, and find a 'sharut' for Tel Aviv. I wait fifteen minutes for it to fill up, sitting in the hot sun, which is a comfort after the cool and dark interior of the hotel and the depressing notes made on Jamal's lecture. I arrive at the Tel Aviv bus station at 11.55 and leave for Haifa at 11.58 taking the last seat in a 'sharut', which is luckily standing next to where the minibus from Jerusalem sets me down. This rolls into Haifa at 13.20. I have selected this mode of travel, as, due to Orthodox influence, there are no buses or trains in Israel on Shabbat. I check out a cheap hotel in the lower part of Haifa and decide to walk up Mt Camel to the more expensive option with better views and a bath. As I walk up the hill, I find a corner shop that has bottles of water to quench my thirst. I go in and realise the language I hear is not Hebrew but Russian. This poorer part of town has been colonised by the latest wave of immigrants, attracted by a better life than in the collapsed former Soviet Union, and the offer of financial support in Israel. Israel welcomes them as part of its policy of increasing its population. I go out for an evening meal. Haifa after dark, on Shabbat, could be any modern European City. Sitting in the restaurant the only real difference is the ever-present security guard on the door.

Sunday 14th December

Early in the morning I walk along Mt Carmel's northern edge, above the gardens of the Bahá'í community and the Shrine of the Báb, which is protected by fences and security guards. There is of course a link here to Dr Kelly, the UK Government scientist who committed suicide[7] in the wake of the 'weapons of mass destruction' debate (debacle), who was a member of this religious group. These gardens are set out on the western slope of Mount Carmel, their formality making a great contrast to the city around them.

I walk down to the station and catch the late running 09.22 to

Akko. I spend three interesting hours walking around the old city, having found my way through the modern Israeli quarter by the station. The old town is history heaped on history. This is an interesting community, which could be a model for the one state solution, with Israeli and Palestinians living in close proximity. I return to Haifa and take the tunnelled funicular Metro to the top of Mt Carmel.

The radio on the station blares out, "We have got him". Saddam has been found in a dug out. He is subject to the humiliation of having his teeth inspected on global TV. While not as bad as things to come (Abu-grade), this treatment by a professional medical man is a disgrace and contrary to medical ethics and the spirit, if not the letter, of international law on prisoners of war. Is it not enough to say he has been captured and has been properly identified as being Saddam Hussein, or can we no longer believe information without the pictures? Each violation of international law reduces its hard-won validity. (Saddam is later hung at the time of the Muslim festival of Eid al-Adha, the Festival of Sacrifice in commemoration of Ibrahim's (Abraham's) willingness to sacrifice his son Ismael. Could this indicate revenge rather than justice, or at best a disregard of the religious sensitivities of others, so reducing the value of claims to moral justification? Indeed some commentators fall into the justification that Saddam himself used this festival for many of his executions. Surely, this reduces those ordering his execution to the same level as Saddam.)

Israeli Railways.

This topic may seem out of place here. However, read on. The train from Haifa to Akko arrives with old French, Alstrom-built, carriages behind a new red, blue and white diesel locomotive. The dark blue coaches have silver reflective coatings on the windows, which makes it impossible to see where the empty seats are from the outside. Indeed, it behaves like a mirror with all the people standing on the platform appearing to be in the train. The train is full of people in uniform: soldiers, air force and police. It takes me a while to find a seat that is not next to a gun. I return to Haifa in a set of 1960s ex-SNCF stainless steel 'firsts', which still carry the French inscription on the door about not going on the "voie" and a blue stripe above the windows to cover up the old yellow first class stripe. The position of the '1' numerals and the brackets for the European 'voiture' number and the destination boards are all still in place. For their age (about fifty years), the ride is excellent, but then they are only going at about half the design speed.

There is an interesting bit of track alignment to the south of Akko, through a tight S bend, with a heavy speed restriction to cross the River Na'aman at a right-angle, but I doubt if it mattered in the Ottoman days, when the journey from Istanbul to Cairo was measured in days rather than minutes. Yes, it was possible to travel from the one side of the Eastern Mediterranean to the other by train before the process of imperial collapse, fragmentation, and international and civil wars cut the route into pieces.[8] I suspect the rebirth of the Israeli Railways since 2000 means this is the best of the remaining sections of the old route that is well and truly cut further south in Gaza.

The modern Israeli railway has a lot of recent track replacement and many automatic level crossings. It appears the whole signalling system has been replaced with German coloured light signals displacing old British semaphore signals. Most lines seem to be signalled for bi-directional running with lots of crossings and loops, just like Germany. Some stations are being rebuilt, while others shown on the road atlas are closed. There is some old equipment around including small diesels of US origin, German railcars and diesel shunters and some wooden-bodied wagons and carriages that could date back to pre-1914 Ottoman times.

One of the problems with being an observer is that it becomes very difficult to stop observing, made even worse in this context by a life-time of train watching; but they say a change (of context) is as good as a rest. However, even railways have a moral dimension: their two great 'sins' being aiding and abetting the oppression and dispossession of indigenous people, as in North America, and the carrying of people to the gas chambers in Nazi Germany. While there is nothing so serious here - the network does not yet extend to the West Bank settlements - the trains are pulled by engines identical to a British Class 67. On this basis, perhaps I should boycott the use of the Royal Mail (my sometime employer). Why? The Israeli and British engines are both made by Bombardier, a Canadian company manufacturing in Spain and the British engines are used on the Royal Mail's Postal Trains that carry (at least before the end of 2005) my letters. Modern boycotts in a globalised world are rather more complicated than just simple boycotting of Caterpillar boots and clothing due to Israeli use of Caterpillar bulldozers, or South African tinned fruit back in the 1960s.

With old French coaches, new Danish diesel trains, German signals and UIC[9] standards, the railway is a little piece of Europe in the Middle East. Is that what Israel is trying to create? After all, it is in the Eurovision Song Contest. Or is it just a little piece of the USA, with the trains providing the context for a rampant display of the 'gun culture'? Or is Israel cleverly riding two horses at the same time; supported by levels of funding from the USA in international aid, some sources suggesting as much as 100 billion US$ since 1949?[10] The link with Europe is through the Preferential Trade Agreement, which must be one of the most questionable aspects of European policy.

Since 1975 and the Association Agreement between the European Commission and Israel there has always been a preferential trade agreement in place.[11] The Israeli economy is reliant on the E.U. as a major trade partner for both imports and exports. The agreement has clauses about Israel's respect for human rights and the origins of produce. While the European Union has similar agreements with other countries with questionable human rights, like Egypt, Syria and even Turkey,[12] the question of origin only arises here. The E.U. states it will not allow imports of goods made in Palestine ("the Occupied Territories") or in illegal Israeli settlements. This is difficult to enforce as such goods may be labelled as 'Made in Israel'. In February 2005, the British Revenue and

Custom service issued a notice to importers stating that proof of place of production must be included in all claims for preferential status and reduced duty. I wonder if British importers have a detailed knowledge of locations in Palestine and Israel and the possible use of three different languages, in three different scripts, let alone different spellings to describe them.

When I questioned a major supermarket about the labelling of organic peppers as being from Gaza in March 2005, I was assured they had been grown by Palestinian farmers. I have never seen such labels on the shelves again.

Monday 15th December

After a train from Haifa to Tel Aviv, I arrive at the Jaffa Street Bus Station in Jerusalem in the late morning.[13] My computer decides to be uncooperative during an unexpected security check to get through the modern shopping centre between the bus terminal and Jaffa Street. I am asked to open it. I hear it click off as I do this, the lid having been closed before it was properly shut down. This means it has been on 'sleep' over night, so the battery will be low. Having opened the lid and pressed the 'on' button, I actually switch it off, which is the last thing I want to do. In this noisy place I cannot hear the start up sounds, but eventually a quick flash of light on the screen is enough for the security guard, who then wants me out of the way as quickly as possible, while I try to replace things in my tightly packed bag.

The last few days seem to have highlighted the division in Israeli society, the non-orthodox (reform), the orthodox and ultra-orthodox. There is Hebrew (divided in itself), German, Russian and many other languages. There is a society of high incomes and people living on the charitable support as students of Judaism and new immigrants. There is high disposable income and poverty as shown by the back-street housing in Haifa and the expensive women's clothes and shoe shops just a few blocks away, near Paris Square; international expensive fashions which might seem rather exotic, or indeed erotic, and certainly too expensive for many in this society. There are some very modern buildings but also a lot of very run-down accommodation and empty shops. This is a uniformed society, of police, military, and security officers. However, the public transport staff are invisible, wearing no discernible uniform. Is it European or American, Developed/Developing? Whatever it is, it is suffering from the grind of keeping down a captive population in the occupied territories that appears to have worn down Israeli society and the economy.

Does Akko hold out some hope as a place where past and present, Muslim, Jew, Christian, and others can live together? However, Akko is in what was designated in 1947 as the third, northern part of the three-part Palestine that was taken over by Israel in 1948.

I go to the little cafe below the Hotel before the evening meeting, having not eaten since the big hotel breakfast in Haifa. Jamilla, whom I met two weeks before in Jayyous, walks by with a friend. She sees me in the cafe and they come in to join me in a cup of coffee. I tell her about some of the things I have been doing in the last couple of weeks. She reminds me that I had said, "I wonder what I am doing here?" when we met in Jayyous. She suggests I seem to be doing quite a lot.

At the meeting in the evening, various members of the team talk about their work in different locations to a group of interested listeners from the many communities in Jerusalem. Shabbat is described as the worse day of the week in Hebron and Yanoun. In Hebron this is when the Israeli settlers, especially the children, come out to torment the Palestinians with name calling and stone-throwing. We are told of the case, in Hebron, of the Palestinian girl who, going to the window to call her father to eat, was shot in the back. She still carries the bullet in her body, it being too close to her spine to be removed.

In Yanoun, the Jewish group called Ta'ayush (which means life in common) helped the villagers back into the valley after they left due to the aggressive settler behaviour towards them. Now the villagers, about 75 people, will only stay there if there is an international presence. One settler, called Victor, continues to be a threat, riding his quad bike into the village, kissing the ground and making a prayer to say, "It's our Land". At different times over the last year, the village water tank has been shot and so rendered useless and the electricity generator has been damaged beyond repair. Settlers, even children, walk through the Palestinian land with their large dogs, carrying their rifles. On occasions, they have danced on the roofs of the village houses in the light of their own searchlights. The settlement stands on the hill above the village, and runs a chicken enterprise. In Yanoun to survive is to resist.

I talk about the structure of land-holding and the way the Palestinians are loosing their one element of stability. Indeed the legal structure of that stability is allowing its downfall. The land holding which was recognised by Ottoman, British and Jordanian Law, is now being confiscated by resort to the Israeli laws and playing old laws off against the new. I also comment that I feel Israel is a society, like so many Western societies, that are now based on fear. Jeremy, from Rabbi's for Peace, picks up my point when I describe the impression I have gained of Israel being a frightened country with frightened people. He says, "... this, the fear, is the real issue, not the occupation."

Silence...

It is strange how the short, intense conversation in the cafe seems to be the beginning of a turning point in my perceptions of what I am doing. This, together with my visit to Israel, has provided a little space and detachment, a chance to 'play trains', a chance to see some history, a chance to see inside Israel and a chance to be more in touch with outside events, has offering me the opportunity to reflect on what is going on. The Greek Orthodox Monk has helped with his comment about "... doing something in the silence; without coercion; working with the spiritual, the practical, and the suffering of humanity."

It is sad to have come all this way to feel that I am doing something useful. I was very happy about being at this meeting.... despite my earlier misgivings of always seeming to be the representative from Jayyous and having to spend more time in Jerusalem. The inner tensions of the last ten days seem to be resolving themselves. The visit to Jerusalem and Israel has helped in this. Perhaps the resolution was only possible by getting away from Jayyous for a while. What is emerging? I seem have developed a 'modus operandi' and a degree of critical insight. I should follow the pattern of an ethnographic study of the situation in Jayyous. In this way, I can become more focused on the process while not seeing the final product, whatever that may be. I will follow the leadings, hopefully with a degree of discernment. The excellent presentation on the Saturday morning by Jamal Juma' has also focused my attention on the real issue and evidence, and ways of working to change the situation by recourse to legal means.

Part Two
The Evidence of Accompaniment

Chapter 8
Working On
Weeks 5-6

"There will be no peace if there is no justice."
Rigoberta Menchu Tum[1]

Tuesday 16th December

I return to Jayyous with fellow EAs Olava and Dorte from Norway. It is a very quick journey, possibly too quick. We leave the New Imperial Hotel at 07.50. The Israeli Police stop the departing minibus in Derakh Shekhem, the street outside the bus station. We change to another service and arrive at Qalandia by 08.15. We quickly find a rather dubious minibus taxi, one of the seats is supported by a concrete block, and the driver is in a hurry so we arrive in Jayyous by 09.45.

I take Olava and Dorte on a tour of the village and spend the rest of the day feeling increasingly poorly. Is this the old stopping problem, slow down and relax a bit and the bugs get in, or is it the hotel food? Having made the transition to Palestinian food without any problems, perhaps I was too casual in my approach to the variety of things available in the Haifa Hotel. Sharif Omar brings news that the South Gate is going to be permanently closed. He says there will be a demonstration on Friday.

Wednesday 17th December

I had a bad night so will be careful today, just writing up my journal and sorting papers, sleeping and eating rice.

Thursday 18th December

There has been big rain overnight, with thunder and lightening. I go to the South Gate early, in very strong and cold winds, with a touch of rain in the air. It is a grey morning, with a moon-like sun rising in low cloud. Grey, olive leaves (as opposed to olive green) and white houses almost make for a monochrome effect, at least a very limited colour range. My favourite rock is rather exposed, so I retreat a few metres for the "protection" of the third almond tree. I go to North Gate at lunchtime in very heavy rain. I talk about mince pies and Okehampton weather and scenery to Ann and Jan on the mobile phone while on the way down to the Gate. I finish my Journal Letter, which has been checked by Abdul-Latif, to make sure the water information is correct. He approves.

Friday 19th December

I wake early with the reconstruction of the Journal Letter on my mind, realising that its weakest point is the photograph. If the photo is changed, the title goes. If the title goes, the final paragraph goes. The other weak element is the lack of characters and names. Which is the best photo that relates to the land and includes a person or people? The answer has to be the picture of Sharif Omar at the Baladiya. If thanks are included to Abdul-Latif and the mayor's name is used, that makes three characters. If the photo title at the top does not mention that Sharif Omar does not have a permit, it will bring a sting in the tail. The new title, "Working in the Silence", will introduce the Orthodox Monk. The body of the text can stay the same. It will be longer, but will still fit two sides of A4; and all this before breakfast.

I have no early duty. Later in the morning, I look for the demonstration at the South Gate, but it has failed to materialise. I go to the North Gate at lunchtime, one farmer in, and one out and some heavy rain, so I quickly return home for a late lunch and some problems with printing Sam's photographs.

I go for a walk at the east end of the village to sort out my mind. The cyclamen are flowering well, having been out for several days. I will check South Gate area tomorrow for further flowers to photograph; thank goodness for the ever present company of the camera, with its touch of creativity. It just about keeps me sane. Another phone call to Ann is a comfort. For a while, I sit in the olive grove with the sound of a wedding in the background and take some more photos.

I walk on through the olive grove, passing a partly built house, and on to a track that leads out to the land to southeast of the village. Here the Separation Barrier twists its way around the head of a small valley, which comes down from the direction of the 'rubbish hill'. This is not made of rubbish from Jayyous, most of the village rubbish being collected in a Japanese-sponsored rubbish cart and taken to a Palestinian dump near the neighbouring town of Azzoun. This is a mountain of Israeli rubbish.

The dump is on land confiscated by the Israeli authorities in 1991. Shortly after this, the rubbish from nearby Israeli settlements, illegal under international law, started to be dumped on the land. No preparation work was carried out, and no control or recording of what was dumped has occurred. This "permanent point of pollution" has the potential to pollute both water and air, the former by infiltration of toxic liquids into the water-table (groundwater) below the dump and the latter due to the deep seated burning, giving off acrid fumes and toxic gases and particles, which affect Azzoun as well as Jayyous. This is an indicator of the lack of environmental care exercised by the Israeli authorities. They may have dumped this rubbish in the West Bank, but the pollutants do not know about Green Lines and Separation Barriers so will find their way back into Israel. Environmental issues are not high on the agenda of either Israel or Palestine, due to the distractions of the Occupation. However, it does suggest that the Israelis do not act in a responsible way that would be compatible with care for the Promised Land.

Back at the house, Rex's return from Nablus is a good distraction from Sam's printing problems. We hear from Rex that Mordecai Vanunu is to be released on the 21st March 2004 after 18 years in prison for knowing too much about the Israeli nuclear installations at Demona.[2] We also hear that Sharon has made a speech that seems to suggest giving away a few remote, militarily burdensome and internationally illegal Israeli settlements, while he proposes to annex more than half the West Bank. He seems to think this proposal is a fair deal.

The situation in Israel/Palestine is like a man holding a bee in his hand. The bee wants to get free so will sting. However, the man says while the bee is in my hand the rest of my body is protected. He could either crush the bee or let it go. The first might be seen as 'genocide' and the second a courageous act.

I suspect most Israelis would see letting the bee go, removing the restrictions and the occupation from the Palestinians, as a reckless act. Recklessness often suggests a lack of awareness of the danger, but here it may be reversed as being an over awareness of the danger. Courage would be based on an awareness of the potential opportunity for peace and the empowerment of the people of peace in both communities. The reckless disregard of the opportunity reduces the chances of peace.

Saturday 20th December

It is very cold in the morning; indeed the house is colder than outside once the sun is up. I go to the South Gate, where there is good light over Tel Aviv that includes a rainbow. The Bedouin family are concerned about something, wishing to phone HaMoked but it is too early. I feel very cold after breakfast but soon warm up working on e-mails. When the computer work is complete in the relatively cold indoors, I go out to enjoy the warmth of the sun to make a sketch of our home in Jayyous Bait Abu Azzam, Sharif Omar's old house.

After lunch, I go for a walk to the western end of the Jayyous ridge. Sitting in the sun, I sketch the view north to Kafr Jamal. Some time is spent watching a display of Palestinian sheep herding, using sticks and stones as two fellows arrive on the track each with about ten sheep. There are no sheep dogs in the "One Man and His Dog" sense; dogs are considered dirty here and are only seen guarding sheep or goat's pens and more frequently running wild in small packs. Several of these feral dogs are able to get between the main Gates in the Separation Barrier when they are shut, and thus are free to move about; while others, too big in the hind quarters, get stuck, having to reverse out. Sometimes they set off the sensors and the I.D.F. arrive to see what is happening.

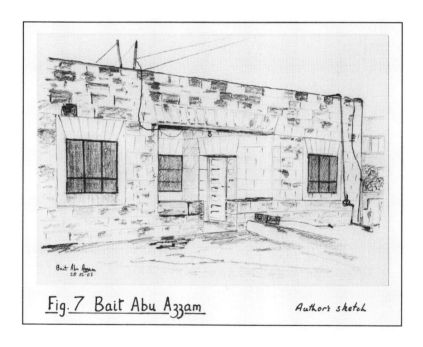

Bait Abu Azzam
20 12 03

Fig. 7 Bait Abu Azzam   Author's sketch

My room is seriously cold so have been working in the main room. The earplugs given to me by John come in useful this evening as the noise level is very high. I make a call to check that the Journal Letter draft got to Ann. It is good to hear all sorts of news from home. It is the longest night tonight. Or is that tomorrow night?

I go to sleep holding some concerns regarding the sort of comments made by the IDF about Jayyous. The comment that, "...it is a terrible place, very dangerous out there: stone-throwing... " There is the possibility the soldiers are starting to punish those who arrive late at the Gate and have got through one day by stopping them the next day. This seems especially so when HaMoked, the human rights lawyers in Jerusalem, have been in touch and asked the IDF to open, or re-open, the Gate out of time. Could it be in effect Israeli punishment on the community for our actions as EAs in helping get more people through? The oppressor will always win. In addition, by keeping one Gate open longer, we only delay the opening of the other Gate. Are we really doing any good by intervening? There is a deep feeling in me that oppressors and bullies need to be confronted, and that nonviolent action includes such confrontation. Without the confrontation, there is no opportunity to change the situation, as it just continues. Some action is better than no action. It is a delicate balance that needs thinking about.

Sunday 21st December

I get to work on the Gate reports for the Mayor, picking out three or four main points for the last two weeks. I will do this for another three weeks historically, which will take the record back to mid-late November. This seems a reasonable starting point. It is a lovely sunny day, with a clear sky at lunchtime. The first almond blossom is out on the way down to the North Gate. This is a simple duty, although the IDF are late arriving from the Jayyous land and heading north towards Falamyeh. I sleep a lot during the morning and afternoon trying to fight off the recurring symptoms of a cold or mild 'flu. My reading of "The Remains of the Day" is going well but also helps me to sleep, which is not a criticism of the book.

Charles arrives back early and independently from his visit to Nablus with Abdul-Latif. He was not allowed back into the city following a visit to a neighbouring village. Abdul-Latif calls in during the evening to see if Charles is all right. It has taken him several hours to get back from Nablus, normally a journey of about forty minutes. He had seen the funeral of the nine year old shot by 'mistake', in what seems to have been part of an Israeli raid on stone-throwers, the day Rex was in Nablus.

Is this a cultural war against the Palestinians? Does the IDF stop the Israeli settler children throwing stones in Hebron?

The last week to ten days has seen an increase in the amount of concrete around the Gates. First came boxes, a little more than a metre cubed, for the soldiers to stand in. Second came self-supporting, inverted 'T' cross-sectioned wall pieces dropped in various locations and now grouped together. At the South Gate, this seems to protect the soldiers, possibly from the stone-throwers. There is also a lot of new razor wire around, both on the Gates and on the hill above the quarry and the site of the planned new Israeli settlement. Despite this extra security, the new gates, erected on the west (Israeli) side of the military road on the tracks leading to the Bedouin house at the South Gate and the farmland at the North Gate, are still not being used. These gates stand without any fence or razor wire on either side, so are easily circumnavigated.

Monday 22nd December

As I go early to the South Gate there is a very cold wind from the east of southeast. It is a drying wind. I return home to do my washing, have some breakfast and finish work on the Gate Logs. These are completed about 10.00, after the return of Rex and then Sam, both having been refused passage to the farmer's land beyond the Separation Barrier. There is no electricity to print the report so I will try again later. I go for a walk up to the 'West End' with Charles, as much to get out as to call on Susan at the ISM house (no reply). We call on the mayor (out of the office) and purchase some cleaning materials. Feeling very hungry and in need of some protein, I buy some bread and sardines, ten and three respectively; it occurs to me that the number of loaves and fishes seem important here.

Working in the Silence

ll funds raised from the sale of this book are to go to the Educational Link with Dheisheh Refugee Camp, Bethlehem in memory of Revd Canon Dr. John Aves of Norwich

January 2004 John Aves, died of a heart attack Bethlehem while serving as an EA. His widow, ne, and their two sons, Ben and Edmund have up a small project to help young people from eisheh refugee camp to study in the UK. We uld be very happy to provide any more infortion about this project.

ou would like to donate to the project cheques be made payable to:-

Norwich YMCA Ltd John Aves Project nd sent to Anne Aves at the address below.

4 Victoria Street
Norwich
NR1 3QX
01603 767773
abaves@googlemail.com

There is an unnecessary argument about who should do the lunchtime duties despite it being up on the list already. I go to the North Gate, but never get there as I see the Gate opening from the lane at 12.23. I wander into the olive grove in search of some flowers to photograph, returning to the lane to find some farmers returning to the village after a second opening.

On the way back to the house, two boys see me writing some notes in the street about Halim. They notice Jayyous in my notes, written from left to right. I write Jayyous and they translate, teaching me to write Jayyous in Arabic, from right to left.

Halim's Story.

"Hallo! Where are you from?" "Engratera." "Welcome!" "Our troubles all started with people from England, not people, government, people get together is very good."

Halim is the barber in Tulkarm, but lives in Jayyous. He has a wife, seven daughters and three sons. He has two brothers who are in Jordan and not allowed to return to Jayyous by the Israeli authorities. The Israelis bring people from Russia, Ethiopia and the other countries, so he says he has to have a big family to balance the populations.

He does not want "shot, kill and bombber"... every day (he) hears on the radio about Palestinian people killed in Jenin, Nablus and Ramallah. "When will it stop? The Israeli government create the"... he pats down his body (meaning checkpoints and searches).... "when people go anywhere."

"They just want us in the towns and villages. They want the water and the land. We need peace between people. The army comes into Jayyous and they have problem with "shooting" stones. In Jayyous they must expect stones, so why come?"

I have this conversation at the top of the hill after the midday Gate watch at the North Gate. This man, in his mid-thirties, can hardly keep back his tears as he tells the story of his pain and fear for the future.

Does the telling of the story make things even more difficult for him, reinforcing his pain, or is the pain reduced by telling more people? This is not a problem that can be halved by sharing. The problem, the occupation, just goes on relentlessly. It is part of the day-to-day reality.

Back at the house, my washing has dried in just four hours, despite the lack of electricity to spin-dry it, before hanging it out on the line. *It is just part of the day-to-day.* I keep dropping off to sleep writing this in my newly sealed room, which feels warmer and a bit less draughty, a plastic sheet being used to cover the slats of the shutters, as the room has no glazing.

With a printer now on the main room table, there is even less space once Rex is working there. The printer has changed the balance of territories on the table, and I have retreated to working on my knees in my own space. What does it say about my character that I keep away from this 'school desk' territorial dispute? What does it say about humanity generally that personal space can become such an issue? Are the kids who mark out their desks, any different from the Israelis marking out their boundary? As a teacher watching, it was always easy to see when trouble would start as the dividing-line was pushed beyond halfway across the double desk. What is there in humans that drives them to expand, collectively as in the British Empire, the American West, the Soviet Union or Nazi Germany, or individually for wealth and power? Where is the spirit of sharing and co-operation, which should be at the core of the spiritual and religious life? Anyway, the space is not the issue when Rex is having one of his talkative moments; 'Working in the Silence!' I had better go and buy something for everyone to eat, sausages again! 'It's all part of the day-to-day."

Chapter 9
Christmas
Week 6

Tuesday 23rd December

I wake late to find my 'flu seems to have gone; the pills from the homeopathic travel kit seem to have worked. The plastic sheet on the window has also made a considerable improvement. This simple installation has changed a lot; the room is mostly warm enough to sit in during the day if dressed for the outdoors, which is the custom around here anyway, as many houses are not heated. It is considerably more comfortable at night and might even reduce the number of mosquitoes arriving in the evening.

Charles, who is first back from the North Gate after an early opening and a running queue of people going through, tells his story simply and quickly over a quiet breakfast. Rex returns with a long story about an old man who was not allowed through the South Gate. He thinks he needs a break, and has plans to go to Bethlehem for Christmas.

I have an interesting morning with Abdul-Latif and the Mayor presenting the Gate Watch Reports. I meet Labeeb, who has just returned from the United States after spending sixteen months in prison, post 9/11, without any charges being made. 'The Land of the Free', unless you are Palestinian, or anybody else the United States does not like! The Mayor is on the phone so Labeeb and I talk. He has returned to a Jayyous completely changed by the construction of the Separation Barrier. The North Gate is in the middle of his land. He has spoken with Yassir Arafat, who, he says, ".... is alert and looking for peace," that he is a freedom fighter not a terrorist.

Charles has experienced another stone-throwing incident returning from the South Gate. He thinks he has a photo this time, but unfortunately, it has not recorded. We decide to report this problem as it has affected both Charles and Sam.

111

Picture 15 The Mayor of Jayyous and the Separation Barrier. The Mayor points, from his office towards his land where the construction of the Separation Barrier has destroyed hundreds of his olive trees.

I have an easy time at the North Gate in the afternoon, with 45 people through in 20 minutes including several tractors, one on-tow, and two vans, one of which provides a lift up the hill.

We talk with Abdul-Latif about the stone-throwing incident when he calls in the evening. Abdul-Latif looks deeply saddened by our story especially when he feels that we may be withdrawn if EAPPI hears about it. I reassure him a few stones will not drive us away. He says he will talk to people about it, and asks us for pictures. To change the subject I ask Abdul-Latif about his education as a hydrologist. He read hydrology at Delft, in The Netherlands, and has since turned down two opportunities of reading for a PhD, preferring to stay in Jayyous where he is happy to be with his family. He was recently in Norway and realised how much he needed to be back in Jayyous. At heart, he is a man who wants to serve his community and is very vulnerable when his community lets him down as in the stone-throwing. His name means a servant; gentle, kind, pleasant and friendly, which seems appropriate.

This incident raises important issues around our status as 'visitors' and Abdul-Latif's position as a host. Despite his care and attention in the matter, he is reliant on the response of his community to the stone-throwing and indeed our response as accompaniers. It may be yet another way in which he, like all Palestinians under the conditions of the occupation, is relatively powerless to take action.

There follows another in the string of, often impromptu, conversations about peace. Within minutes, sometimes within seconds of starting a conversation, often with complete strangers, you can be talking at the deepest level, not just about the situation, but about the human need for peace, and for a peaceful future. We have a report that Sam eventually got to Bethlehem despite being held-up for one and a half hours at the checkpoint. Sharif Omar calls in to give us some special bread from Qalqilya and details of the demonstration on Saturday with a bus from Jayyous at 10.00. It seems that all the great and the good are expected to go, and that includes us 'internationals'.

A good day; and so to bed; I am beginning to realise that the next few weeks will offer a more in-depth understanding of attitudes to the situation.

Wednesday 24th December

Arriving at the North Gate for 06.45, there is no sign of life. By 07.45 over sixty people and a large amount of transport have crossed with just one person being turned back. Walking back up the hill, an old couple on a donkey cart are coming down. I convey to them the Gate is closed, confirmed by him saying, "the door is shut." As they turn back to the village, I am not sure who is getting the most grief, the old man or the donkey, but the woman is not very pleased about the situation.

Breakfast, a shower, clothes washing, journal writing, news from Sam and Rex in Bethlehem and a cup of tea bring me to 11.00. I write some notes on tourism in Jerusalem, especially East Jerusalem, and the impact of the second intifada. This is a good example of how the economy of Palestinian areas is collapsing under the pressure of the occupation.

At 12.15, Charles and I set out for the South Gate, with the intention of spotting the stone-throwers. He walks on as normal, greeting young and old. I follow with the camera taking pictures of any boys, especially those who do not seem to want to be photographed. The jeep turns up with no family ready to cross. The family arrives, with the suspected stone-throwers in tow, and a youth who is helping carry some sacks of animal food. I go back up the lane to help carry the sacks down to the Gate. Da'ud shows up with a pass to go to his land via the South Gate. In the middle of all this, with the jeep waiting and me waving unwanted kids away, the Gate is opened. The sacks are carried through, including a heavy one with goat food being carried, with great difficulty, by the girl. No help is offered by the soldiers. Da'ud, who shows his new pass, is allowed through the Gate. Is this Gate closed to farmers or not?

Returning via the olive grove beside the Separation Barrier, we find an array of Bedouin shacks between the houses on the village street and the fence. As we walk across the little valley to the village, Sharif Omar is coming down the other side. He wants us to find the children who throw stones; "This is very bad for Jayyous." Charles is certain he can identify a pair of lads from the pictures in my digital camera. Indeed the one has already been seen several weeks ago showing off his skills with the stones. The children, who are still standing nearby, are "interviewed" by Sharif Omar and promise to tell if they see people throwing stones. He talks to other children and some adults and finds a witness supporting Charles's suspicions. Sharif Omar will visit the parents tonight. It is fascinating to see how this community controls itself with the interaction of families, leaders, adults and children. We have done enough and hope the problem will go away.

It was lucky we could negotiate our way through this problem without any confusion about our objectives.

Sharif Omar invites us to lunch (15.30). He has been told not to eat red meat, so that makes life easier for me with just chicken and turkey on the menu along with rice and nuts, bean stew, stuffed courgettes and a green bean and squash mixture. When he is told that Sam and Rex have gone to Bethlehem for Christmas he asks, "But why do you not go? We wish you to be happy. You should be near to Jesus at this time." I say (rather to my surprise) that Jesus is everywhere and that we shall be happy in Jayyous for Christmas, probably closer than in the crowded, commercial and militarily-occupied Bethlehem. Perhaps Bethlehem has not changed a lot in the last 2003 years; it is just a different army of occupation. As is the custom, we three men eat together, Sharif Omar's wife only coming to see us off.

Stone-throwing is an issue that will no doubt return to discussions with EAs, village leaders, the Mayor, and the IDF. Da'ud has been talked to by the IDF after using the South Gate today, with them saying the Gate could be opened again if the stone-throwing (at the soldiers) is stopped. Da'ud said to the soldiers that they should talk to the Mayor about the matter, which could then be discussed at Friday prayers in the mosque. I wonder if I need to go and see the Mayor again. There is a fine balance here between doing what the soldiers say to improve access to the land, if that indeed would be the outcome of stopping the stone-throwing, or allowing some resistance to the situation by the frustrated young people.

From our point of view, our stone-throwing incident has been taken seriously by village leaders and suitable supporting action has been taken. Let us hope the matter ends there. It is interesting that the evidence I have gathered photographing, watching and listening to an un-intelligible language allows the identification of the guilty parties. This shows the power of body language and acuity, and years of working with adolescents.

115

Thursday, 25th December 2003.

"A very happy Christmas to all our readers!"

Over-sleeping, as I have not heard the alarm on my mobile phone, I dress quickly by torchlight. In the darkness of the main room, I accept and respond to Charles's Christmas greeting and the offer of a cup of tea. A jeep is seen stopping and checking the Separation Barrier as I walk down the lane to the North Gate followed by a donkey cart. There is nobody waiting when I arrive at the Gate a few minutes later. Like me, the early arrivals have the pick of their favourite places to wait. I lean against the wall where there is a suitable depression for my bottom and some loose stones to prop up the front of my feet. The old man with his wife who were very late yesterday are among the earliest today and full of smiles and waves. His wife still looks as if she is telling him, "Don't be such an old fool". I doubt if either of them are as old as they look. A throat is cleared. It is not cold enough for Ammar to light a fire today. The sky is cloudless and there is a stiff breeze coming out of the hills of Judea to the southeast. The green truck arrives. The light green, almost silver backs of the olive leaves, look like a frost in the distance.

> Last night, walking back from a meal with Sharif Omar, the sky was Christmas-card clear and full of stars. As we climbed the corner into the old village, the same open door cast light across the street as it did one evening towards the end of Ramadan when the hungry farmers made me accept a sweet cake before they would break their fast. This time it stood, expectant, lighting our way. I suspect there might have been room at this 'inn'.

The jeep goes north along the fence, but does not stop. "Good morning. I'm from Canada." A photographer, short and wearing a black leather jacket, is by my side. "Sharif Omar said you'd be here." He goes about his work. The yellow truck arrives empty from the village, and waits for a productive day. A jeep sits on the hill watching. We all wait, expectantly. Another throat is cleared. Ammar excitedly points out soldiers, in the olive grove behind us. Four

116

soldiers, with blackened faces, appear behind the line of tractors, and go down and open the Gate.

The Canadian goes forward to talk with and to photograph the soldiers, who argue with him. The farmers wait. The photographer gets out some papers and phones someone. The farmers wait. The photographer withdraws under pressure from the senior soldier. The farmers start going through, but the soldiers are restless as the photographer works. The farmers have all gone through the Gate, before the old man and his wife lead their donkey cart across. In this world to be early is to be on time, but not always first. Vehicles, including donkey carts, nearly always go last.

Charles calls to say there is no activity at the South Gate. The jeep from the hill arrives to join the argument with the photographer who will clearly not achieve his desired outcome, whatever it may be. I move a little closer to the Gate as the last stragglers arrive and get through. The photographer hears me talking to Charles at the South Gate and says, "How long will it take to get there?" "Twenty five minutes if you are quick", and than realise he has a car parked up the lane and we make it in ten.

As we arrive, the children are coming through with the father and the eldest brother. Da'ud is talking to the soldiers about going across with a fellow farmer. They are given permission but Da'ud's donkey will not go through the narrow space between the inner gate and the wire. When pulled and pushed through this gap the donkey gets its pannier bags caught up on the razor wire between the gates. Charles, Da'ud and several soldiers all attempt to release the donkey. I photograph this distraction from a distance.

After some time, and the further disruption of the arrival of a second jeep that wishes to cross from one side of the fence to the other, the donkey is returned to the Jayyous side of the inner gate. This has been a chaotic start to a day even by 'Jayyousian' standards. The soldiers are edgy and demands are being made on them, of which, they say, they have no knowledge. Is this another case of the decisions made and the

Picture 16. The Jayyous South Gate on Christmas Day. The donkey on the right is caught up on the razor wire. The narrowest part of Israel, the Plain of Sharon, is in the background, with Tel Aviv in the haze behind the open Gate and the donkey that successfully negotiated the razor wire. The senior soldier and the Canadian photographer stand in conversation encircled by a coil of razor wire.

permissions given, higher up the hierarchy (chain of command) not being respected by the soldiers on the ground in this 'democratic' army? That the soldiers on the ground always make the final decision is the basic operational principle of the Israeli Defence Force. Their response to the photographer has been typical. The Gate is shut and locked. Da'ud rides his donkey back up the lane. The jeeps drive off. Christmas Day is just two hours old and it feels as if I have done a day's work already!

Walking to the South Gate at lunchtime the stone-throwing boys say sorry and shake hands, under the watchful eye of a mother, standing in the doorway of the house with the front steps, where the red tractor parks. It seems the incident is over. Let us hope so. This is the response to the pressure put on the community by its senior members. It is interesting how the focus is on an apology to the injured party by the stone-throwers, making them responsible for both their action and the solution. (Just how I used to attempt to work with young people in school, but within a punishment-based system.)

118

Hoping the frayed tempers of this morning are healed, Charles and I present ourselves at the South Gate with a view to crossing to the Bedouin house for a Christmas visit. We hold back while the family go through without difficulty. When we go to the Gate, the soldiers explain to us that we have B2 visas. If we require to enter this area between the Separation Barrier and the Green Line, the "seam zone", we need a B1 visa. We could go into Israel but we would not be allowed back into Jayyous after our visit. Wishing to avoid a walk to the Qalqilya checkpoint, we decide not to leave Jayyous. Whatever the rights and wrongs of the visa situation, 'The soldiers on the ground always make the final decision.' Clearly, the Israeli Defence Force sees the land in the "seam zone", separated from the village by the Barrier, as now being part of Israel. Through such minor incidents, we establish the true meaning of the Separation Barrier. We also establish the true meaning of the pompous demand "to pass without let or hindrance" in the front of the British passport. We return home, via the shop, for houmous, and have our usual lunch.

Some humorous comments are exchanged about how quiet it is, and a more detailed discussion of sensitivity about sharing experiences in stressful situations. For me one of the big issues is the lack of analysis or reflection on experiences and the ability to share the essentials of a Gate Watch, or whatever, rather than the exhausting blow-by-blow accounts. While this may have its purpose to make a point, it is not necessary when we are all experiencing similar situations. Often the account is almost immediately repeated when the next person comes through the door, which suggests we are not seen as good listeners, as increasingly we are not.[1]

I do some very uninspiring watercolours from the roof during the sunny afternoon. I realise I have no white paint with me (not that one should really use it with water colours), so it is almost impossible to achieve the light, olive leaf green. It is a pity I did not notice the omission before my visit to Haifa, where I found a shop with a wide selection of art materials.

I make a Christmas dinner from a mixture of onions, herbs and tomatoes (a present from a farmer), creamed potatoes and sweet corn on the cob, washed down with local fruit juice. This is supplemented by some take-away Falafel from a stand just beyond the village shop and a tin of corned beef for Charles. The food miles for this must be less than ten, apart form the corned beef, and all for inside twenty Shekels (under £3.00). Abdul-Latif comes in the evening. We have a wider discussion than usual that includes talking about the gun lobby in the US. He knows little about this so it is good to tell him something of the background to the culture of violence that "goes for the gun" both at home and abroad.

We finish the day with the news that the West Bank is closed after a bomb in Tel Aviv, which leaves four Israelis dead, following the 17 Palestinians killed in Gaza yesterday. This maintains the normal 1:4 ratio of killing, Israelis to Palestinians.

As it is Christmas, the Berlin Wall comes to mind as I prepare for bed. In the 1960s, I can remember a feature of the BBC Christmas Radio News broadcasts was the number of people that had been allowed through the wall. This was especially to do with Berlin rather than between East and West Germany. It crosses my mind that we may in future hear about the number of Christians allowed into Bethlehem in Christmas news programmes.

I also especially remember the setting for listening to the radio news being the large living room, with, I suspect rather disappointingly insipid wallpaper, but with a bold touch of colour in the dark green and turquoise William Morris design curtains. Add to this the fireplace in Flemish Brick and the simple furniture and of course at this time of year a Christmas tree, decorated to the accompaniment of the Nine Lessons and Carols broadcast from King's College Cambridge on Christmas Eve. However, those childhood days are far from this Christmas set in the land of those lessons and carols.

We hear from our colleagues working in southeast Jerusalem that they arranged for a donkey to carry a local woman, led by her husband, dressed as Mary and Joseph, to approach the Bethlehem checkpoint. They are refused entry. I understand the soldiers did not realise Mary's 'bump' was a pillow; so much for security

Friday 26th December

I am in reflective mood as I arrive at the North Gate. The scene could be from "The Return of the Gate Watcher"; with me and the donkey cart rattling down the lane on this stormy morning reminiscent of Hardy's description of Egdon Heath.[2] *This donkey cart is fitted with an old bus seat complete with arms.*

Also on my mind is the discipline of Gate Watch, a time for observance, both literal and spiritual. (A Humvee goes slowly by on the inside of the fence.) *Time for writing; with the recording of observations interjected into another text.* (The donkey cart driver lights a fire while the donkey grazes the edge of the track. I am invited to share the warmth, but decline.) *Am I too detached, or do I just need to keep in touch with the ideas that are going around in my head and get so easily lost in the everyday?* (Four more men arrive, singing down the lane, including Ammar, also known to me as "Next Week", from a joke about the time for completion of the work on the kitchen. He has difficulty with my name and calls me Mouse.)

There are things to write before going to Jerusalem on Monday, including an article on stone-throwing for the Devon Religious Education website. The David and Goliath tradition continues. I write a newsletter for the Friends Meeting in Exeter, something for general circulation, probably this piece, and to make a final edition of my Journal Letter for Friends House to put on the web site.

The West Bank is closed. We hear this piece of news during a phone call from Charles's wife in Scotland. We hear of the snow in Scotland from Abdul-Latif who watches the BBC news here in Jayyous. He does not know about the closure and Charles's wife did not mention any snow. (Six men arrive on a single tractor.) *What does this closure mean for us? Edgy soldiers after the bomb in Tel Aviv? We might find our movement both inside and outside the West Bank restricted, or, more likely, that if we go outside we will not be able to get back in. It sounds like just another travel problem, like snow at home.* (There is the sound of distant shooting from the direction of Qalqilya. Two men are discussing the harness of a donkey cart, which is allowing the cart to catch up with the donkey's back legs. The problem is solved.) *This closure might cause difficulties for my colleagues who have been to Bethlehem for Christmas. How many aggressive checkpoints will they have to pass through on their return journey?*

Picture 17. The Jayyous North Gate. Women, men and donkeys wait to go to work.

(Two more tractors arrive with a cargo of ten people. As it is Friday, there is no school today so there are more boys than usual. One woman stands detached, like me, a little up the lane from the group by the fire, half sitting against the stone wall. Three more fellows arrive on the "might not start" tractor, which is parked well up the track to give it plenty of rolling space for a bump start. There is a roar of a gas cooker as a brew of 'chai' is made.)[3]

How quickly the everyday takes over. Here I am thinking about the problems of West Bank closure among people to whom it is of little concern. They cannot go to Tel Aviv. Their produce is already effectively banned from the Israeli market. At this moment, they cannot even go to work in their fields. What will a West Bank closure do? While it was 'open' since the Haifa bombing in early October by a young women law student, there have been no Israeli deaths. The four people killed in Tel Aviv in early December were the result of a gangland battle, and not a suicide bomb, although some of the world media assumed otherwise. One Palestinian woman, an unemployed primary school teacher, was caught with bomb-making materials about ten kilometres away from Jayyous. However, in the last two weeks at least twenty Palestinians have been killed in Ramallah, Jenin, Nablus and Gaza, this figure including several children. There has been little or no international clamour to stop this.

(A second fire is started, an indication that this could be a long wait.) *Are we waiting because of the closures? Are the soldiers busy elsewhere? The sun breaks over the Jayyous ridge behind us under the leaden sky.* (Charles phones from the South Gate to check progress. A jeep is heard on the hill and as it appears on the corner, the call goes out. 610657Y, chased by a barking dog on this side of the fence, rolls past the Gate into a turn and comes back to face the rapidly forming queue of 'customers'. Two soldiers go to their concrete boxes and one opens the Gate. The dog is first through but then loses confidence and hangs around the other side of the Gate until some men move forward.

There is no hurry; some still sit by the fire. The "might not start" tractor rolls down the hill and comes to life beside me with the reassuring sound that comes from an old engine sweetly ticking over. The cold and the threat of rain seem to speed the flow. *This bit of the West Bank, for the Israeli soldiers tell us the Separation Barrier is now the border, is clearly not closed. The Gate closes. I walk up the hill wondering if I have done anything significant in the last hour and three quarters.*

The last arrival at the Gate comes down as a passenger in a car. It turns at the bottom of the hill and starts to follow me up. Of course, it stops to offer me a lift. The driver is an elderly man clad in a brown galliabia, which is much the same colour as the car, the dust on the dashboard and indeed his face. He clearly has things to say. "Why are you alone? It is the second time I have seen you alone?" I say some of my colleagues are in Bethlehem for Christmas. "I forget it is your holy-day. Happy Christmas! We must take our joys when we can and celebrate. There is one God and he has enough for us all. There will always be peace and there will always be war but we must take our joy from the peace when we can."

I ask him how many died in Tel Aviv. He says, "It was terrible, four have died. We just ask for peace. We always ask for peace. I did not think the Gate would be open today because they do not want peace." I thank him for the lift to our house, Bait Abu Azzam. *I suspect I also thank him for noticing that I was working alone, for knowing about Christmas, most of all for his visionary words of joy and peace. Here the everyday seems to be more than every day. What a joy to have a lift from this man!*

Most of the morning, indeed most of the day is spent on writing up, checking and preparing files for sending to Robert at the EAPPI office in Jerusalem. If I cannot get to Jerusalem, I will transfer them to Charles's computer and send them by e-mail. A party of 'internationals' arrives during the afternoon from Jerusalem, including Grethe, the medical student from Denmark, Grethe's mother and a man, clearly lacking in perception, awareness and social grace, who, interestingly, is introduced as the head of 'World Vision' in the Holy Land. *Am I the only one to see the irony of this juxtaposition?* Tea is provided, but the visitors fetch their own food from the shop. *Is my private humorous response indicative of feeling rather detached, enclosed in my own thoughts and concerns about a worsening situation? What we need is vision at a human level, not at a global level. Whose 'world vision' is it anyway?*

Rex returns having spent 3 hours at Funduq, caught by flying checkpoints on his journey back from Bethlehem. Rex is also full of his 30 Shekel Christmas meal in Bethlehem (40 NIS with the wine).

This experience may have some bearing on my going to

Ramallah on Sunday. Will Ramallah be open? It appears that it was closed today, but obviously movement to and from Jerusalem is possible, if unpredictable, for westerners. It will also be interesting to see how tomorrow's demonstration goes in Qalqilya.

Saturday 27th December

There is a very cold wind at the South Gate 06.40 - 08.10. This is a long and cold watch. It is a strange time and place to start re-reading 'Brideshead Revisited'.[4] It is very full. Even if I 'ditch' the pages of this broken down copy, held together with a rubber band, I will not throw out the pages marked by Ann describing the failure of relationships by metaphor. It is masterly.

Picture 18. The Younger Generation - Jayyous children going home from Kindergarten. Even in this occupied community it is safe enough for these young children to walk home from school on their own.

We have been invited to Qalqilya for the demonstration. We arrive by the shop at 09.50 and join a crowd of people who are waiting. One of the young children from the village calls me "Papa Noel". It must be the red coat, although I suspect the white hair and beard have something to do with it. There is news of flying checkpoints at Kafr Jamal and Kafr Thuft holding buses going to the demonstration. Eventually at 10.45, we set out in a taxi to Qalqilya. Having got through the checkpoint, we are dropped off to wait for the rest of the

Jayyous people. They arrive, but are not allowed through the checkpoint, so have a demonstration on the Jayyous side. As this causes the closure of the checkpoint, we are unable to return to join their impromptu demonstration. We take another taxi into Qalqilya and join the end of the main demonstration. It is interesting to see uniformed Palestinian Police for the first time. We walk through Qalqilya back to the checkpoint, getting a lift part of the way.

We walk through the checkpoint there being no soldiers on duty and the Gates being open. Just two hours after the demonstration that closed the checkpoint, the place seems deserted. While waiting for transport, we meet three Englishmen who are looking for the demonstration. Two other fellows on big motorbikes stop and ask if I am with the demo. They are a pair of photographers from Ha'aretz, the Israeli newspaper. We exchange cards and I invite them to Jayyous, the village by the Separation Barrier. While talking, I manage to stop a taxi for the return to Jayyous. The same soldier who cleared us through the Qalqilya Checkpoint this morning checks us at Azzoun leaving the '55 Road'. There is a smile of recognition, a small sign of grace. We get through after Charles's EAPPI I.D. card has been carefully studied.

On our return, Charles and Rex separately go walking and visiting in the village. I take an afternoon nap that is interrupted by children ringing the street doorbell.

Chapter 10
To Ramallah with Checkpoints
Weeks 6-7

"The Occupying Power shall not deport or
transfer parts of its own population into the
territory it occupies."
Article 49 of the Fourth Geneva Convention[1]

"…and then you will come to walk cheerfully
over the world, answering that of God in every
one."

George Fox[2]

Sunday 28th December

I am up at 05.00 and at the bus stop at 05.40. I check that this
is the right stop for Qalandia. "Inshallah" - God willing - the
voice from the dark says, "the weather is better after the rain,
not so cold." We head into the darkness, stopping to pick
people up in each village. The only sign on the bus says
"Prohibited Throwing Garbage". Are the English-speaking
people especially known for this? At one stop a smart fellow
gets on, saluting all his fellow travellers with a wave and
kissed fingers. We are back to Kafr Jamal again after a trip up
the side road to Kafr Bush. All this is to the sound of morning
readings from the Koran on the radio, followed by the weather
forecast. Even though I cannot understand it, the pattern of
sounds is the same as any weather forecast; then there is the
news, with a few words I can pick out.

There are wonderful superimposed profiles of the hills, added
to by the grey and pink clouds as day dawns as we travel
through the hills towards Funduq. Here we run into a flying
checkpoint to the west of the town, on the number 55 Road. It
is 06.45. The bus is stopped, but nothing is checked. A soldier
tells us to turn round, helping us make a three point turn by
waving his gun, and we return to Funduq. First we head out

towards Nablus, with the driver on his mobile phone checking conditions ahead. We stop and turn again back to Funduq and take the road we have just come over from Jayyous. He must have been told of another checkpoint blocking his first choice of revised route.

During the stop a few people stand to better see and hear conversations with the soldier. A few people get off the bus at places on the retraced route. Most fall into resigned silence. The radio, turned off at the checkpoint, is not turned on again. The driver, Yusif (Joseph), gets some comments, I guess of support. He continues to use his phone, even on the hairpin bends.

Picture 19. Dawn over the Samarian Hills. The dawn breaks over the northern hills during the bus journey from Jayyous to Funduq

We pass the bus stop in Jayyous at 07.22, having taken 1 hour and 27 minutes to nowhere. At Azzoun, we join the 55 Road to Funduq, arriving less than a 100 metres to the west of the checkpoint after 50 minutes of travel time. We turn right onto the road for Qalandia, Ramallah and Jerusalem. We collect the people seen waiting at the bus stop on our first visit to this junction before heading south. I ring Julia, who by now will be expecting me in Ramallah. We are clearly back on route picking up people, four at Yukur Katan Junction, and onto the 505 Road. Israeli Settlement buses are on the move, without restriction. A fellow boards, in dark suit, white shirt and tie with a golf size umbrella, clearly commuting to Ramallah, on this now very wet morning.

I try to feel centred, (after all I am on the way to a Quaker Meeting) which is rather difficult as progress is hard work especially on the hills. There is a good deal of 'Inshallah' about me - what will happen, will happen and there is not a lot you can do about it. Our western ideas of control, of self-determination, of being in charge are out of the window.

At 08.10, we meet the Tulkarm to Ramallah bus waiting by a junction; the connection has been kept. I take a chance and switch buses; in theory, this should be the shorter route. Yusif, the bus driver, seeing me change buses kindly comes to check I know where I am going. There is a touch of the 'Good Samaritan' in this rocky valley that reminds me of the picture in a childhood Bible story book. Indeed the 'Good Samaritan' and the 'Good Palestinian' is the same thing, for Samaria is now Palestine. By 08.37 this second bus is stuck in standing traffic at a blocked informal road junction. We seem to be on a mud track connecting to roads blocked by dirt banks. As we slip about between cars and lorries, we make progress slowly to the top of a hill and join the second road. It is difficult to monitor the progress as the windows are steamed up and I am standing. Many people get off at the northern edge of Ramallah and more at Birzeit University. I get to sit down for the last few kilometres. I talk to a student who is looking for a job, as an agronomist in a government department in Ramallah. He asks a fellow passenger, who works for the Ministry of Finance, to take me to the Lion Manara, the roundabout that is the centre of Ramallah. I feel welcomed in this strange city. At the first try the instructions to get from there to the Meeting House do not work. The second attempt takes me to the 'Friends Boys' School'. As I turn from the Gate, looking at my watch, there is a yellow taxi standing behind me. "Can I help you?" I say, "I need to find the Girls' School". I later learn these are old titles. The school is now co-educational, the only one in Palestine, and split into upper (11 to 19 years) and lower schools (3 to 11years).

The taxi driver asks where I am from. I tell him Jayyous, and that it has taken three and a quarter hours. He asks how long is it since I have eaten. I suddenly feel hungry as he gives me a hand full of nuts from his door pocket. He tells me he worked abroad before 1990, returning to his hometown of Ramallah having lost a cement business in Kuwait in the first Gulf war. I asked what should be done with Saddam. The response is short and Anglo-Saxon. I ask him which is worse, Saddam or Sharon. "They are both..." and sentence is finished with the plural of the same perfunctory comment. As he drives through the gates of the Girls' School he smiles and says, "Here is your friend." Julia stands by the Meeting House, as I ask him what I owe him. He says nothing. I give him ten shekels saying, "It is for the nuts." He drives away with a smile.

Paul and Mary arrive and talk about other possible people who may be at the Meeting. We end up with an international group of nine; Paul, Mary, Julia and I are joined by Jacob, a teacher at the Friends School, and his parents from the U. S. and Giuseppe from Italy and his friend Zindzi from South Africa. Paul speaks about finding our way quoting from the Old Testament book of Isaiah. I speak about being here and Julia about the lack of hate in Yanoun. We go from Meeting to lunch at the Pizza House, just up the road. Unfortunately, the stalwart member of Ramallah Meeting, Jean Zaru, is unable to attend. She is between visits to the US and New Zealand, and had been told if she comes back to Ramallah she may not be able to get out again to go to New Zealand.

Paul West interestingly says over lunch that he feels the Quaker Truth and Integrity Testimony is the most important of all and that the others on equality and community, simplicity, peace and the earth and environment follow from it. This is a very sound concept, which I will need to ponder.[3]

Love, faith, fear and hate: We find the first three in Palestine but very little of the last. Is it because we are not looking for hate, or is it just that the day-to-day actions of people like Yusif and the taxi driver keep displaying the care of these people, who welcome the stranger in their land?

After lunch, Julia and I go to find Heide and Margaret at the Coffee Shop. Neither the Pizza House nor the Coffee Shop would look out of place in any European city. We then take a taxi to Heide and Margaret's flat that is the base for the Ramallah EAPPI team, who are mostly working in the refugee camps around the city. There is some discussion about Julia joining them after her weeks in Yanoun.

Heide and Margaret slowly, carefully and very much with an eye to process, work through how Julia could become part of the team in Ramallah and what the impact might be. This is excellent, professional reflective practice, and I suspect is an area that needs more consideration during the preparation in Jerusalem, more than just, "sort out what you need to do!"

We all leave together for the Internet Cafe, with Julia and me going on to the Qalandia Checkpoint en route to Jerusalem. This is the first time I have approached this checkpoint from the Ramallah side, indeed the first time I have actually gone through the checkpoint, as I normally skirt around the south side on the Jayyous road. There is no problem for us with our red European passports walking through, although the minibus we catch the other side is stopped at a flying checkpoint on the dual carriageway road somewhere in the north part of Jerusalem, although the soldier only checks to see if we have documents. We arrive at the Damascus Gate at 17.00 and walk to the New Imperial Hotel, which is nearly full. I go for a quick meal at the end of a long hard day. I have a small side room over the alley, and the hotel doorbell and the clank of the metal door initially punctuate my early night.

Monday 29th December

Breakfast is in the main dining room. This is an honour, but then the hotel is full of participants in the International Peace March, so the little breakfast room would not be able to cope. I post a parcel home, and manage to find another chemist (more cough sweets) but forget about the request for peanut butter for the kitchen in Jayyous, as the little shop by the hotel door is not yet open. I arrive at the office about 9.00 and talk to Polly about various things and transfer articles and pictures to the EAPPI computer.

On my return journey, I arrive at Qalandia at 12.00 and find a bus going to Funduq at 13.00. I have a disturbing phone conversation with Charles about the situation in Jayyous. I buy a some ka'ak, bread covered in sesame seeds, from a young bread seller who carries his wares on a stick. While the checkpoints have provided new markets for the bread sellers and other traders, they have added to the time and cost of moving around Palestine. Journeys from Ramallah to Bethlehem have increased from 45 minutes to between 2 and 5 hours. From Ramallah to Nablus from 45 minutes to 3 to 6 hours and from Ramallah to Jerusalem from 20 minutes to at least an hour. The costs have all increased, due to the need to change of buses or taxis, form 8 to 17.5, 9 to 30 and 3.5 to 5.5 New Israeli Shekels, respectively.

The Israelis have safety concerns for the soldiers working on the checkpoints. They are dangerous places to be for lengthy periods, being in close contact with the Palestinian population. There is always the risk of attack. Each checkpoint requires at least six soldiers per shift, which last many hours. This takes up a large portion of the army's personnel. Their work varies from simple pass checking to detailed and some times destructive searching of vehicles like ambulances. A number of Palestinian deaths have occurred due to patients being turned out of ambulances at checkpoints, so the checkpoints are also dangerous places for Palestinians.

Sitting on the bus eating the fresh bread, I wonder how many people have ever sat at the Qalandia Checkpoint reading 'Brideshead', let alone tearing out the pages that have been read. This could be the one truly unique activity in my life; it is a pity it could not be something more directly creative, rather than just a comfort, despite the book's plumbing of the uncomfortable depths of relationships and faith. Does life just end up as a few pages scattered in the dust?

The bus cannot turn left onto the road because of the low concrete barriers, so it turns right towards Jerusalem and after about 200 meters it makes a 180 degree turn in the four lane road, around the end of the barrier, to return to the checkpoint corner and onto the West Bank.[4] It is a good run to Funduq with only a brief stop for traffic at the checkpoint at the junction where the 57 Road to Nablus turns of the 60 Road to the north. I quickly find a shared taxi from Funduq to Azzoun and get straight into another for Jayyous. It is a journey of about 3 hours, but if you take out the wait at Qalandia a very reasonable 2 hours for a total of 21.5 NIS (£3) from the office to Jayyous.

At several points during this journey, and being watched with interest by my few fellow passengers, I am able to take photographs of the Israeli settlements that have been built on some of the hilltops along the route. The number 60 Road, which mostly threads its way through the valleys, has signs pointing up roads to Shilo, Eli and Ma'ale Levona. Other, less formal, signs, point up rough tracks to collections of containers and "Portakabins" on the hilltops. These settlements, which are not named on the map, are clearly recent developments. Indeed my geographer's mind quickly formulates a staged model of development of these additions to the West Bank scenery. First stage elements include containers, caravans and Portakabins, often with a mobile phone mast but always with an Israeli flag. These small groups of structures are often arranged in a circle or oval, not unlike the wagons of the American settlers on the prairies. The second stage might include a better road, a more formal sign and a gate on the entrance. There might also be a high fence around the space for further growth on the hilltop. Then comes the building of houses. There may be just a few houses, or large 'estates' of similar houses or apartment blocks, which have a modern European or American feel to them. They have the distinguishing feature of red tiled roofs as opposed to the traditional Middle Eastern flat roof. Eventually there is an entry checkpoint with guards for the settlement, which in the final stages include shops, schools, community centres and synagogues.

Picture 20. An Israeli settlement of portable homes on a hill in the Palestinian West Bank taken from a bus on the 60 Road.

My mind also goes back to the geography lessons I used to teach about the origins of the location of settlements.[5] In the context of England, references to defensive sites always seemed to puzzle my students. To talk about a town being on a 'defensive site' would seem to have little relevance. However in the schools in these settlements the concept would be quickly understood: height over the surrounding land gives you power. Judging by the posters seen on the doors of a street utility cabinet in Jerusalem (Fig 8), these "outposts" are seen by some in Israel as the way towards the future, the way to realise a stronger grip on the West Bank. In reality it is not just the built Settlement that has a impact on the Palestinian population, for when a hilltop is selected by the settlers they consider the whole hill to be theirs and deter the Palestinians from using their land on the lower slopes with the threat of dogs and guns, as experienced by my colleague in Yanoun. (See 27th January)

WE ARE ALL "SETTLERS"
ALL OF ISRAEL IS AN OUTPOST

SPECIAL TRIBUTE TO SALUTE THE HEROIC HILLTOP YOUTH!

CONCERT!

DAVID   SINAI TUR   V SHURIN   BEN LEVINE

ursday Sivan 19, 5763 (June 19, 03)   KFAR TAPU   - SHOMRON

Fig. 8 Settlers' Concert Poster ~ seen in Jerusalem.

Under international law these neat housing areas, with rich funding and plenty of water, these 'suburbs in the hills', are illegal. The Forth Geneva Convention states in article 49, "The Occupying Power shall not [deport or] transfer parts of its own civilian population into the territory it occupies." Despite this Israel has established some 120 settlements with nearly 200,000 settlers[6] in the West Bank, not including East Jerusalem. These settlements range from the 20,000 people in Ariel to these small, starter settlements of just a few caravans, seen along the road going north through the West Bank. Israel argues that the Geneva Convention does not apply here as the area, despite being called the Occupied Territories, was captured in 1967, and that the settlers are not forced to settle in the West Bank. Indeed, Israeli does not accept the application of any articles of the Geneva Convention in the context of the West Bank. It is estimated that the settlements cost Israel as much as 550 million US$ per year.[7]

Halper suggest there are two types of settlers. The first ideological settlers like members of Gush Emunim (Bloc of the

Faithful) who support the concept of Eretz, or Greater Israel. These are the most vocal, visible and violent, but still a small minority compare to the large number of economic settlers. The latter take advantage of Israeli government loans, tax breaks and contractor subsidies that conceal the political purpose of attracting new populations to affordable housing in the West Bank. Many of this larger group would gladly move "back home", which might provide a significant bank of housing to resettle the Palestinian refugees.[8]

When I reach Jayyous the good news is that a white jeep with the IDF commander, or at least someone linked to the 'DCO' (District Co-ordinating Office), turned up at the South Gate at the same time as the water tanker to supervise the delivery. The 'officer' told the soldiers to remove the razor wire and stakes and allow the tanker through. They returned 30 minutes later to allow it back again. This is excellent news as the tanker is several weeks over-due and the family has been relying on rainwater for nearly three weeks. How much this is organised by the International Committee for the Red Crescent, or how much it is chance we will never know.

We are invited to Sharif Omar's for a meal with Sweden's youngest MP, Gustav Fridolin, (elected at the age of 19 years) who is a member of the Green Party and is on the Middle East Parliamentary Committee and writing a report for the Swedish foreign minister. It is good that Tim, a Jerusalem based EA visiting Jayyous, can enjoy one of these meals, which are becoming a major (in fact the only) feature of our 'social lives'. One of the men at this meal, Shukri, has been refused a permit to go to his land since the construction of the Separation Barrier. He thinks this is part of a *'collective punishment'* for his family as his son was arrested in Qedumin in 1998 on charges of theft. His son was killed in a car accident that occurred when the army was moving him from Qedumin to a detention centre inside Israel. *'Collective Punishment'* is not permitted under the Forth Geneva Convention.

Chapter 11
The Gates and Society
Week 7

"If we do not share life with the oppressed, we do not share life with God."

Leonardo Boff[1]

Tuesday 30th December

A farmer arrives at the South Gate at 06.45 to go out to his land on a donkey. The animal is tied to the twisted olive tree as it is in danger of being tangled up in the razor wire. It is soon in trouble here, its panniers and saddle pad becoming hooked on a branch as it works its way round under the tree. The farmer goes to sort out the situation. The donkey is tethered in another spot away from the tree. It continues to graze.

A jeep goes south at 07.05 and shows no interest. Last night, talking to Sweden's youngest M.P. who was here on a fact-finding visit, I said to him that Sweden seems to grow peace workers. He said that Sweden had the highest percentage of ISM personnel per capita, and that this was not surprising as Norway and Sweden were the first countries to broker a peaceful settlement over the creation of the two states in the early twentieth century. We hear later that the MP had been arrested while travelling to Jenin, and that the Israelis deported him.

The family arrives with a donkey cart at 07.30. The wire, which was removed yesterday to allow the water cart through, has been replaced in a rather haphazard way. I notice that one set of stakes has been "planted" wide enough apart for a vehicle to pass through if the razor wire is removed. Was this part of the original 'design' or just chance?

At 07.35, another farmer arrives from the village. I ring Rex at the North Gate and hear the reassuring sound of tractors moving. It could be another 20 minutes before the Humvee gets here. At this point an empty plastic bottle goes bouncing down the road, making repeated cracking sounds. Rex calls to say the Humvee has gone into the farmland rather than heading for the South Gate. We wait. I ring HaMoked. At 08.11 a jeep arrives and opens the Gate. The farmers go through and Dharifah and daughter come in after considerable discussion about the horse and the razor wire. The soldiers hold the wire for them to pass so the girl can get to the last day of her exams, albeit late again. The boys go home with the horse and cart. Perhaps they do not have exams today.

During this wait, in a weak moment, I resort to a little traditional geography and draw a sketch of a single share donkey plough. This is a donkey plough for two reasons, it can be pulled by a donkey and it can be carried by a donkey on its saddle pad.

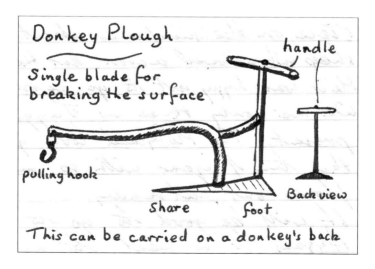

Figure 9 - Sketch of the donkey plough from the author's Journal.

The North Gate at lunchtime was uneventful. A flock of sheep is not allowed through the Gate, but the shepherd does not seem too fussed about it, so does not make an issue of it with the soldiers. Back at the house Rex and I talk about Sam's prolonged absence. Rex still has the opinion that we need four people in Jayyous so we can have the correct amount of "free" time. Our contract from the London office mentions having time off.

In the field, this concept seems meaningless to me. It is rather like saying teachers on school trips can have a day off. I carry the old professional feeling that I am on duty all the time here in Jayyous. Anyway, how can you have time off from an occupation?

Rex continues his excellent work making a video with a group of local young men about how they see the situation in Jayyous. I go to the North Gate in the evening, which is opened late but otherwise uneventful and walk up the hill for the second time today. I need an early night and will leave the Mayor's Gate Reports until tomorrow. Tim has had an interesting day in Qalqilya. *Uneventful seems to be a good word for today.*

Wednesday 31st December

I go to the North Gate early. It is 06.45 at the North Gate. A family with mother, father, and two boys (most likely not the whole family) arrives in a pair of donkey carts. The donkeys stand side by side in front of the Gate as if in some Donkey Derby or chariot race. Ammar tells me an empty car has been blown up by missile from an Apache helicopter in Gaza and an Israeli soldier has shot a baby in Nablus. "It's crazy". A donkey is untied from the back of a trailer as the jeep goes by and on up the hill showing no interest in those who wait. The donkey is retied to the trailer after the false hope of an opening. The men are half asleep, with hands in pockets, shamaghs wound around necks, sandaled feet with no socks, summer trousers, and some in tailored jackets that have seen better days. There is a new tanker trailer with kit for crop spraying.

There is just enough space for another donkey cart to get

through to the front of the queue. The partridge-like birds cackle in the olive grove while a distant dog barks and silence falls. A single voice speaks and a reply is made. A plane drones overhead. We listen for the jeep, forty men and the sound of a flapping plastic sheet. We wait. This is working in the silence. The digger starts in the distant quarry, rata-tat-tat. I wonder if this enforced 'community activity' (the waiting, the inactivity) has changed the social relations in Jayyous. A new arrival leaves a tractor engine running, its nose into the bank, poor brakes or poor starting, or both, and the listening stops.

At 07.40 a jeep arrives, looks around and goes on south, meeting another jeep coming north on the bend at the top of the first hill. They talk and move on. The sun arrives. The jeep drives straight by. This is beginning to be a bad morning. About 60 person hours have been wasted so far today. Fold-up plastic fruit 'chips' are put together.[2] The tractor is turned off. The despair grows. A good fifty people wait. At 07.50 I take a photo. The Jasih (the army) arrives from the north at 07.53. We have an opening. People move forward. They are searching the youngsters inside their jackets and lifting their tops, but today "Big Boy" is not searched. A young horse wanders over to the soldier checking passes. A soldier tells the men he is checking to get it away. The man moves forward without his pass, which is still in the soldier's hand. He stops in his tracks as the other soldiers turn their guns on him. The horse wanders off. These city boys are not used to dealing with animals.

A donkey cart is checked. The next one is told to both wait and come on by different soldiers at the same time. The six tractors move forward. Trailers are checked but the tanker seems to go through unnoticed. The last man is ordered off his tractor to shut the inner gate. It is 08.11 as the last tractor speeds through and the Gate is closed. I ring Rex at the South Gate to say the jeep is on its way and gladly turn into the warmth of the sun for the walk up the hill.

While at the North Gate today I have written the following although it is about the South Gate yesterday.

140

Land Rover

I listen to the silence at the Gate,
Freedom comes with the sound of a jeep,
I hear the swish, the whine, a different tone,
That icon of British design, the Land Rover.

A proud vehicle, built to last,
Resplendent in UN white or,
More humble national park green,
Here prostituting in military olive,

The jeep has a roar, a crudity.
The Humvee, wide footed, ugly,
Became a fashion symbol in New York yellow,
"To support our boys in Iraq".

The Land Rover, designed for war,
Used for oppression, driven by economics,
How sad this excellent vehicle could not
Be solely used for productivity and peace.

Back at the house, I complete the report for the Mayor. I then get side-tracked after a phone call from Susan about the Bedouin family having been told they must leave their house. This is just part of the ongoing switch back ride of the soldiers and the Bedouin. Again the soldiers seem to be "getting their own back" after the officer told them to let the water through.

This adds to our concern that the chain of command in the Israeli Army may not be very strong. There seems to be a so-called 'democratic approach', with the soldiers on the ground making the final decisions. Is there some internal power struggle going on with the soldiers trying to score points off the command when they have to do things they do not like? Does this have implications for us when we ask the soldiers to be told to do things by ringing HaMoked requesting them to ask the District Co-ordination Office to open or reopen the

141

Gates?

How can people live with this uncertainty, this ever-changing set of rules and demands around their most basic needs? Even here, we have enough anchor points to ride out most situations; and ultimately we are able to leave.

At 12.40 the Jeep 610657Y arrives at the South Gate and the family is still in town. It goes away again. I sit and wait under an olive tree and wonder how I would have coped in the summer. Presently the diurnal range of temperature is around 25 degrees C, with lows of about 4-5 degrees C and early afternoon highs in the top 20s.

At 12.56 a jeep goes north, pausing slightly as it passes. An Apache flies over from the northwest to the southeast. The flies are bad today in the heat. The family walks down from the village. At 13.05, a man arrives on a donkey. Dharifah hands round bread to all those waiting, including us. At 13.10, I ring Feras, the human rights lawyer, as suggested by Susan, but he is out of the office until 14.00. I ring HaMoked to get the Gate open as soon as possible.

For something to do I inspect the area around the Gate. There are a lot of stones and some large rocks about on the dusty inner track, indicative of stone-throwing practice. The clematis is flowering on the nearby rocks. The Dharifah goes to sit in the shade. I think the mosquitoes must have been inside my sleeping bag last night as the heat makes the bites more irritable. The boys, ever restless, bring me a sprig of olive and put it in my top pocket while their mother moves back to sit by the Gate.

The jeep 610657Y returns at 13.55, an hour and a half after its first visit. The soldiers get out and cock their weapons. The Gate is opened with difficulty. The family go through and a man with a donkey comes back from the land. One soldier uses his weapon to move the wire for the donkey to pass, and gets its shoulder strap tangled up in the barbs. The jeep goes at 14.00.

I take a nap in the afternoon after some writing up and

142

processing this morning's pictures. I will possibly put some notes into the Apple computer this evening while listening to some music. Rex has visitors again working on the video. Ann will ring about 21.00 if all goes according to plan. Abdul-Latif comes this evening for nearly two hours, so not much of what I intend to do actually happens.

Abdul-Latif's questions and comments include; "Can a society survive when you pull away the reasons to work? There are now 'food baskets', a social change to charity: the pride in not wanting charity now becomes a demand to have charity whether it is needed or not. We have become a 'dependent society'. People's attitude is changing, altruism changing, "We did not have a basket"". He talks about the social and psychological effect of curfew. When under curfew he dug a cistern (an underground water tank). Your brain goes "like jelly" you cannot read or work. He quotes the former Israeli Prime Minister Netanyahu who says, "We have no problem with the Palestinians any more", but "We have a problem with the Palestinian Arabs in Israel". His solution would seem to be the removal of all the Arabs in Israel, including those in the Occupied Territories. Abdul-Latif says there is a new relationship between industry and income, and between income and dependency on Israel. Some 120,000 Palestinians from the West Bank worked in Israel before the limits on work permits after the start of the second Intifada in 2000.[3]

Abdul-Latif goes on "There is the metaphor of a wound with the danger after the knife has been removed; the pain is not over. The 'youngs' (sic) have all their power inside. The Palestinians are in 'boxes' and are broken people. Will we become like the Native Americans, living on reservations but without the solace of the alcohol? The occupation has driven the focus onto the individual, away from the land, from the family and the community. This focus on the individual is against the Islamic creed of caring for others. You do not eat your neighbour's hunger. The principles of Islam; peace, charity, integrity, honesty, faith, care of the poor, care of the environment, care of society, hard work, are being diminished".

Why does Christianity have the right to convert the world? It would be good if some of the Christian neo-conservatives in America considered some of these Islamic ethics more carefully; the world might be a better place. Proselytising religion is what is wrong; it certainty gets in the way of the ultimate faith and understanding that is behind and beyond day-to-day religion.

If we perceive a situation as real, it is real in its consequences. Changing the way we understand situations changes our perceptions and therefore may change the situations we find ourselves in. Changing understanding and awareness may lead to pressure, personally or collectively, to change the situation.

Science Fiction has a tendency to be prophetic, with soft boundaries between reality and invention. "1984" was prophetic about the great power blocks and the surveillance society. When people write about peace it does not seem 'to come true'. Gandhi's writings on peace could not bring Indian independence without violence. Is this violence all a problem of power, of men, of territorial needs and the thrill of the fight, all of which may be the basis for leading countries to war?

The Occupation of the West Bank has run parallel to the great shift from the sense of the collective good in societies, during the third quarter of the twentieth century, to the focus on the individual demands. This has it origins in the work of people like Hayak, which become popularised by Margaret Thatcher, with such comments as "... there is no such thing as society". It has its origins in the distrust of the Cold War, which was based on 'Mutually Agreed Suspicion' as much as 'Mutually Agreed Destruction'. Surely, Abdul-Latif's outline of the principles of Islam closely match the principles of Christianity or indeed any religion, which can only function, as indeed humans can only function effectively, with a sense of co-operation and community. The alternative is barbarism.

After this evening's discussion, there are again concerns in my mind about our role in accompaniment. We are clearly

144

providing an audience for Abdul-Latif. Are we listening for information, or to develop a sense of having an important role in these people's lives? It could be suggested we like having people dependent on us and thereby making ourselves indispensable. What happens to these people when we, or other EAs, are not here? What support will they have then? The extreme case of this is the village of Yanoun to the north west of Nablus, where the seventy or so Palestinians will only stay when' internationals' are present. However, this is a decision for the villagers. The problem for me is more to do with the 'confessional' researcher. Is it a legitimate way of gathering information to be here as a listener, and by listening do we become indispensable to these people? What duty does it place on us to use the information? What happens when there is no one to listen? The Palestinians are used to having no one to listen, both individually and collectively.

What a way to greet the New Year, "You do not eat your neighbour's hunger".

Thursday 1st January, 2004

I am early to the South Gate, where it takes an hour and a half for two fellows to get through. I only get half way down the hill to observe the North Gate at lunchtime. The visit of Giuseppe, Zindzi and Mary West from Ramallah Quaker Meeting meant I was late leaving for the Gate. Giuseppe said how much Jayyous reminded him of the Southern Italian hill towns in the 1950s, socially, economically and environmentally.

It was good to show these folks around, and getting some very sensitive responses to what they saw. Zindzi and I discussed the comparison of Palestine under occupation with South Africa under apartheid. She suggested the situation here was worse than apartheid, more walls and less space. There was no occupation in the military sense, but a Police controlled separation in South Africa. It was a short visit, as they needed to be back in Funduq for the bus from Tulkarm at 13.00. I took them to the main road and in ten minutes they were in a shared taxi en-route to Azzoun, with many thanks and invitations. What an interesting day!

Picture 21. The Older Generation - Two men, one the owner of a vegetable shop and the other our neighbour, have time to talk. The traditional dress, the galliabia, contrasts with the ubiquitous white plastic stool.

Giuseppe set me thinking. I first came across the work of Danilo Dolci in the mid sixties when at school. Rather dull English lessons were suddenly brought to life by a student teacher who asked us to read and write about this man who was taking on the Mafia in Sicily and saying, "to achieve peace we need to be nonviolent revolutionaries."[4] In my geography lessons I taught about the "Cassa per il Mezzogiorno" the Fund for the South, or literally "for the midday". This was set up in 1950 to attempt to correct the imbalance in the Italian economy with its affluent north and poverty stricken south. These considerations seem like the economic and welfare concerns of a different age; a different age due to the rise of the free market that did much to remove the regional aid agenda, especially under the Thatcher

146

Governments in the UK. There is still cohesion funding for the periphery of Europe, for example in the southwest of Ireland. There have been moves to stem poverty in Africa with financial support, "a fund for the south", which I suspect is as much to help keep Africans in Africa, by reducing the increasing numbers of migrants moving north to rich Europe. This topic was dealt with in a BBC film of the late 1980s called "The March" which depicted the movement of people from Africa to Europe and included the memorable line from one of the marchers "I would sleep on your mat and eat the food you give your cat". This challenging film never seems to be repeated, unlike so many less challenging pieces.

Chapter 12
More Gate Watches
Weeks 7-8

"… The despoliation of the landscape is not only inexpedient, but wrong."

Aldo Leopold[1]

"Freedom begins when we share our bread with others."

Rabbi Jonathan Sacks[2]

Friday 2nd January

Ammar has a good fire going and is singing well today. Clear skies and a cool breeze make it a chilly start to the day. A donkey canters in, followed by a tractor lightly loaded with just three men. A second donkey arrives, kicking up the dust, braying at the first one and giving its rider a rough ride. The donkey in the shafts of the cart continues to look away with an air of condescension! At 07.05 the Jaish (Arabic for army) go north in their jeep, moving slowly along the inside road, making their daily check of the inner razor wire and culverts. After a steady flow of people, we have the novelty of the arrival of four cows and a calf. These are herded off to the right but climb over the stones into the olive grove where they graze the leaves and drink from a large puddle. The Humvee comes to open the Gate at 07.25 and starts a donkey chorus. Everybody is up and ready to go. The cows are herded back, along with a roaming donkey. A queue of at least forty is formed. The cows are now passing the queue and onto the inner road walking away from the Gate. With great agility the herdsmen drops into the ditch, and up to the inner road, to turn them back to the apron area. Here the lead cow sizes up the situation and decides to go and investigate the soldiers' activities, with warm breath and beady eyes. Being too close for one soldier's comfort, he shouts to someone to drive the cows on, and they are all through the Gate and across the road

148

before the herdsman's pass is checked.

The donkeys are eager to get to work, as their owners pull them back in the queue. The third soldier is watching me through his gun sights from the concrete box the other side of the road. I put my camera away, suddenly uncertain if the bright, low sun behind me offers as much visual-protection as I think it does; how blinding is the blinding light? The last tractor driver goes up the slope quickly to avoid being told to shut the inner gate but slips off his tractor to do this task much more quickly than the soldiers would be able to do it. I get a wave from one of the soldiers, as the Gate is closed.

The midday turn at the North Gate involves achieving a second opening to get Nadeem back from the fields. A youngster tries to get out, racing the Gate and upsetting the soldiers, causing a problem and not being let through. However, I close the inner gate with Nadeem and I am offered a lift home on the lad's donkey cart despite telling him off for rushing the Gate. Charles has returned from Jerusalem with his family, so I had better go and shop for a meal. We have an interesting evening with Charles's family, eating fruit cake from Scotland; a little bit of late Christmas, and most enjoyable.

Saturday 3rd January

With no early duty, I shower and do my washing, which are all part of the same visit to the bathroom. I put the clothes to soak in soapy water while I shower and then rinse the clothes before spinning them, if the power is on. One morning having taken a shower, I put my hand in the bowl of clothes and felt something in a shirt pocket. It was a camera memory chip in its plastic cover. While the cover is not intended to be waterproof, the surface tension had been enough to stop water going in. I carefully place it onto a piece of loo paper to attract the water away from the case. I then take it away from the bathroom before trying to retrieve the chip. Strangely, the best place to finish drying it out in a warm environment was the top pocket of my shirt, so long as I remembered to take it out next time. After a good time drying, amazingly it still worked.

I go to the Baladiya with the latest set of Gate Reports. In the Mayor's office I join the queue at the table while the Mayor talks on the phone. This is a good time to arrive as no time is wasted waiting in the outer office. Two men are talking to the mayor about IDs, over a heap of photocopied documents on the Mayor's desk. After a while, the Mayor asks me, across the two men sitting at the head of the table, what I have to report. He interprets some of my comments. He returns to the phone and a discussion about the paperwork while I am offered coffee and more people arrive and wait behind me. He puts down the phone and asks me about the Bedouin family. We talk about this and other matters, including saying we are all away from Jayyous next weekend. This is unfortunate as it is the limit of the time given for the Bedouin family to move out. We shake hands and I wish him well in his efforts to get new 'tasreehs' for the farmers.

It is interesting to watch the Mayor's process. Issues bought to him are in the open and therefore public and to some degree democratic by virtue of the openness. It is very interesting to see how this public access to village power works.

Abdul-Latif calls in the evening while Sharif Omar and his wife come to see Charles's wife and family. There is much consternation that they have already returned to Jerusalem on the early bus. Abdul-Latif talks about things going on in Nablus, 3 killed and 40 to 50 homes in the historic Old City destroyed by the occupying forces. He asks, "How can this be a security threat?" He and I also talk about the Khula Valley, in northern Israel, where Lake Hula on the headwaters of the Jordan has been completely drained. There are soil problems with salinization as the result of evaporation of water from irrigated land, the erosion of unprotected soil in the winter rains and the summer winds, mud traps in the rivers and swamp conditions that attract insects. Bird migration patterns have been interrupted and plant communities have been destroyed. This is an example of how the "greening of the desert" has become something of an environmental disaster, the arrogant use of the land having resonance in the controlling arrogance of the occupation.

> This notion of arrogance towards the use of the land is founded on the geographical concept of 'carrying capacity'. The concept of 'carrying capacity' has its origins in the observation of the impact of grazing animals on their environment. If the number of animals in a herd is increased and the area held constant, the amount of grass eaten is also increased, which will eventually lead to a reduction or destruction of the food supply. In the natural world, this results in a drop in population size, the changing sizes of deer herds on islands often being used as an example. In the human context, there are two classes of carrying capacity, the biophysical and the social. The biophysical capacity suggests the maximum population that can be carried by a piece of land with a very simple harvesting relationship and a low standard of living. The actual carrying capacity is determined by the quality of the land, not simply the space available. The social capacity sets out the number of people when a higher standard of living is developed and demands on the land, the 'ecological footprint', are increased. As the demand for resources, food, water and minerals, increases so the population that the land can support is reduced. Whereas the carrying capacity in the context of herds of animals is a simple relationship between the number of animals and the availability of grass and water, the carrying capacity for humans becomes much more complex, as it extends into a wider range of factors and resources.

> The 'ecological footprint' of different human societies is critical in using environments without degrading them in the present or diminishing their carrying capacity for the future. Indeed this becomes an ethical issue, with all land being sacred, a resource that needs to be nurtured. It is one of the paradoxes of the modern world that as we become more 'developed', more detached from the simple 'man - land' relationship, we need more space because of the increased demand for resources. The perception of more space being available historically underlies the great migrations of people from crowded areas, like Europe, to those, which were seen as

151

being empty, like North America. This has increased demands on sometimes-fragile environments which have not been managed with as much care as the indigenous people have used.[3]

The recognition of the concept of carrying capacity has important implications for the conservation of land and resources and, indeed, for the control of population size. If these matters are not addressed, we will not only have conflict over the availability of oil, but even the most basic of resources. Indeed, in the geography lesson mentioned in the Introduction about the River Jordan taught in 1973, I mentioned the possibility of people going to war over water. The occupation of Palestine is, at its simplest, a war over water. Not only do the Palestinians have part of what the Jewish people see as their God-given and sacred land, but also they have the best part of the water resources in the area. The increasing population of the area by inward migration to Israel and 'resistance birth rate'[4] in Palestine are putting the resources for all these people at risk. The unequal sharing of what is available is not only contrary to Marx's dictum, "to each according to his needs", but is contrary to the ethics of the religious groups who aspire to control this land.

The assertive approach to 'greening the desert' with its accompanying environmental problems does not seem to fit well with the Jewish duty of care for God's creation. The Palestinians, albeit due to the restrictions of the occupation, seem to be living more within the carrying capacity of this marginal, almost desert, land. The modern assertion, rooted in Judaeo-Christian origins of having dominion over the earth, that the creation is there for us to use, has no place in the management of this fragile environment. We need to listen to the environment as much as to the people that live in it, and develop a wise stewardship of this land. This issue is a real threat to the security of all the people of both Israel and Palestine.

Land announces citizenship so the farmers without passes have their citizenship denied.[5] This becomes the geography of permission; a human landscape shaped by permits that *maintain the domination of one group over another. This domination is a problem of the 'acquisitive society' in that possession does not bring joy, cooperation and peace. The possession of 'The Land' for Israelis is to do with power, the 'given right' and exclusivity and the heroism of warfare. For the Palestinians 'The Land' is simply tradition, a tradition of holding their 'stones' for others. They also hold onto their humanity in caring for others and maintain the great sense of place found in traditional less geographically flexible societies. More on the 'Geography of Occupation' can be found on the web site of Basem Ra'ad of Al Quds University in Jerusalem.* (6)

Picture 22. Newly-terraced farmland in the West Bank, with an olive grove in the background.

Sunday 4th January

At the Gate - Part One. One man, a donkey and a fire of thorn twigs greet me on arrival at the South Gate. The skies are clear with a pink tint to the east and a grey haze to the west over the coast. There are sounds from the quarry and cockerels crow in the village. One of the 'stone-throwing' boys turns up with a plastic bag containing some food. Is he going to go to the land?

The man walks off to bring back a straying donkey. There is a weak yellow sunrise behind the fence as it curves over the hill to the southeast. The occasional bird sings. The wild clematis, with creamy flowers not much bigger than large bluebells, climbs through the small almond tree beside the path. The dry wood burns freely and I am offered its warmth, which I accept.

A jeep arrives at 06.52 going south. The old man watches but does not move or make a sign. The jeep goes on south. The Gate stays closed. A donkey arrives from the village making a sound like a broken hinge opening. Light smoke drifts across the track from a fire, which has more embers than flame. A stone is prodded with a stick. There is no need to hurry about anything. The hopeful sound of a jeep is heard, but it turns out to be a vehicle in the village. Spit is gathered, projected, and followed by a bout of coughing. The tops of the olive trees turn silver as the rays of the rising sun touch them. The second donkey, tied to a tree, sounds a "death rattle" of a bray.

A man and a dog come out of the olive grove. He talks to the boy trying to keep the fire going. The first man returns with his donkey, recovered from the better grass yet again, and carrying wood for the fire. The boy loses interest and goes to stand by the men at the inner gate. The first man continues to make up the fire. The sun comes blindingly over the hill. In the economic sense, working time is perishing as we wait.

The donkey complains again. It is 07.15 and the Gate should be open, so indeed should the North Gate, which is ten minutes away and is opened at the same times by the same jeep! There is no Bedouin family today as it is the school holidays, the children getting the first two weeks of the New Year off. The pollution haze hides the high-rise offices in the coastal towns, as a man strolls in from the village. He wears a Shamagh, a blue-grey jacket, and navy trousers and carries a stick and an empty sack. He talks to his friends and clears his throat. The boy listens intently. Again, the donkey questions why we are waiting so long. The sun glints on the razor wire as the fire is made up yet again. A jeep? No its the Humvee that drives out of the sun on the inside road, as the man who arrived with the dog heads for the village. The soldiers move the razor wire blocking the inner road by the Gate. The Humvee drives through, and stops for the soldiers and drives on. The movement of expectation becomes the resignation of waiting, again. A throat is cleared. The boy returns to the fire.

It is now 07.33 and the sun is warming now, but my rocky perch is still cold. Village life can be heard behind us; the land lies silent beyond the fence. Is this the intention? To silence the land and then recover it for the state according to Ottoman Law, which says that land not used for 3 years must revert to the State: now the State of Israel. A survey plane has been seen flying over in parallel lines, photographing. Is this silently mapping the new Israeli border? We are told the Israelis take aerial photographs twice a year, usually in May (after the harvest) and in November (before ploughing) as these times do not show clearly that the land is being worked. A contractor's pick-up goes by. Charles rings to say he has forty or more at the North Gate and no joy.

A boy appears with his sheep on the hill beyond the fence. He calls to the boy with the bag of food by the fire. Another little boy comes bare foot from the village. A jeep comes over the hill, slows and stops by the Gate. The men and donkeys move forward. On the hill, the sheep are quietly herded. The bag is given to one of the men going through the now open Gate to be taken to the waiting shepherd. The donkeys are walked around the wire and through the Gate, which is then shut, with the usual difficulty, at 07.52. The sheep graze on the hill, while the shepherd has his breakfast. The children walk back to the village, and all that is left of the scene is a small pile of ashes and a blackened stone.

At the Gate - Part Two. At this point. I would usually ring Charles to let him know the Jaish is on the way to him at the North Gate. However, my phone chooses this moment to fall to pieces, the battery on the ground and the back missing a clip that holds it in place. I rebuild it as best I can in the 'field' but really need some sticky tape or a small rubber band to do the job properly. I am just about to walk back to the village after this delay when I hear a voice from beyond the Gate. The Bedouin family is arriving on their way to the village. It is 08.00. I walk towards the Gate and carefully call HaMoked, asking them to contact the District Co-ordination Office and get the jeep to come back and open up. I walk up to the Separation Barrier to tell Dharifah, that I have phoned HaMoked and the Jaish are at the North Gate using a mixture of words and gestures to communicate the news. It crosses my mind that it would be better if Dharifah were able to speak directly to HaMoked, but the Barrier is in the way. If I were to pass the phone through the fence this might set off the sensors, which would most likely cause the soldiers not to open the Gate. It would attract their attention but not get a positive result.

Suddenly we are back in business. I am glad I had the warm pitta bread, heated on the gas ring, before leaving the house this morning. Charles phones to say he has an opening. At 08.16 the Humvee comes up the hill, stops and three soldiers get out and the Gate is opened. The family walk forward. The boy shakes hands with the soldier holding the Gate, while another soldier checks the adults' permissions. It appears that the soldiers enjoy opening this Gate for the children. Dharifah starts to talk to them with some persistence and continues even when she is moved through and the Gate is shut. The Humvee goes at 08.22. The girl tells me to be here for 13.00, as this is the time arranged for the soldiers to open the Gate. Surprisingly I am back at Bait Abu Azzam for a second breakfast before Charles. I pass on the message about the lunchtime opening at the South Gate

At lunchtime, the North Gate watch becomes protracted with a visit from 12.30 to 14.50. This includes a final half hour with five jeeps around the Gate, three of which come through the Gate. One of these, a clean and dark blue vehicle (they are normally dirty green), stops immediately in front of me as I lean against the wall beside the lane. It has darkened glass in the windows, so I cannot see who is inside. I decide that I should just stay where I am, but resist the temptation of getting out my camera to record the event. I try to enjoy the warmth of the sun and not spend too much time either looking straight at the windows of the Jeep or at the green van, being checked just up the lane. I assume they have stopped for this obstruction to clear, although it is well over 30 meters away, rather than stopping beside me for any sinister reason. The next Jeep is a similar distance behind towards the Gate. I wonder if they keep a regulation distance between them, (*that would be uncharacteristic of this army*) and if I am just unlucky to be on the mark. I was later told occupants included the regional director of Shin Bet, the Israeli Security Service.

Was this direct intimidation? Why do these people need to hide behind a 'veil' of smoked glass? Why indeed do motorists at home hide behind darkened glass? Perhaps the black windows are like the Separation Barrier. The windows give security to those on the inside, allowing them to see, but keep me out. They make me respond in the way the Palestinians do, in that I would not go away, staying by the wall in this no eye-contact, no word said confrontation. I have no idea how long this incident lasted, but it seemed longer than it actually was. Perhaps understandably, this incident has added to my aversion to large vehicles with darkened glass.

However, the Gate has been opened and all those who want to have been able to cross. The green van, having given up before the arrival of the Jeeps and the opening, has been stopped and its driver questioned, going back empty up the lane to the village. I meet the jeeps in the village by the barber's, where I intended to call and get my beard trimmed. With the Israeli Army on the streets comes the stone-throwing, which is often followed by Israeli 'fireworks' or tear gas. I cannot support stone-throwing, so a 'retreat' to the Bait Abu Azzam seems sensible. Any intervention, without sufficient language skills, will probably be misunderstood. Like the old European adage you sell in the customers' language and you buy in your own, neither the over-excited stone-throwers, nor the Israeli Soldiers are likely to listen to a foreign language intervention.

We go to Abdul-Latif's for a meal in the early evening. The discussion covers marriage, family and grand children. Initially his three children are very shy, but are egged on to excitable behaviour by Rex, who says he has been told off by parents for stirring up their children. It seems Abdul-Latif is too polite to comment. One of his many great disappointments in life is not being able to take his children out of the village. They see the animals on the television, but they cannot go to the zoo. They can see the Mediterranean from the top of the house but he cannot take his children to the beach. Because of travel restrictions, he is not able to go to Israel, or to Palestinian Gaza which has beaches.

This again makes me wonder about the way EAs are encouraged to travel around and visit other locations. If we are truly accompanying we should live within our designated locations and be subject to the same restrictions as the host community. However, this is at odds with the need to gain a wider picture. My feeling is that a wider experience should be achieved at the beginning and end of our time in Palestine/Israel with consistent presence being maintained in the host communities. I could easily have made my visit to Israel at this time.

Monday 5th January

I am early to the North Gate. There is no problem, apart from late arrival of a truck, which is eventually allowed through. During the morning, I work on Gate Logs. I get half way down the hill to find the North Gate open at lunchtime, it being closed before the official opening time! It is worth noting the only indication we, or the farmers, have of the Gate opening times is scrawled on the lid of a pizza box, left by the edge of the track in front of the Gate. Hardly a formal, let alone an official notification. I return to the house to finish the Logs and start making an analysis of North Gate openings; work on making the records more accessible and meaningful is moving on apace.

Picture 23 Sharing the pitta bread cooked in our neighbour's oven.

On going to the shop to buy a couple of shekels worth of vegetables for supper, our neighbour calls me into his garden. His wife is baking pitta bread in a wood fired oven. With wood blazing at one side, the uncooked breads are put on a large circular metal sheet. This can be moved in and out of the oven as well as turning round on a central spindle. This allows the pittas to be moved around in the heat, without having to be picked up. The breads go in as creamy coloured disks, rise up almost like balloons and come out flat with a mottled brown surface. Each batch of four 'breads' takes about three or four minutes to cook. It tastes very good straight from the oven. These people will share anything and everything. I ask if I might photograph the scene. Supper is not delayed by this sharing as I am well ahead of time, but the meal is enhanced by the gift of fresh bread.

Unexpectedly, Sam returns to Jayyous expecting a full account of the last two weeks! Rex rings from Nablus needing some support. He has seen some bad things, similar to those described by Abdul-Latif several days ago, and I am happy to listen, Rex being on his own, so making his situation more difficult. My report to the others on our conversation is minimal.

Chapter 13
The Incident, a review

"Without forgiveness, there is no future."
Desmond Tutu[1]

The request from Sam for a detailed report of recent events poses a problem. Over the period from the 27th December to the 2nd January an 'incident' had been running that Charles, Rex and myself decided should only be known about by the three of us directly involved.

On the afternoon of the 27th, after our return from the demonstration in Qalqilya, I was alone at Bait Abu Azzam, taking an afternoon nap. The street doorbell disturbed me several times, with children ringing and running away. On the third or fourth ring, there were three young men at the door. They wanted to come in and I thought this was to see Rex about his video interviews. I suggested that they go away and come back later when I expected Rex to be here. I went back to bed. I must have appeared rather grumpy.

A little later, while I was beginning to prepare some food, Charles returned. He carried a piece of paper with a message scrawled in red biro ink, and in reasonable English, that suggested that if we did not leave the village in three days we would be dead. Charles and I quickly agreed this was a serious matter, but we also thought it did not seem to be a genuine note. Despite being signed Hamas, it looked like children's handwriting. We decided that I should continue with the preparations for our meal while he took the note to Sharif Omar.

Charles returned without the note, having left it with Sharif Omar as evidence for him to show the Palestinian Police in Qalqilya. Rex returned from his conversations in the village. The three of us discussed the situation and decided to carry on as normal and not to tell the office in Jerusalem or other members of the team about the situation. We reviewed the planned activities of the next few days, and it was agreed that I should go to Ramallah as planned and return to Jayyous and that Charles would go to Jerusalem to meet his family, arriving for a visit. The only alteration to our plans was that Charles would put together a case of his things to be taken to him in Jerusalem if we felt the situation had become too dangerous to stay in Jayyous.

On the 29th, during my wait for the bus to depart from Qalandia back to Jayyous, I had a rather disturbing phone conversation with Charles; I was concerned about his report of Rex's robust attitude to dealing with the situation and some of the young people who had come to the house.

Tim, a Jerusalem based EA, was in Jayyous on my return and we talked about various things, including what was happening in Jayyous. I felt he had to know as, due to his unexpected visit, he had walked into the situation. It also felt re-assuring to know that someone reliable on the team outside Jayyous knew what was going on.

In the following days, Sharif Omar first called at the house with a detective who looked at the street gate and the front door. He also said we must have a meeting when Charles had returned to decide on the punishment we required. This could be an interesting cultural experience, a challenge or a problem. There was talk of someone going to prison. We needed to tread carefully.

Sharif Omar later called in to tell us that the police had some suspects who had admitted to putting the note on the door. Any sense of relief at the writers of the note being found and the end of the possible danger quickly evaporated at the realisation of the task ahead, to gain agreement about a resolution to the matter: a resolution that would test the different cultural and faith origins of the three of us.

Returning to my Journal for the 1st January: Having just settled down to some work after lunch, Sharif Omar comes with two adults from a house across the road about the young man being held in relation to the threatening note. I say we will need to discuss the matter and that he should come back in an hour. "Is an hour enough?" he asks, with possibly more understanding of my task than I have.

Clearly Rex wishes to be robust about this, "What do they mean chase? We are not guilty." I do not know about a chase either. Have I misheard something, in my disturbed sleep? Am I going deaf? He talks about being an extrovert and what extroverts do. He makes several judgements about my character, suggesting I take on too much guilt. This is all very interesting but does not bring us towards a solution. I develop a set of questions we need to ask in order to gain a better understanding of the context in which we are working. Eventually we agree on the questions. This re-focusing brings us back to the issue and a tacit agreement that forgiveness seems to be the only option, without any real discussion of the practical, philosophical or moral reasons why. At least this pragmatic decision provides the foundation for the next move.

We await the return of Sharif Omar and his friends. This means I am not able to go to the North Gate this evening. This is possibly not a bad thing, as I feel very tired: is the underlying stress getting to me?

I am challenged by the suggestion that I am not being robust enough in the situation; that I am taking on the 'guilt' of the situation. I am looking for a calm, reconciling solution, which will allow us to carry on with our work here in Jayyous.

Sharif Omar returns. I ask questions about the process and the tradition of the 'victim's involvement'. We are told more about the background, and it appears when the young men called and asked about playing 'chess' they were upset by my response. We quickly establish that we will forgive the young men. However, we also find out more about the process this forgiveness will take. We are to see the local Chief of Police at his house in Jayyous this evening with the father and uncle (one of the fathers is working in Jordan) of the young men. We are to discuss the case and to agree to forgive the writers of the note. The following evening we will again meet at the house of the Chief of Police and the young men will make their apology to us. We will all shake hands and the matter will be closed. I say that we will forgive the young men and accept their apologies for what has happened

In the first meeting, Sharif Omar interprets for me. We again agree to forgive the young men who made the threat. There is much shaking of hands. The meeting is an interesting experience with the Chief of Police talking about the moving checkpoints that encircle Nablus. He also says how impossible it is to effectively police the West Bank when the Israelis arrest your officers (15 in Qalqilya alone) and raid your offices as many as six times in one month, let alone reportedly smashing up police vehicles, paid for with funds from the European Union. I ask if there is any paperwork in connection with the case, saying how the British Police are tied down with paperwork. He laughs and says much of the Palestinian police work is still based on the British model from the time of the Mandate and that we cannot be responsible for the actions of our grandfathers'. "Anyway, you are here to help and support us so there is no paperwork". This also means there is no official record of these events. This may be how they like it to be.

Sharif Omar takes me to one side to thank me for not pursuing the case as one of the young men is a student at university and the other training in a job and that both would lose these positions if we pressed charges.

By the time of our second meeting, which includes the young men, Charles has returned from Jerusalem. We walk to the meeting through the village, passing a house open for a funeral gathering: a Ta a'ziea, a paying of respects for the dead. This event will have an impact on our meeting as many of the people who might attend are relatives of the dead man and must go to the funeral. We quickly accept the apologies of the culprits and the young men are given a very strong telling-off by the Chief of Police. Asking Charles to interpret for me, I say, "I think it is about time I learned to play chess and do the young men know a good teacher?" There are smiles all round and the matter is closed.

Should it be an eye for an eye, or forgiveness and apology? It seemed to start with a note on the door. It ended with a visit to the local police chief where we forgave the young men and they apologised. It actually started with me going to the door from an interrupted sleep. I was not aware of the previous EAs "tradition" of playing chess with these young men who had just returned to Jayyous from their studies and expected the same social activity to be available at the EA's house. We were breaking that tradition following a collective decision not to have such an 'open house', feeling the need for a little of our own space.

My reaction to their request for a game of chess, which must have seemed to be dismissed out of hand, initiated the problem. Another factor was my ignorance of the importance of the relationship these young men had built up with the previous EAs. As I was reflecting and reviewing my behaviour, I realised it was my response that had annoyed. That I was also responsible, through my sleepy and grumpy response, for setting up an unpredictable reaction to the situation. I am glad to have stuck to my own feelings of uncertainty, feelings of working through dynamic, changing situations that offer new insights to our behaviour and so move us on: in this case moving me on to find a chess teacher, and trying to modify my abrasive and grumpy responses to situations. I wonder if it will work. It is the process as much as the learning that is important here. My only, and feeble defence, is that it is human to be grumpy when repeatedly woken from an afternoon nap. Am I the one who needs to be forgiven?

I find it rather surprising how I have reacted to this whole episode. I have not lost any sleep over it. I have kept calm during the days with the possible exception of Rex's attempt to tell me about my problem. The process has worked well and brought out a Gandhian solution, turning the issue round and offering the opportunity for the young men to teach me to play chess.

In his chapter "What about Justice?", Desmond Tutu comments, "retributive justice, in which an impersonal state hands down punishment with little consideration for victims and hardly any for the perpetrator, is not the only form of justice". He contends that there is another kind of justice, "restorative justice". Here, the central concern is not retribution or punishment but healing of breaches, the redressing of imbalances, the restoration of broken relationships, allowing forgiveness and reconciliation. Forgiveness gives people resilience, enabling them to survive and emerge still human despite all the efforts to dehumanise them.[2]

The western view of law and punishment, spread with the Christian message of right and wrong and handed down to the relatively weak by the powerful, all-controlling colonial governments, often destroyed established systems of community-based justice and conciliation.

I was especially interested in the way this incident was handled. There were strong elements of Restorative Justice to be found, in the sense of the well being of the victim, the offenders and the community. Care and support was shown to us. The offenders took responsibility for their offence. A dialogue was established and attempts made to put right the harm done. As victims, we were offered a role in resolving the case. Although this seemed a serious case, it was formed on a simple misunderstanding, a lack of listening and a lack of realisation of the needs of others. It resulted in a spirit of mutual forgiveness.

On a wider scale, such forgiveness breaks the vicious circle of repeated violence and revenge, provoking more violence. That is the problem with the philosophy of an eye for an eye and a tooth for a tooth. It responds to attack, to violence, to threats with the same vocabulary and actions, just in the way President Bush responded to the attacks on the World Trade Center, with threats to "smoke them out" and in the same way as the Israelis respond to stone-throwing Palestinian children, piling aggression on aggression. Restorative Justice on any scale, be it the classroom, the community, the nation or between nations, requires a starting point of listening and understanding, of dialogue and moral code. At the international level such a code must be international law, *which only has any strength by its observance. Each time it is broken, and those breaking it are not challenged, the law becomes weaker. It is no good having a fine set of rules if people and nations are not prepared to live by them, which is where Restorative Justice works in another way. The more it is used, the more it restores justice for all.*

Chapter 14
Back to the Gates
Week 8

"We look not for the things that are seen
but to the things that are unseen;
for the things that are seen are transient but the
things that are unseen are eternal."[1]

Tuesday 6th January

This is just an ordinary morning, so why did I record it in detail?

I take the offer of a lift down to the Gate on a donkey cart, with a young donkey running alongside. I arrive at the Gate feeling I have used more energy than if I had walked, due to the effort of hanging on as we sit on a board over the sacks of manure on their way to improve the land. As soon as we stop, the young donkey is quickly, selectively grazing among the rocks. At 06.52, an Israeli jeep passes on the inner road checking for any over night damage to the culverts and razor wire.

I think there is only really enough room for two on the seat of a donkey cart. The next donkey cart arrives with three, two facing forwards and one looking backwards in the middle. The donkey is tied up by the inner gate. It starts to bray. This noise is discouraged by a few carefully aimed stones. Ammar starts a fire with a piece of plastic sheet. If smoking does not get to his lungs, his habit of burning plastic sheet to start fires most likely will.

At 07.00 on the dot, jeep Y610657 arrives to open the Gate with only 12 people present. The soldiers work quickly with two of them checking ID and permissions, something I have not seen before. Do they plan not to come back and so cause more frustration? Mubarak, the tractor driver with a faded orange hat, tries to slow down the process by hanging back and phoning his fellow farmers who have not yet arrived. Once he is being checked, another farmer starts an argument in the gateway and slows things down yet again. This is to no avail as the Gate is closed at 07.06.

As I wait to be present during the 'official' opening time of 07.15 - 07.45, more people start arriving from the village. At 07.12, there are twelve discussing what to do. Some men on the other side stay to see if the jeep comes back and then drift off to the fields. The fellow in the orange hat is on the phone again. A donkey brays at the razor wire, where the grass is better, if dangerously out of reach. No one notices. A dog lies down under the inner gate. There is much shouting and debate. Another donkey is silenced, by a stone on its flank.

> *It is at times like this that I wonder if just being there, accompanying, is enough. I challenged the soldiers as they shut the Gate but only get the response that "We will be back when you see us". Should we be doing more? As I said to Jamilla in late November, "At times I don't know what I am doing here". What benefit is my presence to anyone?*

At present, there are three possibilities. The Jaish will return. I can phone HaMoked in 35 minutes. The farmers will decide not to stay. I assess the odds of each of these and settle down to an uncomfortable 35 minutes, the rocks being too cold to sit on. By 07.30 the numbers have grown to twenty-four including some women and girls who sit apart.

There is the sound of traffic on the military road at the top of hill, but like a mirage, it could be something else. The yellow truck comes down from the village. We are now thirty standing together in the sun in several small groups. The sound comes to nothing. Half the time has gone. I see a few glances of expectation in my direction to see if I am doing anything. There is nothing to be done at present.

At least it is not raining. However it would bring joy to the hearts of those round me if it were, as this winter is seriously dry. Are these people going to suffer climatic change as well as occupation and the theft of their water? If, as a result of long-term, continuing dynamic changes in the earth's climatic pattern, the climate does change in Palestine, it will mean less winter rain as the dry zone to the south extends northwards. It would be a double tragedy if nature inflicts more pain on all the people of this environmentally fragile region. Climate change will not discriminate between the Israelis and the Palestinians, and neither will be able to control this threat to their security.

At 07.53, I decide to try HaMoked, who will ring back. There are still people arriving at 08.00 and the Jaish come down the hill watched by all. It is the same jeep. *Perhaps it was all planned just to make us, and more particularly me, feel powerless by not saying they will come back.* The men are told to open the inner gate and start going through. Only one soldier checks the permissions this time. Checking stops and gun waving takes over, as the queue gets too close to the Gate. *When will they learn?* The soldiers are clearly jumpy today. The donkey carts are called forward as the group of young men stand and watch. The men are told to move back yet again. There is still a lot of gun waving and fingers too close to triggers for comfort. The soldier in the jeep shouts at those at the Gate. They start to close the Gate in front of the queue, still telling them to move back. I move forward and ask, "What is the problem now?" As the soldiers close the Gate, their guns are pointing at the ground. They say, "We will be back in five minutes. Something has touched the fence and we have to go." Having opened for ten minutes, the jeep drives off to the north leaving another twenty to cross. I gesture to people to move back and indicate that they say they will be back in five minutes with much shrugging of shoulders and unsaid Inshallahs.

Having said they will be back, amazingly at 08.14 they are back and unlocking again. A women and a girl are first through, as much as to say, "Don't you men mess up my chances again". The guard's gun is still too high, but they do not fuss about the queue being on the ramp. The problem of under-18 year olds without permissions always takes time. By 08.22, all are through. I shut the inner gate to save the tractor driver having to get off but he still comes to help and say thank you. *I am not sure why.*

> *Gate work is plodding work, like me walking up the hill to*
> *Jayyous, thinking of a second breakfast of yogurt, honey and*
> *pitta bread from the neighbour's oven, reheated on the gas*
> *ring. It is slow and sometimes seems to have no purpose. It is*
> *observation, but for what, a source for future historians*
> *writing about the end of Palestine, for the mayor to have a*
> *record, or just for me to tell others about what is going on? Is*
> *recording enough? Would recording have been enough in*
> *Germany in the 1930s? To me recording has become part of*
> *accompanying, whatever that is. Accompaniment cannot be*
> *easily measured; like so much in life it is the domain of human*
> *relationships: the smiles of the tractor drivers once on the*
> *move, the helping to shut the Gate, the "shaloms" of the*
> *soldiers. What does any of it mean?*

Polly arrives from the office in Jerusalem. We walk to
Baladiya for her to meet Abdul-Latif. This allows me to
witness an opening of the North Gate at 14.30 for a tractor and
Donkey cart. We go to Sharif Omar's for a mid afternoon
meal, cooked by Abdul-Latif's wife. We hear there has been a
visit from the Senior Officer in charge of the Separation Barrier
to discuss passes with the Mayor. This meeting took place
through the Separation Barrier, as the Senior Officer had not
been given the right key to open the Gate! The Mayor said to
him without fear, "You were tricked by the IDF!" We return
home laden with citrus, illuminated by a vivid sunset. That
the clematinas are over and mandolinas are just starting is of
no matter; they are all full of taste and wonderfully juicy.

Sharif Omar says, "The land is like a woman. If someone stole
your wife no compensation would be enough. Therefore there
can be no compensation for the loss of the land, ... trees, ...
stones, etc." While this metaphor might tell us about attitude
to the relationship between husband and wife, it also
illustrates the great affection these people have for their land.

We have a long talk with Polly during the evening, about our
work in Jayyous. Some interesting issues arise around the
headings of group/individual work, future requirements and

plans and orientation of the next group. There is a requirement for us to write a report on the work of the Jayyous team between November 2003 and February 2004. This report needs to include information as a platform for the next group of EAs to build on, without having to go back to start at the beginning again. The evening closes with an interesting discussion about the distinction between fear and anxiety in Israeli.

> *Fear has always been an important factor in human society. At the most basic it is the motivation to protect oneself or one's community. Fear gives us the fright and flight reaction. It also gives us what may be seen as the 'fright and* **fight***' reaction. Fear needs an object. Fear can become the motivation to action, so sometimes the most frightened become the most powerful. Such fear may be used to develop mistrust and even hatred. It has happened with such groups as Jews, Gypsies, homosexuals, communists and Muslims, or with people who are just different, all being made the focus of hatred; hatred in the name of an ideology or in the name of security.*

> *Anxiety may grow out of fear. The anxious have an excessive uneasiness, an uneasiness that feeds on the dark-side of the mind. Anxiousness is there, independent of an object of fear. It is the emotion of the uncertain situation. In the individual, it may result in setting a defensive posture of detachment, self-absorption and self-reliance: of a search for security. Fear and anxiety can lead to the need for security and control. These words may seem compatible, especially if paired in the conventional way. Israelis have a legitimate fear of being attacked by Palestinians, the most likely method being the suicide bomber. There is an object; there is the accumulated experience that this can happen, which can be assessed as a risk, rather in the way we all, at some level, assess the risks of everyday life. Having established that the risk to Israel is unacceptably high, fear has motivated control; the additional military control in the Occupied Territories, together with the construction of the Separation Barrier: the 'Security Fence' to most Israelis. This, together with the limited access, due to*

the issue or non-issue of passes to Palestinians to travel or work in Israel, may provide some security. It might keep the fear out of Israel, or at least keep it at bay. However, it does not necessarily remove the anxiety.

There is another possible means of achieving security, a security where fear is not converted into control, a security built on reducing fear by developing a greater understanding and a greater friendship. As the British Chief Rabbi, Dr Jonathan Sacks says, "The greatest single antidote to fear is friendship."[2] At present experience and propaganda stimulates fear and anxiety for the future. The self-absorption of people narrowly grounded in the history and rights of this young state limits knowledge and understanding of the 'other', and may become a tenacious motivation to blindly protect. The situation needs a new way to develop security that turns these negatives into positives, to provide security for both the Israeli and the Palestinian. The experience of cooperation that dispels fear, the honesty of understanding of the others' heritage, position and feelings might be the basis for an accommodation for the future. With the need to find solutions to wider problems, for example the care for a fragile environment, the self-absorbed could be brought into a wider debate in an attempt to create a peaceful future for all.[3]

On a number of occasions, it has been suggested to me by Palestinians that we must, "Make our enemy our friend". This comment seems to have it origins in both Islam and the speeches of Martin Luther King. Indeed, it has been used in many ways by many people. Here is Gandhi's version, "It is easy enough to be friendly to one's friends. However, to befriend the one who regards himself as your enemy is the quintessence of true religion. The other is mere business". Moshe Dayan the Israeli General said, "If you want to make peace, you don't talk to your friends. You talk to your enemies." It is not important to know the 'reference', it is important to attempt to live by the sentiment.

Desmond Tutu asks, "Do the Israelis realise the depth of the Palestinian hurt in the situation?"[4]: the dispossession of people and the creation of the refugees in 1948-49, the *occupation since 1967 and the construction of the Separation Barrier on Palestinian land since 2002. The deeper the hurt inflicted to gain Israeli security, the greater will be the fear and anxiety for the future. I have heard it said that the Separation Barrier will be removed when the Israelis have a feeling of security. How can a feeling of true security, lasting security, be developed if people are separated, unable to meet and to build friendship? As an observer, I can see the impedimenta of the occupation, the Separation Barrier, the passes, the checkpoints. These things may be transient. What I cannot see as an observer or accompanier is the fear and the need for security, things that may be everlasting.*

Wednesday 7th January

There is heavy rain over night that continues to the start of midday watch, with a torrent flowing down the lane. There is the beginning of a 'wash-out' on the inner right hand side of the Gate just next to the drainpipes, the water preferring to follow its own route rather than that provided for its 'control' by the engineers. Just one young farmer goes out to the land. I walk back up the hill after 12.50, when opening time expired and find the flow of water significantly reduced after the cessation of the rain about 30 minutes earlier. It is also interesting to see the amount of water standing in the farrows under the olive trees where the small patches of soil have been ploughed. This water will eventually soak in where it is needed, ultimately to feed the deep aquifers.

The barber is not open so I will find somewhere in Jerusalem to trim my beard tomorrow. There are more conversations with Polly. I spend some time sorting things (papers, books and other bits and pieces) into three boxes: things to go home in luggage, others to be read before going home and things to be sent home by post. I estimate one more, large box from the Israeli Post Office will be fine for the last posting. I had better go to bed, as it is a 05.00 call in the morning.

Chapter 15
A Reflection on the Situation
Weeks 8-9

"What is my witness? What is the witness of my
community, my people? In the light of the
challenges we face, what responsibility do we
bear? We have to bring forth true justice to all."

Jean Zaru[1]

Thursday 8th January

Polly, Charles and I leave Jayyous at 05.50 and arrive at
Qalandia at 07.45 and on to Jerusalem at 07.50. We are held at
the checkpoint until 08.15 including waiting in the traffic
queue. We are at the Damascus Gate by 08.35 and the New
Imperial Hotel at 08.50. We have come early in the day, as this
is the only direct bus to Qalandia, others from Funduq
requiring possibly two taxis, as well as the potential for missed
connections. In the rain, I visit the Post Office, Tourist
Information Office in West Jerusalem (not very helpful), the
British Airways Office and HaMoked (it is very interested to
see the faces we speak to on the other end of the phone). I call
in at the Educational Book Shop, where I buy "I Saw
Ramallah"[2] and return to the New Imperial to dry out and
start reading my new purchase.

Later I find a barber to get my beard trimmed in David Street.
This is the best beard trim I have ever had, the work being
done with a cutthroat razor. There is no room for fear here,
the trimming of my beard becoming a definition of trust as the
blade, sharpened on a leather strop, flashes around my face,
and all for 15NIS (£2).

As it is still raining, I go to the Tower of David Museum and
back to the hotel to warm up again. I have a chance meeting
with Tim, which allows us to exchange notes on our
'professional' conversation in Jayyous. Having missed their

phone call, I reply to Sophie and Louise by e-mail. I say I am fine, if rather wet, which might seem like obfuscation and double-entendre. This arrangement of weekly calls to the staff in London has pretty much broken down. On occasions, I have managed to make contact with Beryl, in the London office, which has been administratively useful and pleasantly encouraging. On a strong recommendation, I go to Papa Andrea's for supper, but it does not live up to expectations, so I will return to using the Armenian Restaurant or the Palestinian Samara Café under the hotel in future.

Friday 9th January

We have a good run north up the 443 and 40 Roads on the Israeli side of the Green Line, but have trouble finding the western end of the 55 Road to the southeast of Qalqilya, where the map does not seem to relate to what is on the ground as the result of new road construction. Eventually, as voluntary or self-appointed navigator, I get my bearings mostly from the landmarks around Jayyous, which is on the hills above us. It is interesting to have the Israeli view of Jayyous from below. We drive into very poor weather as we head north after picking up Sam and Rex, who have walked through the checkpoint on the 55 Road, having come by taxi from Jayyous. The mist is down at Mount Tabor so we drive straight on to Tiberius on the Sea of Galilee. Some of us find an excellent vegetarian restaurant, called 'Apropos' on the 'sea front'. We spend over two hours eating and relaxing, our meal only coming to an end for the Shabbat closing at 16.00.

The retreat accommodation does not live up to expectation, being little better than a third rate Youth Hostel in the 1960s. All the men are accommodated in a separate building; a box with windows would be a better description, with some bunk beds and mattresses on the floor and no plumbing. There is hardly any room to move. There are clearly very different views of what a retreat should be, with some focusing on spiritual comfort while others clearly think a little rest and relaxation would be good, or indeed both. The former military mind says, "You should never move your men to inferior conditions for rest and relaxation". What is on offer here is not as good as our simple accommodation in Jayyous. I would appreciate the physical comfort of an armchair, which would provide a good start to some spiritual comfort.

Saturday 10th January

I have probably my worst night's sleep since we arrived in Israel/Palestine, trying to keep myself in a non-snoring position. There is a lot of talk in the morning about snoring, mostly by those making a good deal of noise themselves. Tim says it reminds him of a concentration camp. While not totally disagreeing, I think more of Gilbert and Sullivan's "...steamer from Harwich".[3]

Before breakfast, I walk up to the Monastery and have a conversation, around the fishpond, with a monk and the gardener, unexpectedly using some basic German. As I sit and write in the Church of the Bread and Fishes at Tabgha, it is overwhelmed by a large number of pilgrims who show little respect for the Germanic requests for silence.

How glad I am to have come in earlier while trying to get 'started' on the day. I will return later, when the tourist buses carrying the pilgrims have gone. Sadly, the retreat has caused me to become a tourist again. As a tourist it is frustrating to be so close to Nazareth and have no means to get there. John says Nazareth would be like Tiberius without the lake (sea). However, as a woodworker, I would like to have seen the place.

I spend most of the day keeping out of the way, apart from interjecting that people should be able to do as they wish, for which I am told to mind my own business, which is most likely a fair enough comment. My understanding of retreat is to be in a 'supported space' to attend to one's own spiritual needs; to have quiet space and people prepared to listen; to have space to walk, space to think and space to talk quietly. Here there is a programme to follow and expectations to be part of it all. One becomes obvious if one drops out of group activities. The old Quaker problem of not taking communion comes to light again, so I stay away from worship sessions. What can I say in the inevitable evaluation? I wonder if I should ask if I might skip some of this weekend. It would be more interesting to be in Jerusalem on a Sunday and spend time at the different church services with one's own spiritual company, being recharged with simple experiences and new observations.

The Church of the Beatitudes does not over impress me. It is another relatively modern shrine with rather shady origins.[4] It is full of Russians and Nigerians, which is fine, but it tells one a lot about the changing face of religion and economies in recent years. The signs at the entrance tell one a bit about modern Israel - red, European style, prohibitive circles with diagonals that proclaim no ice creams, no smoking, no phones and no guns. The tee shirts in the souvenir shops include several with pro-Zionist (Christian Zionist), Pro-Greater Israel slogans. While the visiting pilgrims are aware of the religious significance of this place, I wonder how many are aware of the human situation of this Land.

John joins me in declining to attend communion, but no doubt for different reasons. We sit under the Aleppo pines, with him reading from "The Innocents Abroad" by Mark Twain, me doing some sketching. This is about as close as he and I are going to get to a 'retreat'. He talks and laughs; I listen and smile, communing with the paper. The sketches are poor and disappointing, which is possibly the best evaluation of the situation.

In the 'free' afternoon, I walk north towards the ruins of Capernaum along the western edge of the Sea of Galilee. The scale of the place impresses me, as here one stands at the northern limit of one of the largest physical features on the earth's surface, the Great Rift Valley. This stretches south for thousands of kilometres to southern Africa. This is the beginning and the end of it, depending on your perspective. In the great scheme of things, whatever that is, I find being in touch with this piece of geography more spiritually uplifting than much around me. To see the feature I once taught about using maps, diagrams and later satellite images, almost makes me wish I were still teaching. How much better it is that most new geography teachers now see much more of the world before they teach.

I find my fellow EA, Maria, bird watching on the beach near the Church of Peter's Primacy. We talk about being near the end of our time here and arrangements for going home. I have clearance to leave two days early on the 7th February, if I can get the ticket changed. The evening meal in Tiberias is something of a disaster for vegetarians, and indeed rather sad on a number of fronts: noise, service and cost, which is more than the allowance for an EA each month.

Perhaps I just find it difficult to let my hair down - too serious all the time - but then we are engaged in a serious endeavour. Perhaps I have started to feel the whole experience of being in Palestine is a retreat; a time for personal reflection, which may just be reinforcing my prejudices about all sorts of things, ranging from relationships with colleagues, through to matters of personal faith, belief or non-belief. I begin to feel one does not need a retreat from a retreat.

Perhaps I have not realised how much spiritual energy I have gained from the work of accompaniment. My rules have changed. I came to accompaniment with the idea of accomplishing something. Life in the western world is largely measured by accomplishment and acquisition: what have we done and what we have materially. Here, perhaps for the first time, my life is being measured by its spiritual dimension, whether the measurement is being made by oneself or others. To some extent, I have escaped from the issue, from the concerns about the impact of the occupation and one's inability to do anything about it, by coming and living under it. Rather like the old piece of travel advice that says we should travel light as most of the essentials of human life are available where people live, so the essentials of living under an occupation are found with the people here. The essentials are not so much the material things the traveller may carry but the spiritual things of relationship, of respect, of care, of

179

identification with and watchfulness for the other. There is no need for a retreat as there is nowhere spiritually better to go than the day-to-day focus of the work here. I am accompanying the people in Jayyous, people who cannot 'retreat', so why should we?

Eckhart suggests, *"Without personal attachment to things and people one is no longer swayed by one's emotions. Hence, one can confront the world calmly. Borne along now by an inner quiet".*[5] *This realisation brings me to a new mental satisfaction, which is unrelated to external circumstances. A new spiritual modus operandi has come into play in this different situation in my life. This is more than just a focusing on the issue; it is seated in a changing relationship with my own degree of attachment and my desire for accomplishment. This changing relationship amounts to a growing detachment, but an even greater detachment from the generalities of the world; a detachment that, paradoxically, seems to allow a greater engagement with the work of accompaniment. It provides a greater clarity about what needs to be done and great simplicity about how to achieve the desired result. I am accepting the situation on faith and, in so doing, letting concerns go.*

I seem to gain a spiritual uplift by detachment from the distractions of visiting other locations and the material things of normal life (although the laptop and the digital camera are a very real practical aids and comforts for the task in hand). Is my spirit lifted by the engagement with the farmers, mostly an engagement not in conversation but an engagement through presence, rather in the way of the Quakers in a meeting for worship become 'gathered' without any initial need for speech? The feeling of being 'gathered' at the Gate is very strong for me.[6] *There may be little if any verbal conversation beyond greetings, but I believe we are 'together' at more than a physical level.*

Sunday 11th January

I take an early walk by the water, the Sea of Galilee, and have some quiet time in the Church before making contact with the Exeter Friends Meeting Sunday School class by way of a text message but, disappointingly, no questions come back as previously planned. Rather than returning directly to Jerusalem, we travel via Akko, where I consider taking the first train south and a bus to Jerusalem from Tel Aviv. This would have got me to the New Imperial Hotel two hours earlier, and provided the opportunity to witness some church services in the Old City. It would also have avoided yet another bunch of pressured invitations to go visiting other locations.

Monday 12th January

Some time is spent at the EAPPI office, collecting our subsistence money. I take a 'service' to Salah Eddin Street and quickly walk down to the BA office, but it is too early to change my tickets. On the way back to the hotel, I visit the Palestinian Pottery, where I find some items of interest. The Pottery opened in 1922 when the British Mandate brought Armenian Potters to renovate the tiles of the Dome of the Rock. The owner tells me this was the, "... first Armenian Palestinian Pottery... there was nothing like this". I walk through the Suq, disregarding several pottery shops, to the galliabia shop, where the shopkeeper is full of recognition and welcoming handshakes. "Yes, I have a grey one for you in my store". I say I will be back in a couple of weeks. I go to the hotel and then walk to the New Gate to avoid walking through the Suq with a rucksack.

I have the second chance meeting with the Franciscan who attended the gathering of clergy to hear about EAPPI. He says it is going to get cold again. I catch the new bus service, complete with a 'green stripe' bus with a dedicated route number painted on the side, from Damascus Gate bus station to Qalandia. Arriving at the Qalandia checkpoint at 11.50, I depart for Funduq at 12.00, arriving there at 13.00 and get straight into a taxi, quickly changing to another at Azzoun, and getting into Jayyous at 13.25 in just over 2 hours from the

Old City. This is possibly the best journey yet. Pedants may like to note that this interest in transport schedules is an old railway observation habit and is about 'transport', not 'tourism'. Transport is a matter of movement, while tourism has questionable baggage of prurient interest in the odd and the different. It is also a reflection of my habit of recording everything. Please rest assured that there are many other details recorded in words, pictures or in my head, which have been left out of this work.

On my return, I fax HaMoked with the Gate Observation Reports using the machine at the Baladiya. Abdul-Latif arrives in the evening and is excited by my idea of distributing the Gate Observation Reports and offers to help put them on his computer. He has spent the day walking into and out of Nablus to get to his work visit. He says, "Life is becoming impossible."

I wonder what we can do to help this deeply thoughtful, moderate and dignified man, who this evening seems both excited and close to despair. Ultimately he, and all the Palestinians, have to bring the conditions of the occupation to the light for themselves. The situation reminds me of the scene in the film Gandhi, when the English Reverend Charlie Andrews is told by Gandhi he can help no more, because he is not Indian, he is not truly part of the matter.[7] Andrews has to use the rejection to let go, and realise he can only go on to support the great cause from the outside, the future being in the hands of those who desire the change. Many in India considered Andrews had 'gone native'. When he preached of Christianity standing in support of Gandhi, against Imperial rule, his congregation walked out. In a more recognisable way Lawrence of Arabia went 'native' but still came to the same conclusion, if in a violent context, "Do not try to do too much with your own hands. It is their war, and you are to help them, not win it for them".[8] This suggests that all I can do is to report what I see and to bring the circumstance of the occupation in to the light, as those who are trapped in it are less able to do.

It has been strange how the weekend, focusing on the children, (even if it did not work according to my plan) and attempting to re-date my ticket, has made me feel very detached from the whole thing. It is rather like when I came back from Haifa when things started to happen after a break away. Were it not for the retreat, and I had therefore not visited the British Airways Office to make arrangements to travel home two days early, I might not have gone to the HaMoked Office, which is just round the corner. If I had not gone to see the staff of HaMoked and made a chance comment about the Gate Reports I would have been totally unaware of the Palestinian case at the International Court of Justice. The preparation for 'publication' of the information collected on the Jayyous Gates as part of the evidence for the Palestinian case will become my focus for the next couple of weeks. It appears that another piece, perhaps the most important piece, of the jigsaw has fallen into place with this realisation of the need for evidence.

Perhaps, if I was a Muslim I would say, "It is written."

Part Three
Finding a Purpose for the Evidence

Chapter 16
How does all this fit together?
Week 9

"Both past and future remain in some sense hidden from the present. The past 'refuses' its presence whilst the future 'withholds' it."

M Heideggar[1]

Tuesday 13th January

The morning is spent working on Gate Reports for the Mayor and Gate Observation Reports, ready for Abdul-Latif to find suitable computer software to handle the evidence. This is the first problematic washing day, but I only need to have a couple more as I have a maximum 'range' of about ten or twelve days without doing any washing. I do two North Gate watches with a tractor ride down and a trailer ride up. This has been an easy day.

Wednesday 14th January

Gate Watch often gives one plenty of time to think. As it is pouring with rain, I stand below the dome of an olive tree and rehearse the arguments for and against standing under trees in heavy rain. I even begin to construct the basic form of an experiment to settle the issue once and for all.

However, this train of thought soon gives way to other more pressing issues. I am here at 06.40 on a normal working day and there is nobody else around. Where have all the men gone? A jeep passes at 06.38, just before the official (or at least what we have been told is the official) opening time, this being from 06.45 to 07.15.

184

I am waiting in the silence. The water drips off the tree onto my waterproofs and I remain dry. This will not be the case for the average Palestinian this morning. Often one sees them on a day after rain wearing jackets that are still wet from the previous day. Their defiance of the rain is almost equal to the defiance of the occupier. However, rain is an important element in "paradise". I hear a dog barking in the village. Is someone coming down the hill? It is 07.03 and feels very strange not to have any, for want of a better word, 'customers'. *These people are not customers, as there is no payment in the conventional sense in this relationship and I offer no material good or service. I use the term more in the sense of custom, of passage through a port.* At 07.10, a Humvee drives very slowly by, going northwards, clearly checking something as the door on the fence side is opened for a better view.

> *I reflect on the way the team has worked. I am sad at my sense of failure, that yet again my objective to be part of a co-operating team seems to have come to naught. Is the aspiration just too much to be able to achieve or is there some problem with me? After all, I am the common factor between all the teams I have worked in. As a teacher, I worked my way through different positions in teams, which worked with varying degrees of success. In these situations there was possibly a lack of reflection on the task in hand and understanding of the different characters in the team. The issue we are working on is well understood, but the way each of us works is less well accommodated. This fragmentation is the greatest sadness to me about the whole endeavour. Perhaps it is inevitable in a team of people who have not worked together for long and who are working under a range of unpredictable situations and pressures.*

It is 07.23, and the dogs are barking again. At 07.36, a tractor shows up with driver and three passengers. *Are passengers people with passes or people passing, or just travellers? If so, should I call them passengers rather then customers? This is a fruitless debate as both customers and passengers imply payment.* The Humvee is back at 07.40 checking the culverts on the west side of the fence. It stops and a soldier gets out to check and then it slowly moves on. We can be sure that somewhere in the Humvee is the key to the Gate, the Gate that remains closed.

The tractor driver shows me his key ring, the fob of which has the word peace in English and Hebrew on each side of a dove. He sits covered in a plastic sheet. There is a lot of coughing, sniffing and nose blowing. At least it has stopped raining for a moment, but the wet is still penetrating. There is a roar as the Humvee goes over the top of the hill above us to the south. At 07.45 I try Rex and get a polite woman, who tells me the number is not available, or something, in Hebrew.[2] The rain is back and we sit under the wall in a line to shelter as best we can.

I try Rex again, but he has seen no activity and has no one waiting to cross. Is it the weather that has put them off going to work in the fields, or have they all gone to Qedumim, near Nablus, to sort out their new permits needed from Friday? At 07.55, I phone HaMoked who talk to Naji. Increasingly, I do not talk to HaMoked, but just dial the number and let the Palestinians speak for themselves. It is better for them to present their own case. He is a small, compact man, who wears a tailored dark navy jacket over his working trousers, complete with designer label at the cuff. This smart jacket is a contrast to Ghassen, the tractor driver, who wears a piece of plastic sheet, which is tied at the top, has armholes in the sides, and is tied round the middle. It almost touches the ground and offers considerable protection while driving a tractor, with an 'apron' over his legs. This enforced wait will make most of them wet for the day, even if they are working in the greenhouses.

It is decided to light a fire. Wood is gathered from under the nearby olive trees. Strips of card are torn off a box and one is dipped into the tractor fuel tank to act as a lighter. This is eventually ignited and the fire started. A small piece of plastic sheet is held in place to help the fire draw and when it starts to melt is dropped on, giving off acrid fumes. In a sudden campaign to tidy up this corner of Palestine, one of the farmers puts an old broken pair of trainers on the fire. Thankfully, Ghassen quickly removes them and throws them well into the olive grove. One small environmental disaster does not need to become a bigger one for our lungs. He gestures to his nose and we laugh together about the possible smell.

Picture 24. It could be a long wait.

The designer jacket is now being protected by the plastic sheet as the rain comes on very heavily again. By 08.20, there is a roaring fire and steaming trousers, but no jeep. At 08.30, I ring HaMoked, who say they are working on it. The fire is remade several times. At 09.25, I ring HaMoked to check the situation and they say the Gate should be opened. At 09.30, a jeep comes down the hill and passes without a pause.

Sunflower seeds, sweets and cigarettes are consumed. The rain has stopped and there is even some blue sky. A jeep arrives almost unnoticed and stops. The Gate is opened. The pedestrians walk through and the tractor eventually starts down the hill. The Gate was opened at 09.40 and closed at 09.43. I gave the last tractor driver a hand to shut the inner gate, which was wedged in place with a stone acting like a cam, the greater the pressure of the swinging gate, the tighter it shuts.

Through all of this two-hour period of waiting, I heard nothing that sounded like an angry word. No one shouted at me to do something. They talked calmly on the phone to HaMoked and looked on with resignation when the jeep did not stop. No one went to kick the fence. No one seemed to suggest going home. There were some long faces and some jokes about the rain, but then farmers have a mixed view of rain anyway.

This is perhaps a reflection of the nature of Islamic culture. The word Islam signifies submission or resignation to the will of God. It is easy to see how this trait becomes central to day-to-day life, often with the attachment of the word 'Inshallah', God willing. Culture is not hanging onto things; it is more the hanging onto the ethics or principles by which one lives one life. This seems especially so with this group of farmers who despite the potential loss of their land still display their humanity.

There is no way I could have walked away from these four men waiting to go through the Gate, not because I feel they are dependent upon me or that I am responsible for them, but because I am here to accompany these people when their way of life and indeed their culture is under threat. Part of my culture is the principle of human rights, therefore it is my duty to do what I can to draw attention to the failure of respect for human rights. These men are being punished by a State, to which they do not wish to belong, that has fenced off their land. This restricts their movement and is destroying their society and economy. The one thing it seems that this State is unable to destroy is the faith, resilience and patience of these people.

My account of this gate watch chimes with Rachel Muers' notion of "Quaker accounts of the need for silent worship (which) have often described silence in terms of a performed interruption", a silent interruption that helps to discern the significance of whatever is interrupted, and leads to the consequent liberation and transformation of one's concerns.[3]

While the discussion on customers and passengers seems of little significance, it rests on a major concern of the labelling of people, individuals and groups and the ease with which an attitude can become attached to that label. The labels students and pupils, Christians and Muslims, Jews and Gypsies, blacks and whites, fascists and communists, all carry attitudes that may be negative or positive. My concern about the cohesion of the team has perhaps put the matter in context and possibly transformed it by bringing it to the surface and 'discussing' it, if only with myself, so that it might be set aside for a while.

At 12.25, I return to the Gate. The rain has stopped and the sun is hot. The rill in the road is still running but it is not the torrent of this morning. At 12.40, a soldier is seen on the hill above the Gate and the eight men waiting all shout to remind him that they are waiting.

There is a discussion with me about the problems caused by the fence and how long we will stay in Jayyous. I tell them that in a couple of weeks we will go and new people come. I say that we too are subject to Israeli permissions, not being allowed to stay more than 3 months on a tourist visa. However, I do not say that we are illegal according to the latest Israeli notice handed out at the airport. This tells people on tourist visas they must not enter the West Bank against a threat of deportation.

We talk about the local domestic cigarette industry. This cottage industry produces packets for just 2.5 shekels rather than the ten of the commercial varieties. These cigarettes come in polythene bags and need to be handled with care, especially for those with the habit of keeping their 'fags' in the back pocket of their jeans. Some fellows have little plastic boxes to put them in to keep them dry and straight.

One of the smokers is the caller, the muazzin, at one of the mosques in Jayyous, one Abu Talib. He tells me a little of his time at college in Nablus training as a translator, and of the many problems with the "sheeps". He has 120 sheep and they have no permissions to cross to their pasture. Many sheep in the village are seriously underfed at present despite the rain having encouraged the village grass to grow and provide some grazing. This is not enough and the sheep rely on the land that has been cut off to provide enough fodder to sustain them.

The Gate is opened at 13.00, just as I call HaMoked, a call that I cancel, as the jeep comes into view. As the men walk forward, Abu Talib invites me to go and see his land. I decline his offer: that I am cooking to night being my only, rather feeble, excuse. This invitation puts me on the spot with regard to going to 'The Land', a matter that takes another fourteen days to resolve. The jeep leaves at 13.09 after nine men have gone through. Abu Talib and the fellow in the Islamic hat are both searched while the others just show their permissions. The soldiers take more time shutting the inner gate than they did to check the men through. When will they learn how to close their own gates or provide some wire or rope to tie it shut? They are most likely city boys, so they do not have the wit to use a stone as the farmers did in the morning despite it being placed on the ground near the gate latch.

I reflect on a quote from this period of conversation with Talib.

"We are stuck between the past and the future. The past is no longer in our hands, neither is the future since it does not exist yet. The only time we have control over is the present. It is now; it exists. It is not heavy to bear, and it is liveable by all, on one condition: that we let the past go, and not be impatient for the future. The present moment passes quickly. Before you know it, it's in the past while another present takes its place, as light and narrow and fleeting as the preceding one."

The Separation Barrier is here today but it was not here in the past and need not be there in the future. We have to work through past changes to understand the present and to use the past and present as potential to unlock the possibilities of the future. If the past and the present seem hopeless then it is difficult to see how hope can be made in the future. Living in the now is a survival strategy if the future seems too hopeless. However there is always potential for the despair of the present flooding the now of survival.

Chapter 17
Reports One
Week 9

"O friends, no more these sounds! Let us sing more cheerful songs. More full of Joy."

Schiller[1]

Thursday 15th January

Between Gate duties, I get started on the 'Jayyous Report' for the office in Jerusalem and the replacement team, doing some more writing and sorting out of papers, and spend much longer than average on today's crop of ten e-mails.

Friday 16th January

Going to the North Gate for 06.45 there is a ruddy sunrise reflected in the clouds to the west, with a breeze coming in from the east possibly good enough for washing if I get in quick on my return to the house. The rill in the track is now completely dry and the gullies on the edge of the inner road by the fence have grown since last inspected on Wednesday morning. The situation is unstable. The cyclamen are bravely flowering amongst the rocks.

The gentle sound of crunching stones tells me of the approach of a donkey cart, indeed two donkey carts. The materials for a fire are quickly gathered and in less than a minute flames can be seen leaping from behind the rocks. The remains of Wednesday's fire and the plastic sheets I put under a stone on the wall are still there. It has stopped raining so the sheets are thrown to one side, no longer needed, being part of the past. This is a good illustration of the tendency here not to think of the future, which seems to be deeply ingrained into this culture and faith. Living in the present may lead to problems or at least not having a plastic sheet handy next time it rains.

It is on my mind that I am too much the observer and not enough the participant. There is an interesting relationship between being a participant observer and being an accompanier. Add to this relationship the barrier of language posed by my lack of Arabic (not something I could have realistically done a great deal about), and my reticence about pushing myself into other peoples' activities, and the relationship becomes more complex. These factors, along with my increasing focus on trying to record as much of this experience as possible, make it more difficult to get more involved. Whatever my thoughts, I am still an accompanier: I am still here, with these people on behalf of the many people, known and unknown, who supported my coming here as part of this programme to witness this situation.

I am offered tea. A donkey cart arrives with what I recognise as the back seat from a Fiat Uno, the pattern in the fabric showing through the grime. Perhaps it comes from "one careful owner", the wrecked car body, dumped up the track, that has become a landmark on the way up the hill to the village. At 07.12, the first tractor of the day comes down from the village, complete with small tank for crop spraying. The donkey that is 'parked' next to me brays, and is hit for its trouble. There is a bloody mark on its nose just below the lump caused by the harness chain, which today is placed above the ridge of skin. There is more braying as further carts arrive. The cart closest to me moves forward and I see the harness is in part made from recycled car seat belts, but I do not think the buckles still function.

A quick count at 07.20 reveals over 30 people gathered to go through the Separation Barrier and four more arrive on an 'express' donkey cart, which comes to a fairly sudden stop at the end of the queue. The cart near me moves even closer as the donkey takes a passing interest in my note pad. At 07.25, the Humvee arrives and there is a general move forward. Some men still sit around the fire knowing this will take a while. At 07.26 the Gate is pushed back, followed by the inner gate and the checking starts. This is the group of soldiers of whom one has taken to waving to me at times. He has a round face with glasses under his helmet. Unfortunately, (or possibly fortunately) we have no opportunity to talk face to face, partly because this patrol does not seem to cause problems. I wonder if by chance he is one of the students, also a military reservist, who may have visited Jayyous a month or so ago and was due to be called up. I watch from a distance and suck a Swiss mint cough-sweet purchased in Jerusalem. The bicycle is through with its young rider followed by a man with a carefully furled, black umbrella. There is a hold up over the permission of the woman from the family that was among the first to arrive, but eventually she goes through. The delay allows another tractor, in this case out of time, to join the queue unnoticed.

The young pedestrians are standing too close and the equally young, round faced soldier rather half-heartedly waves them back. They stop creeping forward. The soldier picks out men to go forward to show their permissions, and some paper work is taken by the third soldier to the Humvee. One person is allowed through but the donkey cart and three fellows wait just inside the inner gate. At 07.45 a jeep heads south at speed and Charles rings from the South Gate. He has nothing to report. A donkey rider departs from the checking area at a gallop to his land as the tractors move up to the Gate. A lad returns to shut the inner gate, which seems hopeful for the donkey cart still waiting. The Gate is balanced in place against the turning piece of the latch mechanism. At 07.48, the Gate stays open with two soldiers around the Humvee. The three men and the cart wait, talking to the other soldier, but I am out of earshot.

At 07.55, the Gate closes after Yusif is called towards the Humvee to collect his green ID card, being the last of over 50 people who have gone through the Gate this morning. I attempt to call Charles to tell of the joys that are coming his way as the Humvee leaves. I cannot get through. As I walk back up the hill, the flowers are opening to the rising sun as the scene becomes clothed in yellow, pink and orange.

I return at lunchtime. The Gate is being opened early at 12.15 by the same Humvee 'crew'. There are four people coming back to the village and 15 waiting to go out to the Jayyous land. The ever-courteous man with his woolly hat waves at the soldiers and yet again does not seem to show his permission. He is waved on. The friendly donkey from this morning does not wish to return home, having to be pulled down the slope away from the Gate. An older couple give fruit to the soldiers. A Volkswagen van arrives from the village, but only to pick up some of those returning. A boy gives the checking soldier some fruit still on the branch and offers more to the guard on the other side of the road. The last person going out is checked at the 12.27 and the Gate shut by 12.28. The Humvee goes south. The Gate should open at 12.30. I decide to stay until the official closing time of 12.50. I think this would be a good time to telephone the UK to see how things are at home if only to compare the weather on what is like a good summer's day for England. I am soon joined by three women, a man and a boy.

I ring HaMoked at 12.40 and the man talks to them. This timing would allow for any others coming before the official closure time of 12.50; it always takes ten minutes for the Jaish to get back after a call. HaMoked will call back. The man goes to inspect the Gate and the new boxes installed to the left. He has not been around as he is a student at university and realised this was the last day to get to see his two clementina trees. At 13.00 I call HaMoked to tell them that those waiting have wandered off and do not now seem to wish to go through. They say the Gate is about to be open so I call the people back.

A tractor arrives at 13.08 which is well out of time for the opening, but then these people should be allowed to go to their land at anytime, so that is not a problem. A donkey cart follows at 13.12 arriving smartly painted in a mixture of blue, red, yellow and green with an equally stylish driver in a smart jacket and quasi Elvis hairstyle. HaMoked tell me at 13.20 the Gate should be open by now. Seven minutes later, the Humvee comes out of the land and slowly roars off to the north, only to return in a few minutes, stopping to talk to three people who have turned up on the other side of the fence. It continues south.

The Humvee is seen sitting on the top of the hill watching. It is now 13.37 and there are now eleven people waiting to go to their land. The Humvee returns at 13.45 to end this game of cat and mouse. The Gate is open and those coming in are checked first with those going out being told to get back from the inner gate. Both soldiers are checking. The inner gate is open for the donkey to come in and the men are called up to be checked one at a time. The first one called up comes back for his donkey cart. The tractor driver has a long discussion with the soldiers about his permission, which runs out today. His passenger comes back to shut the inner gate behind the tractor and the Gate is shut at 13.55. In all 11 people have gone out and two people have come in, having waited over an hour beyond the official closing time. They will have to be back by 16.30, so what was a four-hour work session has become two and a half hours.

I will go and have a small picnic before going back to the house, using the sweet bar and some water in my bag as refreshment before going back up the hill. I walk along close to the Separation Barrier to photograph the gully damage to the edge of the inner road where the runoff water has declined to use the pipes provided and to inspect the large culvert at the bottom of the hill just north of the Gate.

I continue through the olive grove veering towards the village. Just before joining the track that has been cut-off by the Separation Barrier I come across a heap of olive prunings, one of which includes a straight piece about six inches long and about an inch and a half diameter. Now all I need is a saw to cut it off. Unbelievably, as I turn round looking for somewhere to sit for a minute I see an old, rusty and indeed broken saw lying on the ground next to the wall. Within a couple of minutes, both ends of the piece of wood have been cut and my souvenir is ready to carry home. Back at the house I seal the ends with candle wax to prevent splitting as I suspect it is this year's wood, so is still drying out. I do not know what I will make out of it, but it will be of more value to me than all those crosses and cribs with Jerusalem or

Bethlehem on them, as this piece of olive wood will have Jayyous running all through it.

I write up the two visits in the Gate Report as follows

Morning

FIRST DAY OF THE NEW PERMISSIONS

> Gate opened at 07.26 and closed at 07.55. Over 50 people pass through to the fields. All very normal apart from one young-man whose ID is taken to the Humvee to be checked while he and his donkey cart wait inside the Gate, while others are checked.   MH

Midday

EARLY OPENING AND REOPENING

> The Gate was opened between 12.15 and 12.28. Four people went out to the fields and 15 returned to the village. At 12.32, five people arrived from the village to cross in the official opening time. After many phone calls to HaMoked, and much passing of jeeps, the Gate was eventually reopened at 13.45 with 2 people coming in and 11 going to the fields.   MH

In the evening, I cook a meal that keeps the colour of the individual vegetables despite the use of tomato paste. This is accompanied by a packet of sausages for the meat eaters. Indeed I taught this word to several children on the way back from the shop as they were interested to know the English names for the items in my bag; peppers, tomatoes, onions, courgettes (cucumber), aubergines and sausages (sours-a-giss!).

There must be many very depressed people in the village community today, especially those who have not been able to obtain new permissions to go to their land. It will take a day or two for us to know who has permissions. There is a very depressed fellow, who spends much of his time sitting in the shop, who has been refused twice. It will be interesting to find out about Sharif Omar, Assama and others who did not get them in the first bunch. I photograph an old pass thrown on the track by the Gate. There is nothing so useless as an out-of-date permission and there is nothing so valuable for these people, who want to quietly carry on their lives without interference, as a new permission. What will those who have no pass feel? There will be the uselessness of not being able to uphold family honour and one's own honour in the family. How will this frustration find an outlet? For the young there is always the possibility it will be all too horrible.

I spend part of the evening listening to Beethoven's No9 Symphony, a recording made by Bernstein and the Berlin Philharmonic at the time of the fall of the Berlin Wall. In this recording the word 'freude', joy in Schiller's Ode to Joy, is changed to 'freiheit', freedom, as was appropriate for the 25th December 1989. The piece is also a metaphor for my time here, indeed for life. In the first three movements Beethoven seems to wander, directionless, disconsolate, sometimes almost in torment as he starts and rejects one theme and moves on to another, often in a different key, which in turn is left for something more hopeful. Finally, he moves towards the great conclusion, the foundations of which we realise are there from the beginning. This recording, not the best, could be seen as a 'victory' rendition until we read in the sleeve notes that players came from the Soviet Union, the United States, Britain, France, and from Berlin, Dresden and Munich. Here the hand of friendship was extended to the collapsing adversary. For a while, I have a moment of respite from the reality of Jayyous.

Chapter 18
Reports Two
Weeks 9-10

"We should not have rich and poor but measure
people by their degree of empathy."

Theodore Zeldin[1]

Saturday 17th January

After working through a 'mountain' of paperwork and
wondering if I have made accompaniment too bureaucratic, I
go to see Abdul-Latif at 09.00. I give him the Gate Evidence,
which I send on to HaMoked, and he sends to many others on
his E-mail circulation list. By the end of the day, he has
responses and questions.

*I woke last night to the sound of a mosquito. I wish, not for
the first time I had brought at least a small mosquito net for
my head, as it gets rather hot sleeping under the hood of the
sleeping bag. Thinking about this it occurred to me that a
mosquito net is rather like a fence. I wonder if the Separation
Barrier is rather the same for the Israelis, just a means of
controlling their environment.*

*This idea makes Abdul Latif laugh when I tell him after our
early morning meeting. Having transferred the Gate
Evidence to his computer, he asks if he can send it to other
people. I say, "Why ask, it is your information, Palestinian
information, as much as it is mine; I am not going to put a
'Fence' around it". We laugh again at the ridiculousness of
the idea - 'the accompaniment of laughter'. I thank him for his
help distributing this information and the honour for having
both our names on this small but now joint work.*

*He says the honour is his and that this is good work. I say to
him that there are days when I find it difficult to see how he is
able to continue his work. He says we have to stand by what*

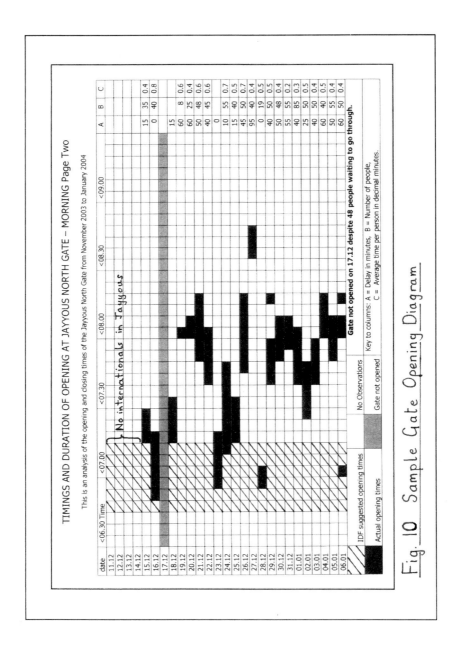

Fig. 10 Sample Gate Opening Diagram

we believe and that we have to work for humanity. I say that I feel he is both hugely resilient and brave in the situation. He says how important it is to have the support of those who call on the conscience of humanity, those who are prepared to leave their families, their homes to come to Palestine.

He changes the subject by asking if I heard the gunfire last night, gaining comfort by moving back to factual rather than emotional territory.

Arriving at the North Gate at 12.15, there is a breeze from the south, sun and broken cloud. A group of farmers is waiting on the other side of the Separation Barrier, by the outer gates. A jeep arrives at 12.22. The soldier calls up the first man with his donkey and check his permission. He then appears to give the farmer the Gate key and tells him to open the Gate while he checks the donkey. Indeed the man unlocks the Gate, which the soldier then opens. This man rides his donkey around the end of the inner gate and canters off up the track to the village. The second man through is told to open the inner gate. Checking is taking a long time, with just seven people taking nine minutes, the Gate closing at 12.31.

All is quiet. I will wait up the lane just in case of any latecomers who arrive in the official time-period, up to 12.50. It is an easy watch, apart from the wait at the end for any latecomers. I go and sit on a heap of rocks in a field next to the track, enjoying the sun, with only the distant rattle of the Gate in the breeze to disturb the peace. I finish my writing, have a snack and a drink and walk back to the village.

As I approach, I get a call to say there is a flying checkpoint about 300 metres beyond the eastern edge of the village, on the road to Azzoun. I drop off my bag at the house and walk down to the back of the traffic queue. A group of youths is hanging around the end of the queue and attempt to throw stones at a jeep that comes from the direction of Kafr Jamal. There are too many people about for them to have clear shots and only one stone is launched. I walk along the queue until I can see the soldiers in the road, and the people being checked. The ubiquitous 'services' minibuses and old German yellow, seven-seater taxis from Azzoun are dropping their passengers, who then have to walk through the checkpoint and on to the village. If the flying checkpoint were further out in the country a collection of yellow taxis would soon appear on each side of the blockage to maintain a service to and from the checkpoint, the drivers not wishing to waste time in the queue. This shows flexibility in accommodating the occupation. It also shows the flexibility of a population with a low level of car ownership and a culture of shared transport.

It is taking a long time to check the vehicles and the queue does not move while I walk up and back. Surprisingly, I decide to take a few discrete pictures and get out of the way. I walk back to Bait Abu Azzam and start writing this journal account.

> *This may seem a bit feeble but it is a recognition of the limit of the "jurisdiction of good will" and the lack of any authority to do anything in this situation. An expression of moral authority would simply be dismissed as partisan argument. It is better to leave this checkpoint without adding to the delays by having 'internationals' getting in the way and slowing the process. Perhaps it is a reflection of having become too focused on the Gates and a lack of flexibility to accompany in wider situations; or is it just a reflection of limited energy? With many things still to follow up, time is running out.*

I work in my room, which has more light and less interruptions during the afternoon. I complete a lot of word processing and have a short sleep. This included some work on the 'Jayyous Report', but I must do more on this tomorrow.

I spend the evening putting some text messages into my mobile phone ready for a second attempt at making a link with the Sunday School class tomorrow. HaMoked phones for the ISM telephone number in Nablus. Good to have them call us for once, but it is about a problematic incident, which does not sound too good, and probably relates to the flying checkpoints and the general tension of the last few days. This has been a bad day in terms of the situation, but a good day in terms of getting things done.

Sunday 18th January

I very much enjoy helping with the Sunday School Class. I just hope it worked at the other end. It becomes a quiet moment in an otherwise hectic day. Morning and evening at the North Gate are normal; one donkey cart driver is turned back in the morning and the green truck is towed in from the land later in the day. There are checkpoints all around Jayyous and out towards Nablus, stopping teachers and students getting to school, college and university. A teacher is told he will be shot if he does not get away from the checkpoint. Abdul-Latif has cancelled his visit to Nablus tomorrow. He calls in relation to events at the South Gate where the Bedouin family has to wait until 17.05 to go home. Dharifah has been told at lunchtime that she is forbidden to go back to her house. Things are getting bad in all directions.

Abdul-Latif has passed the report on the Gate Opening on to many people, including the Palestinian Authority, the Civil Administration and various Human Rights Groups. I am very pleased about this useful development. It makes use of the evidence and may feed the information into the challenge of the legal status of the Separation Barrier. Is this why there is a clamp down around Jayyous; does somebody know? I doubt if the Israelis are too concerned about our work.

The main elements of the case for Jayyous in the Israeli High Court or the International Court of Justice are:

1 The provision of a permanent checkpoint, to replace the Gate, so that movement to the 'Land' is possible at anytime

2 Direct access to Qalqilya for markets and services

3 Proper access to water resources

4 Allowing farmers to stay overnight on their land behind the wall

5 Access for traders to/from Nablus, the economic centre of the northern West Bank.

To get permissions the farmers require deeds, ID, land ownership proof from Ottoman times from at least 85 years ago, plus a security check.

> *I wonder how we would respond to this sort of demand to claim ownership of a piece of land? The Israeli Minister of Justice says the Separation Barrier is bad and in the wrong place, but I suspect changing its location is as likely as the Okehampton By-pass, (a structure of similar size and planned with a similar degree of misjudgement), being re-built outside the Dartmoor National Park.*

This is our life, arbitrary decisions at checkpoints, changes in security levels and interruptions of movement. Several young men call about a problem of two of their friends being held, 'retained', by the permissions issuing office in Qedumim. I give them a HaMoked card.

> *After his greeting yesterday "A thousand good mornings", this morning Abu Talib says "You're the joker; you always have a smile, but you are serious; it's so complex." It is strange that over the last few days, the more tired and weary I have become, the more people seem to want to engage; Talib; the farmer on the tractor who stops to talk, the fellow on the donkey cart, who says, "Hello Maurice".*

> *Does it take ten weeks to really feel as if one is just starting? Perhaps Abdul-Latif has also let it be known that the information we have recorded has been passed on to support the Jayyous claim for better access to their land. This could have made a big difference, the recognition that the one who just watches, has indeed been working. The comment by the artist Rothko comes to mind, that "Silence is so accurate".*

> *This has been a good day (for me).*

Monday 19th January

I cover the morning duty at the North Gate. It is normal, if late and slow. I spend the morning on Gate Reports and going to the Mayor, returning for an early lunch and a walk in the north eastern valley. This is a little gem and provides good territory for photographs. I find a lizard basking in the sun on a rock only to see it slip off before I can take a picture. I also find a grasshopper jumping along the lane, and take a picture. Caves on the north side of the valley could be worth investigating on another occasion when I have more time.

I return to the house and work on the Jayyous Report for most of the afternoon, getting it checked by Charles, who approves. I must get the others to do their contributions.

I cook a magnificent cauliflower for supper, by just putting the whole thing in a pan, with a little water and a lid on. This boils the stem and steams the top. When it is cooked, I drain off the remaining water and serve it in the pan. There are other vegetables in a homemade tomato sauce with herbs and Indus Valley Basmati rice. I have not recorded the meat I provided for the carnivores; sausages I expect.

> *This has been a day for some geographical study; released from other activities by the feeling that I have achieved something by being here. I will have to make time to visit this valley, full of limestone features, again before leaving Jayyous.*

Tuesday 20th January

I spend time finishing the Jayyous Report and tidying up my 'Apple' (computer). There is very much a feeling that our time here is nearly over. I decide to walk to the North Gate via the valley to the north east of Jayyous, visited briefly yesterday. My early start allows me to investigate the large cave on the north slope and to walk down the dry valley to join the road from Kafr Jamal. Here I am greeted from a distance by some boys sitting in a cave high up on the hillside. As I walk towards the North Gate across some rough ground and through an olive grove, a Humvee sits on the hill by the Separation Barrier.

Being Watched?

I walk along the track,
They're on the hill,

I walk through the olive grove,
They're on the hill,

I climb the wall,
They're on the hill,

I take the pictures,
They're on the hill,

I wave at the family,
They're on the hill,

I look for the flowers,
They're on the hill,

Sitting in their Humvee,
They're on the hill.

Wednesday 21st January

I arrive in Ramallah at 08.45 after a good run with Hans, one of the Danish Medical Students. I have time to walk out to the Muqata'a, Yasser Arafat's head quarters. The Muqata'a is too depressing; a prison for the leader (no matter how good or bad) within a prison of a city, within the prison of what should be a country. Some of the buildings look as if they have been hit by an earthquake, but it was just a few helicopter gun-ships, ironically called Apaches, the name of another oppressed native people. Across the town, I find some small workshops on the edge of the old city including a woodwork shop. It would have been good to talk to a fellow woodworker but, unfortunately, there is no one around. By chance, I meet the taxi driver from my previous visit, his greeting being accompanied by much tooting as he blocks the traffic for a minute or two.

I join other members of the group at the Palestinian Embroidery Co-operative, which was started in 1989, at the beginning of the first Intifada. At that time, people came from the surrounding communities to seek charity from the Greek Catholic Church, which responded by setting up the Co-operative. It now has 500 women members, building on the long Palestinian craft tradition.

As Qumsiyeh says, 'examination reveals fascinating stories and facts about the ancient heritages of this society... each district and town in Palestine having its own traditional fabric and dress design.[2]

The cooperative's designs have been developed from the patterns on the bodice, side and around the headpieces of traditional Palestinian dress and applied to items such as bags, purses and waistcoats. There are 25 members between the age of 75 and 85 years and some of them have been provided with glasses. Those women with sight problems make pieces to designs with white backgrounds, which can be worked in poor light conditions. The different colours found in the designs relate to different areas with brown and ochre being traditional village colours.

This is an excellent example of a charity becoming the promoter of skills, self-respect and confidence. There is great difficulty getting goods to the post in Jerusalem for the international market, due to staff not having Jerusalem IDs. There are also big difficulties with earth barriers and checkpoints in moving materials to the outworkers in the surrounding villages. Some women have stopped working for the co-operative due to these problems. Equally, there are difficulties in payment for international orders.

The afternoon is taken up with a meeting of the General Union of Palestinian Women. I am the only man at this gathering attended by a group of women EAs, which is a strange switch from the male dominated social environment in Jayyous, but Ramallah is less conservative in these matters. We are made most welcome and the audience is so keen to hear what we have to say that our comments are interspersed with questions and statements to 'encourage' us. This powerful group amounts to the great and the good of Ramallah's professional women, both Muslim and Christian, university staff, doctors and teachers.

We are told, "You are a distinguished band of people. We need proper Christians who believe in peace... as Gandhi observed." "Justice, Peace, Freedom is what we wish." "Speak truth to power." "We are in a situation that is bereft of principle."

> *I close the day reflecting on the thoughts expressed by Hans during our early morning bus ride. He says his time here has changed his 'helping and doing' attitude to an 'engaged, developmental and supporting' stance. We do not do to the people, we are part of the people. He says, "There is the task to make one question in the forest of it all." I have found my 'question' in the collection of Gate Opening Evidence.*

Chapter 19
Bethlehem and the Children
Week 10

"We hear of the 'Conflict of Civilisations.' It isn't faiths that are at fault; it is the faithful; no faith propagates injustice and violence."

Desmond Tutu[1]

Thursday 22nd January and Friday 23rd January

On Friday morning at 04.45, in the Knights Palace Hotel, I write the following as a piece to send home.

My time here is nearly over. I write this from a comfortable Jerusalem hotel, retreating from the foul weather outside. Indeed the wind howling around the corner of the building has woken me yet again. Despite the early hour, I will not sleep again tonight. The rain yesterday cancelled the olive tree planting planned in the hills near Bethlehem.[2] One has to remember that both Bethlehem and Jerusalem are between 700 and 800 metres (2300-2600 feet) above sea level and have a winter climate that can be as wet and cold as the hills of South West England.[3]

Like much here, the weather changes suddenly. In Ramallah, it was very hot with glorious sunshine, but Thursday dawned very wet so gradually the text messages and phone calls build up a picture of people not going to plant olive trees. Another session is cancelled in the afternoon for lack of interest, or rather, I suspect, failing energy and too much to do in the last few weeks. So unexpectedly, I have a 'free day'. I decide to go to Bethlehem.

Standing just 11 km and one checkpoint to the south of Jerusalem one takes a 'service' (minibus) to the checkpoint, at 4 shekels. I walk through. "Where are you from?" The soldier holds my British/European passport in one hand and a bagel in the other. "England." "OK. Go." The security arch sounds as I walk through but nobody notices so I walk on, trying not to think about the soldiers' guns behind me. I slowly pass a line of locals trying to get out of Bethlehem and rather surprise them, and myself, with my Arabic greeting.

A taxi driver approaches "You like a tour?" "No, just take me to Manger Square, please. How many Shekels?" "Twenty, I make you a good price for you in Bethlehem." "Just Manger Square." "OK." It is not OK for as soon as we are on the move he is planning my morning's itinerary. I open the door and tell him to stop. I do not wish to be hustled around all the sites, or sights, with "I wait for you at each place", and the clock running. I am afraid my sense of charity, so alert at the women's co-operative yesterday, is lost as I hear about feeding this aggressive man's family. No sooner am I walking towards Bethlehem, wondering how far it is and how wet it will be, than another taxi draws up. "Manger Square" "OK, 30 Shekels" I take it, and he does not try to show me all the 'birthplaces' of Christendom in a morning.

As I was not expecting to be a tourist and my guidebook[4] is in Jayyous, so I acquire a map from the tourist information in the Peace Centre on Manger Square, and quickly design a short walking tour. Going past the mosque on the corner of the square, I go up a narrow street to the Lutheran Christmas Church. I return down a back street where the rain is blown upwards by the wind funnelled up the side alleys that steeply descend the hill to the south. During this 'shower bath', I have to change both batteries and memory chip in my camera, without getting it wet! There are signs telling of the regeneration projects conducted by the UN and sponsored by Norway and Japan. In eleven weeks, I have still to see a project sponsored by the UK government.

I go on to the Milk Grotto, the first stopping point on the flight to Egypt. The steps of history are retraced as I head for the Church of the Nativity (Franciscan). As I go in, an Orthodox (but I don't know which particular orthodoxy) funeral is coming out. Bethlehem is a sad place that I fear does little for my soul and increases my concern about the future of the Palestinian economy which is increasingly under a strangle-hold. Tour guides to tourist seem to be in a ratio of about 2:1. However, it does provide me with some much needed hot falafel before I find a taxi back to the checkpoint (20 Shekels... so I was 'Done' earlier). Yes, it is a bit like Exmouth or Weymouth on a bad day out of season, but I think Agatha Christie would have described it as "tawdry". The Christmas all-year round shops, broken decorations still up and an illuminated sign (not switched on) welcoming Yasser Arafat who did not get there this year. My 'prison visit' to Bethlehem is over and I am back through the checkpoint. As the soldier is busy trying to keep his hands warm I show him the photo and the visa in my passport. I assume his nod is an indication that I may pass "without let or hindrance". This is clearly not their favourite posting.

After going to Jawad Abden, the galliabia shop in David Street, I spend the afternoon drying out, warming up, having a bath and sleeping in my hotel room. I have been recommended a good vegetarian restaurant in West Jerusalem, so in the evening I cross the road into that other modern, international (i.e. it has the Golden Arches and Burger King), and expensive Hebrew Jerusalem. It is somewhat like going from the old East to West Berlin, but without the wall. I put my hand on the door of the restaurant, which brings forth a challenge by the security guard. I forget that in Israel you have to approach any public places like the farmers sometimes have to approach the soldiers back on the Gates in Jayyous, with your jacket open ready to be searched. Perhaps this is why this all seems normal behaviour to soldiers on the Gates. At least it has stopped raining as I am blown back to the hotel.

After writing the above, I have a leisurely start to the day. I meet Charles, just in from Jayyous, at the BA office. We are told there is no space on the early flight on the 7th February, so we will try again later. I quickly catch the departing bus for Qalandia. As it is Friday, there are no buses back to Jayyous so I elect to pay 100NIS and share a 'service' to Funduq with a nursery teacher, travelling to Tulkarm with a minibus full of educational toys, and in so doing cut the cost of her journey in half.

We discuss the impact of the occupation and the Palestinian Refugee Camps on children. She is travelling to a camp in Tulkarm, where, she says, all normal aspirations are cut off. Education is supported by the family and the culture, but it does not offer the traditional way out of poverty and the political situation. The occupation brings increased poverty, restrictions on movement to school, to hospital and limited water supply, all having an impact on children, and that is before the deaths caused by the violence of the occupation. Children have been shot for throwing stones, for being in the wrong place, for being a threat.

I tell my travelling companion about my colleagues in Hebron who take the children to Cordoba School, negotiating the military checkpoint and the daily abuse of the Israeli settler children. These settler children throw stones and eggs at the Palestinian girls in their smart white and green striped school uniforms and this, under the eyes of Israeli soldiers who seldom intervene. On some occasions, when the children are not allowed through the checkpoint, Mrs Feriel the headteacher holds her classes in the street, watched over by gun-carrying soldiers. Experience suggests many children in the West Bank cannot express their wishes and dreams or even sleep because they feel threatened and traumatised.[5] These children are unable to face the stages of healthy development without the over-arching impact of the occupation. Despite the care of their parents, these children have lost their right to childhood. I also speak about another colleague in Ramallah, who is working with children through therapeutic drawing in one of the refugee camps. The images drawn by the children include house destruction, tanks, guns, funerals and other symbols of the occupation. Some of the mothers also draw similar pictures.

Nightmares, bedwetting and sleeplessness all add to the burdens of the day for Palestinian children and their parents. We agree both Palestinian and Israeli societies have become "trauma organised", societies where violence is tolerated as a normal way of life.[6] In any breakdown of society, the vulnerable suffer first. Here the vulnerable are the largest element in the population, children under 16 years of age. In 1996, children amounted to 51% of the total Palestinian population of about 2.1 million in the West Bank (compared to 1.9% over the age of 65). The birth rate at that time was 44 per thousand of the population and the infant mortality was 25 per thousand births, both high by international standards. The main cause of infant death was acute diarrhoea.[7] These figures will have changed little over the intervening years. Birth rate is kept high by the tradition of having large families and by the desire to increase the Palestinian population to build a bigger "state". The infant mortality figures will not have improved due to the increased difficulty of access to medical care and restrictions on access to water.

If children successfully complete their school education and move on to college or university, they are confronted with more problems. A report from 2002 paints a picture of obstacles to learning both psychological and physical.[8] There are travel disruptions and economic restrictions as family income drops, and campus disruption caused by Israeli military incursions that threaten both students and teachers, to all of which is added the anxiety and distraction of life under the occupation and the collapse of motivation and an uncertain view of the future. While the Israelis are not responsible for the education system in Palestine, they certainly have a duty not to impair the system, as it has done since the Intifada erupted in 2000, thus violating the basic right to education.[9] Indeed the Fourth Geneva Convention stipulates that the occupying state must facilitate the proper working of all institutions devoted to the care and education of children.[10]

Our discussion ends on a hopeful note, talking about Neve Shalom ~ Wahat al-Salam, a school community southwest of Jerusalem, that offers a small oasis of educational peace and a possible vision for the future.[11] Here, Arab and Israeli children learn together to develop trust, equality and self-respect. Unfortunately, this is a very rare opportunity.

In October 2002, the United Nations General Assembly adopted resolution 27/2 "A world fit for Children". The principles outlined in the resolution include access to education, protection against acts of violence, abuse, exploitation and discrimination, and protection from the horrors of armed conflict and foreign occupation, in accordance with the provisions of international humanitarian law.[12] The Israeli constitution says the country upholds the principles of the United Nations Charter,[13] but it does not seem to respect the United Nations resolutions when applied to the children of the West Bank.

I wait half an hour at Funduq for enough people to go to Azzoun and pay for an expensive taxi to Jayyous. This is not a good journey, long on both time and money. Friday is as Sunday used to be in Scotland, at least in the Highlands, no public transport, and indeed like Israel is now on Saturdays.

On my return to Jayyous, I check my guidebook for information on Bethlehem. Despite its title, Israel and the Palestinian Territories, this is really a guidebook to Israel with, for example, half a page on bus services in Israel and just four lines on the services in the West Bank. As with the maps there is confusion over the location of the National Border, some showing the Green Line and some not, some showing the Golan Heights as being in Israel and some not. Some show the 'Area A' zones of Palestinian responsibility and the 'Area B' zones where Israel is responsible for security. On Israeli maps, names are in Hebrew rather than Arabic versions, both old and modern Palestinian names being replaced. This chimes with a study by Dr Basem Ra'ad that recognises the exceptional problem of attempting to establish a Palestinian tourist economy against the background of Israeli bias in tourist information.[14] He suggest Palestinians have become invisible, their history is ignored or lost in fabrication of an inaccurate and invented Israeli past, and the confiscation of Palestinian culture, history and achievements. Naming places on the map is only the beginning of the issue. It is not for the first time that maps and guidebooks have been* *used for asserting dominance and propaganda. *Please note there is a difference between an Israeli past that is to do with the country and a Jewish past that is related to the people.*

I go to the afternoon watch at the North Gate in the cold wind and the rain.

Saturday 24th January

I am at the South Gate early and the North Gate at midday. I go to see the Mayor about the visit of some Human Rights Activist on the 29th January. He would like me to be there. I need to re-draw the original graphs to show the evidence in a more understandable manner.

Returning 'home', I hear that more farmers have been told they will have to prove ownership of the land before they can get a permit. Once the land is identified as theirs by the issuing of an Israeli deed (for land that is not Israel's under international law) they will have to pay Israeli taxes. These taxes will be charged in arrears, and one can only assume will go to the coffers of Israel, the occupying power, and so have no benefit to these farmers. One farmer is talking of 40,000 shekels (about 10,000 US dollars). This would clearly have very serious implications for the financial future of these farmers.

I speak on the phone to John Aves about his coming to Jayyous the following weekend. We agree, with much laughter, it would be good to have a 'pastoral visit' from the 'Bishop of Bethlehem'.

Sunday 25th January

I have a busy morning redrawing Gate Opening Evidence graphs, which present the information with greater clarity. I also sort out Gate Watch files in Charles's computer, which departs on the 28th and so becomes unavailable. It is good to get this material presented in a way that is easily assimilated.

215

I go to see Susan after lunch and discuss the Gate Evidence and the life of women in the village. She has found it easy as an 'international' woman, to have access to both male and female members of the community. She has worked with a number of women and families in ways that would not have been possible for me as a man. I am able to learn from her a little more about women in this society. "There is privacy and freedom in the Hejab, the headscarf, and the Abaya, the long coat buttoned up to the neck. Women wear makeup at home, but not when going out. They are more respected by their husbands there being less competition with other women, less comparison, less commodification of women. These are highly intelligent, well educated, women, who like to be thought of for themselves, for what is inside them. The women tend to view the Second Intifada as going nowhere and that there must be another way out of the situation. They turn to their religion and the will of God, Inshallah."

The position and attitude of Palestinian women, especially in rural areas, is such a contrast to western, and indeed Israeli women, with their fashion for tight trousers, short skirts and bare midriffs shown in public. It is clear from my observation of the shops in the Arab Suq in Jerusalem that there is no lack of variety in women's underwear available for the Palestinian market, and it is not all sackcloth and ashes.

This is a useful insight into the female side of the village, which takes me past the barrier that women will not talk to men in public unless they are a close relative. This cultural tradition of 'privacy' for women has made this work, a study of the men of Jayyous. This is a weakness that it is impossible for me to overcome. We must leave this issue for another time, as we are here to accompany people under occupation, not to change a society or the position of women within it.

Generally, this has been a very pleasant, quiet and productive day. We have had a message from Polly that we are not to be replaced by another Jayyous team. As a result there will be no immediate future support for Jayyous. Perhaps they are just over stretched. If we had had enough time, we could have supported the farmers set up their own recording and

216

reporting system.

I am surprised how calm, even flat, I feel. There is so much of other people's anger about; there is no point in adding my own, even if it was there to add.

In conversation with Charles about the situation, we share a mutual concern about whether we can keep the news from the people in the village until there has been a confirmation of the situation direct to Sharif Omar and Abdul-Latif. We are also concerned that Abdul-Latif and Sharif Omar should be aware this has nothing to with the problems we had, reinforcing with them that the office in Jerusalem and Sam do not know about 'The Incident' (Chapter 13). I suspect there are other factors that relate to this matter. These range from external direction by the World Council of Churches, people dropping out late from the new team (later confirmed), new demands to be met and even changing requirements for the support offered by the Accompaniment Programme.

Polly from the Jerusalem office phones at 23.00 for the telephone number of the UK Programme Manager. Due to the bad reception and the heavy rain I can only respond with a text message and go to sleep again, wondering why this number is needed at this time on a Sunday evening.

Chapter 20
Israeli Human Rights Groups
Week 11

"The problem is not how to wipe out all differences, but how
to unite with all differences intact."

Rabindranath Tagore[1]

Monday 26th January

I return from early Gate duty to the tragic news that our
Bethlehem-based colleague, John Aves, has died. Now I
understand the phone call late last night and the need to
contact London.

Charles and I spend the day with the Mayor and the Governor
of the Qalqilya District and three hangers on. We start at the
town hall at 10.30, go to a meeting held at the boys' school in
Falamyeh and back to Jayyous for lunch at 16.30 and home at
17.30. Charles says there was not a lot that was new, apart
from the issue over land ownership and the payment of Israeli
taxes.

At the meeting many of the voices from the floor ask about
why the Palestinian Authority (PA) does not support the
Palestinian farmers with economic, tax relief, social and
practical support, let alone political support. This seems to
raise the question about how strong the PA is. How much is it
desperately hanging onto power, especially its leader Yasser
Arafat? Is it well organised enough to be able to run an
effective policy on anything? The response from the panel is
about having good relationships between the PA and the
people in the Qalqilya and Jayyous... and Azzoun (they
remember there are people from Azzoun in the audience). I
suspect the majority of people in the room do not see the point
of these political words. They just want some concrete
support in their terrible predicament. The meeting seems to
be about 'pressing the flesh' but also a degree of direct

democracy with the great and the good exposing themselves to public examination. Those in the line up include the police chief, the civil servants for education, agriculture, health, interior and the local representatives in the Palestinian Parliament. I am not sure if any of the groups here, farmers, politicians, civil servants or 'internationals' find the meeting satisfactory.

It was however an interesting opportunity to see inside a new Palestinian School. It could have been mistaken for a typical newly built English secondary school in the 1950-60s. It has rather plain classrooms of a good size with big windows. There are chalkboards and rows of chairs and tables ready for a traditional style of teaching from the front to large classes. The toilets were spotless which would be an improvement over English schools.

> *This has been a busy day, frequently punctuated by thoughts of John and his family. It is rounded off with Abdul-Latif reading (and simultaneously translating) a paper on the situation, which he will send us when it is translated. It is good that he wishes to keep in contact. His thesis is that Israel means war, and that war means economic destruction for their Arab neighbours, and therefore there is no social or economic development. "The one who grows thorns will never harvest flowers." The "jadar" (Separation Barrier) is a physical manifestation of a culture of division. I wonder if Abdul-Latif ever thinks about the consequences of speaking (writing) out against the Israelis when we know that one can be put in prison for relatively minor public comments.*

Tuesday 27th January

It has been a very wet night and there is water everywhere on the way to the 05.50 bus, for a day trip to Jerusalem to address the next group of EAs on the work being done in Jayyous. There is a feeling that this journey is rather pointless if we are not being replaced. There are few people travelling this morning and it is a quick run. It takes just 15 minutes to get through the Qalandia Checkpoint in a torrential downpour. In the chaos, I eventually get a place on a number 18 minibus to Jerusalem. I arrive at the New Imperial Hotel at about 09.00, after walking through the Suq in an attempt to keep relatively dry. (Jayyous to Qalandia, c80km, two hours, and Qalandia to Jerusalem, c8km, one hour.)

It is interesting to talk to the new people about Jayyous. I offer any support that might be needed in making arrangements for John, but the Jerusalem team seem to have it all in hand.

I just catch a bus for Qalandia and straight onto the bus for Funduq. With quick connections, I am back in Jayyous in just under two hours. On my return journey, I reflect on some of the other work being done by the wider team that has been spoken about in the meeting. My thoughts focus on the Israeli players in this situation with whom I have not had much contact while in Jayyous, with the exception of HaMoked, the Israeli Peace and Human Rights Group. These Israeli groups, that standout against the culture of military control and repression in the Palestinian Territories, include Ta'ayush, a group of Israeli citizens who volunteer to work with Palestinians in such places as Yanoun.[2]

Another such group is the "Women in Black", inspired by the Women's International League for Peace and Freedom, which was established in 1918 and formed in Israel in 1988. Over nearly twenty years, its members have stood for peace in weekly vigils, usually at busy road junctions in Israeli cities and towns. The focus of the vigils is precise, "End the Occupation". The women wear black. While not being silent there is no chanting. The public reactions, often in the form of verbal abuse like 'whore' and 'traitor', are received with silence and dignity. This simple movement also works with Arab Israeli women and Palestinians in Israeli prisons. There is an international support network. [3]

The Women in Black are members of the coalition of women's organisations called Women to Women for Peace, formerly know as Mothers for Peace. The group is based on the concept that peace will come through the will of ordinary people working in independent grassroots organisations. Their work to promote understanding of the situation includes helping people comprehend the reality of living in this land, and breaking down the stereotypes to allow individuals to be valued despite different ethnic origins, cultures and beliefs.[4] Another member of the coalition is Bat Shalom or Daughters of Peace, which works for the self-determination of both communities, in two independent and secure states, with Jerusalem as the capital for both of them. A prerequisite of this solution would be a final settlement of many issues under international law.[5]

Two more members are New Profile and Machsom Watch. The first works towards a civil rather than military society in Israel and supports young Israelis who become "refusers", by declining to serve in the Israeli Defence Force or in the Occupied Territories.[6] Some EAs have attended the trials of Israelis who are resisting the actions carried out by their government. The second is a group of Israeli women volunteers who conduct daily observations at military checkpoints to monitor Human Rights abuses.[7]

Finally in this list, which is by no means complete in its coverage of Israeli organisations, comes Rabbis for Human Rights. This is the rabbinic voice of conscience in Israel, giving voice to the Jewish tradition of Human Rights. Just one example of their work brings me back to my own work here. They help guarantee Palestinians access to their olive trees during the harvest, reducing the number of violent incidents and acts of theft and vandalism. It also helps market Palestinian Olive Oil and so stimulates the economy.[8] It may be interesting to note that many of these groups were formed around 1987, the date the first Intifada, or 'Palestinian mass non-co-operation' started, after twenty years of occupation.

These Israeli peace and human rights groups are not 'armchair' protesters. They work alongside Palestinians on a day-to-day basis and are prepared to confront other Israelis with the policies of their government. One such incident is recorded in 'Security or Segregation', when Israeli activists were attempting to protect the olive trees in Falamyeh, just north of Jayyous. When asked to stop cutting down the trees an Israeli contractor with a chain saw said, "If I don't do it, someone else will". Such individual responses illustrate how moral, political or economic attitudes support the government policy in the oppression of the weak.[9]

These groups welcome outside support for their difficult and dangerous work. The individual members, be they on a vigil in fashionable West Jerusalem, watching soldiers at checkpoints or questioning the orthodoxy of political or religious leaders, are standing against the conformist culture of this youthful State; standing as individuals against power. It is an honour to be linked to these groups, if only by association, especially as they have to carry on, while we are able to leave this land that needs their work so much. My time here would not have been so purposeful without the day-to-day support of HaMoked[10] and the information from B'Tselem[11] and Israeli Campaign Against House Demolition, [12] to name just three more Israeli groups already mentioned above.

Chapter 21

Nothing To Do - a day for a play

Week 11

"We need to see how each of us is caught up in the other."

Desmond Tutu[1]

Wednesday 28th January

All three North Gate watches end up as my duty today. It proves to be a good chance to witness the three 'acts' of gate opening during the day.

Act One - Morning

I arrive at the Gate at 06.42, taking only twelve minutes to get there from the house, all the walking of the last eleven weeks having greatly improved my level of fitness. It is dry, clear, still, indeed dead calm, and there is a yellow glow to the sunrise over the Jayyous ridge above and behind me. There has been heavy rain overnight.

I hear a tractor coming, one I have not seen before, a Massey Ferguson with a cab and pulling a very respectable green and yellow trailer, full of sacks, covered with tarpaulin and plastic sheets. The driver is also new to me. Has he only just been given a permit to go to his land? The silence is interrupted by my coughing and then the sound of another tractor. It arrives a minute or so later, complete with transport box and a driver wearing a red shamaq. Greetings are exchanged between the two men. The donkeys in the village do likewise, but without such reserve.

At 06.55 a Humvee comes from the north and stops at the Gate. One of the soldiers comes to open the Gate at 06.57. He just flings the Gates open and they bounce back towards him. The men in the shamaq walks slowly forward to open the inner gate and the other tractor moves forward. A man comes running down the lane followed by a cantering donkey and another man walking. I move towards the Gates. The inner gate is shut but the Gate is still open as papers are checked.

Another man deftly takes his donkey around the end of the closed inner gate without dismounting. The next walker is another new face to me. He does not know the ropes and stands in front of the inner gate uncertain what to do. He than decides to go under and walk towards the soldier checking papers. He is the last through and the Gate is shut at 07.04, eleven minutes before the end of the time it should be open. I make no comment as I cannot see or hear anyone coming down from the village. At 07.05, the Humvee leaves as quickly as possible up the hill to the south. The hydraulic rock chisel starts work in the quarry, with its relentless tap, tap, tap. At 07.08, I hear voices up the track amongst the bird song.

Two young-men arrive at 07.10. The sound of a tractor is heard and it shortly appears in a cloud of exhaust fumes, with two men on board. This could be a long wait as HaMoked do not open until 08.00. The Humvee is sitting on top of the hill, no doubt watching the scene of its own making. All these people could have gone through if the Jaish kept to its own times of opening.

The regular tractor and trailer belonging to Mubarak, with Ammar in the trailer, are the next to pull in. When he hears the Gate has already been opened it is the first time I have seen this usually very calm man get angry. The tractor, with the homemade cab, comes two minutes later at 07.19. While this time is out of the official time slot, it is well within the customary opening time, which at the North Gate has normally been up to about 07.30. Ghassen, the driver of this novel piece of automotive engineering, looks up the hill and turns to me, saying, "Very bad soldiers".

Later I hear from B'Tselem that since January 2005 the Israeli Civil Administration has refused to issue permits to Mubarak and his sons. As a result, only his wife who is in poor health is permitted to go to their land. Despite an arrangement with another farmer, who has a permit, to work Mubarak's land for one third of the crop, production has suffered. Mubarak and his sons sit at home detached from work and income, while crops go to waste.

Picture 25. A group of farmers wait at the North Gate.

At 07.25 ten men, three tractors and one donkey are waiting. As I ring Rex at the South Gate, a donkey cart comes down the hill. *It is strange to think that in a week's time I will be unlikely to see any of these people again, except in my pictures.* I take some more pictures. By 07.35, we are 14 men, all of whom would have got through the Gate on a normal day. There is a lot of laughter from Ammar and his friends as three separate groups form around three seated tractor drivers. A piece of wood is used to keep the brakes on when another tractor arrives at 07.37 with a three-man cargo.

The donkey with the cart finds a good patch to graze that the restrictions of the cart will allow it to reach. I try Rex again, but there is still no reply. It is now completely overcast. Ammar asks me about how many and which tractors went through at seven o'clock. I tell him, and he knows to whom they belong.

I wait for HaMoked to open in Jerusalem and the farmers wait for the Gate to open. At 07.47 a jeep comes slowly down the hill from the south, stops and switches off. This seems hopeful but it has stopped too close to the Gate. A man is called forward to the jeep. He is told the Gate will open at 12.30 and not before. The jeep goes. A contractor's open-back pickup goes north at speed. At 07.50 I start to ring HaMoked. At 07.58, I get through and Ammar talks to them.

While we are waiting for an answer from HaMoked Ammar talks a little about economics. He gives an outline of Israeli policy (even if it is broken English) "They don't want us to be going to the land for potatoes, clementinas, olives, cucumbers. They don't want us to have money for the house, for the boys, for the gas, for the food or for the *'womens'*." (In the way that 'sheeps' are plural, in translation 'womens' seem to be both singular and plural.)

At 08.00 and jeep goes by going south. There are now 18 men waiting. Since the visit of the jeep at 07.47, everybody is standing around, and the tractors and donkeys wait alone beside Ammar and me. More men gather around the fire. On average, these men have waited 40 minutes so far this morning (08.15). This works out at 12 hours of wasted time. I ask Ammar how much he is paid an hour. He says 5 shekels (70 pence) an hour, and 50 shekels a day working on the land. This works out at about 300 shekels a week, in a good week. (I have about 900 shekels in my pocket to cover the last eleven days of my time in Palestine!) He also proudly tells me he has saved 140 shekels for the Eid festival to buy clothes and sweets for the children.

At 08.20 I check with HaMoked. There is no news yet. One group of men is round the fire. Others walk about aimlessly and another group stands around, a few sitting on the rocks. Ammar cannot believe it is nearly 08.30 when HaMoked rings and says, the Gate will not open until 12.30. They also give me the contact details of Faras the Human Rights lawyer. Ammar tells the waiting farmers the news. At 08.38 an army truck speeds by. The men are milling around at the news. The lone man on his donkey is the first to canter off up the track. He is followed by some walkers while the tractors turn round. Nadeem says I should go and that I have done enough and stops a tractor for me. I indicate that I wish to stay.

We are left together, Nadeem and his donkey cart, Mubarak and his tractor and trailer, Ammar and me, as the final tractor leaves with six young men holding on where possible. Ammar talks to HaMoked again and I phone Faras, but he will not be in the office until 10.00. *Is he ever in the office?* There is a ray of hope as a jeep goes north, slowly, but does not stop. Nadeem knows it is not going to stop before it reaches the bottom of the hill. You only have to listen to the engine note to have a good idea if you are going to be in luck. The fire is built up and Nadeem's trousers are nearly incinerated because of Mubarak's over enthusiastic fire building. Ammar shows me his feet in plastic bags because his boots leak.

There is a final conversation with HaMoked at 09.00 and Rex is still not replying. Another jeep comes quickly down the hill at 09.07 and yet another from the north at 09.08. It is getting busy around here, but all of them are too busy for attention to human rights. I wonder, has something happened to distract them and if the South Gate has been opened? The fire crackles and the donkey grazes. We wait. We wait, Nadeem with his characteristic woolly hat on, Ammar in his brown open-faced balaclava and Mubarak in an uncharacteristic blue baseball cap. I expect his normal faded orange cap is still wet after yesterday's torrential rain. They sit quietly around a fire of large olive logs, the younger pair chatting while Nadeem listens. Mubarak takes a mobile phone call.

Having not seen a jeep for nearly twenty minutes, these last stalwarts give up waiting. Nadeem turns his donkey cart to home and the Mubarak offers me a lift up the hill. This is only the third time I have had a lift up the hill at this time of day since we arrived in November, and the other two times were with fellows who did not wish the go to their land. After nearly three hours, 'Act One' is over.

Act Two - Midday

"There is nothing to do!"

The title for this act is a quote from one of the farmers returning at midday when I say to him "Are you trying again?"

Scene: the same as this morning, a track running between stone walls leading to a pair of bright yellow gates in a fence that stretches across the landscape. There is a scatter of olive trees near by. Unlike this morning, the scene is now in strong sunlight and the temperature is relatively high. Most of the men sit in the shade of the narrow row of olive trees (front stage right); and so our scene is set for this unfolding human tragedy.

At 12.00, there are 10 men and two tractors.

Scene 1 On being sensible.

One of the men gets up and goes towards the inner gate. He starts to open it. The other men tell him to leave it alone, waving him away and knowing that if the inner gate is open this is enough for them to be punished by not opening the Gate. One must not touch Israeli military property, even for a reasonable act of preparation to save time.

Scene 2 The Humvee

Enter from the north (stage left) a Humvee at speed. It goes past the Gate and swings into the Jayyous land. Some of the players, who are the audience (chorus) to this scene, raise a shout or two.

Scene 3 The prayer scene.

Mubarak arrives on his tractor and trailer at 12.12, but without Ammar. A fellow in a white shamaq goes to pray a little way off (down stage right) and is joined by Mubarak and another, younger man who wears an Islamic style pillbox hat. A donkey cart stops up the road, with a man and his wife, waiting near the trailer of building blocks left there since this morning. Some cloud breaks the bright light and heat. A tractor arrives to pick up the trailer full of blocks. The driver calls for some help and one of the other men walks up the track. Once hitched up he moves towards the Gates. It is 12.25 and we are promised that the Gate will open at 12.30. The scene continues without much action. The donkey cart moves to a better place for grazing, indeed the donkey seems to be the only 'player' who is free.

A tractor arrives from the Jayyous land and (behind the fence, back stage right) joins another already waiting. These are the two tractors, which went through the Gate in the first part of 'Act One' of today's drama and are waiting to return to the village. The scene returns to inaction, while the three men still pray. A dubious tractor arrives and parks up the lane using stones as brakes and keeping enough gradient in case it will not start. (Directors should note here that this production needs a large stage of international proportions. There is more to this simple scene than there appears to be at first glance. This is not just about donkeys and farmers!) The men return from their prayers.

Scene 4 Calling for help.

The narrator telephones HaMoked to request some help to get the scene moving. It is 12.50. There continues a period of further inactivity. (Director should be careful about reducing these periods of inactivity to keep the audience's attention. They are a characteristic part of the situation.)

Scene 5 The 'opening' scene. (This seems a bit late!)

There is the sound from the stage right as the Humvee appears, slows, stops and switches off. It is 2 minutes to 1 o'clock. The leading soldier's gun is cocked (made ready to fire) while it points at the sky. The Gate swings open. The inner gate is opened by a farmer and things start to happen all of a sudden. A boy arrives from the village, almost unnoticed as the farmers move up to the Gate.

A farmer with a donkey carrying two panniers, and with a

sack of fruit on top tries to control the animal as he picks out some fruit for the narrator as a thank you. He jumps on the top of the panniers still holding the sack in place on this beast of burden. The last young farmer has difficulties with his papers; he has been turned back before, but to day he is allowed through, but only when he has shut the inner gate. To do this the soldier has to put his foot on the tractor accelerator to prevent the engine stalling. At 13.10, the Gate closes. The scene ends with the Humvee leaving the stage (left) as quietness falls and the bright sun light has gone.

The narrator may be seen sitting on a boulder eating a small orange citrus fruit.

Dramatis personae ~ In order of appearance

The narrator

Farmers 1-10

A farmer's wife

Farmers 11-16

Donkeys 1 and 2

Humvee Driver

Soldier 1 - 3

A boy   **End of Act Two**

Notes towards Act Three - Evening

The old stone-throwing problem occurs on the way to the Gate this evening. Having passed a group of likely lads, greeting them with "Mahubers" and "Hellos" I walk on a few paces only to hear the clatter of a stone on the ground behind me. Mind you, I did get an interesting reaction from a dog at about the same place at lunchtime. It was standing too close to the edge of the path for comfort, as I remembered my decision not to have a rabies injection. I bent down to pick up a stone, which was enough for it to run off into the fields.   It clearly associated my move with pain in the past. I turn and photograph the boys who run off into the almond trees.

Anyway, I arrive at the Gate just after 16.00 in bright afternoon sunlight with long shadows forming. There are several farmers already waiting on the other side of the fence. The jeep roars down the hill from the north at 16.33. The Gate is quickly opened and the tractors start to move forward. I am glad to see Mubarak's is at the back so I can take a lift. The Gate closes at 16.45. I ride up the hill on the coupling bar of the trailer, as there are "*womens*" inside. Does anyone need a white-knuckle ride when you can ride up the Jayyous North Slope on the outside of a trailer? (Directors, please be careful of making this a more dramatic ending; it seldom happens like that.) On this day one of the farmers tells me thirteen Palestinians were killed in Gaza by the Israelis.

Thursday 29th January (morning)

I arrive at the Gate 06.47. The Humvee comes north slowly on the Jayyous side of the fence at 07.14. It is a busy morning before the Eid holiday. There are already two vans, eight tractors, one donkey cart and three donkeys. There is also a bicycle that is seen to disintegrate under its rider as he stops at the top of the queue, the front wheel folding up as he goes over the handlebars and somersaults to a stop. The broken bike is thrown over the wall. There are also three women. There is no sign of the Jaish, having got everybody out early just in case there is a repeat of yesterday.

At 07.42, Rex rings to say the South Gate has been cleared and the children are on their way to school. The jeep is coming my way. It must be coming very slowly. It must have stopped. No, here it is. It goes straight past at speed, northwards to Falamyeh.

07.53 sees the Humvee, again at speed come from the north and disappear in a cloud of dust down onto the farmer's land. There is a lot of 'chai' being drunk as we hear the sound of the boys' school this morning on the breeze. The teacher's orders and the national anthem drift down the hill. At 08.03, when all is quiet again, I phone HaMoked. At 08.05, the jeep appears and the soldiers open the Gate. They make the waiting people move back away from the Gate. The little fellow starts picking out farmers to check. This is one of the more unpleasant soldiers. It takes nearly half an hour to check 44 farmers' permissions to go to work.

I return to the house and hear the news that there has been a bus bomb in Jerusalem.

... And, so this human tragedy will continue: if not here then somewhere where the interests of the rich, the powerful and the over-armed are threatened by the weak, the dispossessed and the peaceable people of this world. During the morning wait Abu Talib says what an excellent man Sharif Omar is for the village. He says everyone will tell you how hard he is working for the people, for the village, for the land, that he always cares. I tell him about Sharif Omar and the arrival of my bed. It seems a long time ago, but he always cares.

Chapter 22
The Evidence
Week 11

"...the inadmissibility of the acquisition of territory by war and the need to work for a just and lasting peace in which every state in the area can live in security."
UN Resolution 242 November 1967[1]

Thursday 29th January (afternoon)

Picture 26. Sharif Omar (left) with Jamal Juma' in Jayyous. Jamal is holding the evidence provided by the 'internationals' in support of the Palestinian case that the Separation Barrier is illegal at the International Court of Justice in The Hague.

I have a call from Susan that we are to be at the Baladiya for 14.00 to meet the human rights visitors. We meet at her place at 13.50 and quickly decide that if these people seem to be the right ones we will give them the Gate Watch Records,

233

compiled by ISM and EAs since August. Jamal Juma' of Palestinian Environmental Non-Governmental Organisation Network (PENGON) is present so we give him the pile of paperwork to add to the evidence for presentation in a human rights case in the Israeli High Court and later in the International Court of Justice in The Hague. He is very pleased to have all this supporting material and says he will pass it on to the legal team. We have confidence that our work will be of use to the Palestinian case in finding justice in the matter of the location of the Separation Barrier. Susan is pleased with this outcome.

In the meeting session, the Mayor talks about "Making peace between peoples". He also talks about the 'Rajka' or financial deed required by Israeli, as they do not recognise Palestinian Authority documents that are based on the Ottoman, British and Jordanian land registrations. To get the deed the farmer must pay tax and then they may still not get a permission, a tasreeh, to go to their land.

The Mayor continues to use the opportunity to make the case for Jayyous and Palestine to the visitors. There are 420 unemployed young men in Jayyous. Only 40% of farmers have permissions. The Mayor says the visiting Israelis wish to make peace. Neighbouring Azzoun has lost 12,000 dunums of land and has no Gate. He says, "Visitors give us hope". It is good that these Israeli lawyers say 'No!' to Sharon and his policy of violation.[2]

The Policeman asks, "Who needs security? The people with the ID, howada or the people with the weapons?" There have been agreements on security and within hours they are broken (by the Israelis). Security should be mutual and integrated with social and economic issues. Sharif Omar says "Visits strengthen the land of the just and the right; there should be no walls between people".

Azhar says, "The Israeli who killed Yitzhak Rabin, the former Israeli Prime Minster, is given an excuse by the Israelis. (A right-wing Israeli radical who opposed the signing of the Oslo Accords assassinated Rabin.) Why does the Israeli

234

government not do a study of the cases behind those who make themselves into bombs? I am totally against killing, but we need to know why it happens. I am reminded of the comparison in the way people are treated by the Israeli Courts. For making public comments about the Israeli occupation, a Palestinian policeman's son is given 23 months in prison, but an Israeli soldier who is charged with shooting a Palestinian is fined one Shekel (14 pence or 30 US cents) and the world is told he has been convicted. It's a joke." (He is a teacher and it shows.)

We suddenly find the meeting is over, ending in the characteristically abrupt style, and that the whole group is going to the Mayor's house for lunch (15.30). We arrive to find plates set out for us. While walking to the Mayor's house, Bergitta of Norwegian People's Aid says she has seen other people with the EA jacket. I tell her about Dorte and Olava (also from Norway) in Hebron and mention that I am a Quaker. She says Inga, who is here today, is also a Quaker from Oslo Meeting. We sit together for the meal of rice and lamb. The Mayor asks me to tell the departing guests about the heap of olive-tree trunks in his front garden. I say, "The trees are 'members of his family', brought home having been uprooted to make way for the Separation Barrier. Mayor Salim had 800 olive trees, but 700 of them were on land taken for the construction of the Separation Barrier. He now has no more than 100 trees. This is his reality on the ground." He turns his face away while I speak, and a hand moves to his eyes.

Some months later I think of the Mayor, when I hear that olive trees, uprooted from the Jayyous Land to make way for the expansion of the Israeli settlement of Zufin, are put on lorries to be sold to people in Israel. Indeed, I also read at this time of a group of mature olive trees being planted in a West Jerusalem park. Do the people sitting in the sun looking at these trees ask themselves where they came from? I am reminded of the Mayor's words, "It's difficult to think of peace and negotiation in a situation like this. This is our reality, our facts on the ground. I want peace with the Israelis and to live beside them."

Picture 27. The Mayor's olive tree trunks.

Perhaps it is difficult for those who are not Palestinians to understand the place of olive oil and therefore olive trees in this society. As the poet Mourid Barghouti says, "For the Palestinian, olive oil is the gift of the traveller, the comfort of the bride, the reward of autumn, the boast of the storeroom, the wealth of the family across centuries."[3]

After the people have dispersed, I leave the Mayor with his grief and walk back to the house with a great sense of achievement, but a concern that I do not say too much. I ring Ann to share my joy and reduce my enthusiasm! This seems a very fitting finale to my time in Jayyous. There is little point in coming here to accompany people on the daily wait to go through the Gates, if we do not attempt to remove the cause of this injustice. In some small way this we have now done. Will our evidence be the straw that will break the camel's back?

236

Part Four
Reflections on Accompaniment

Chapter 23
A Quiet Place
Weeks 11-12

"Security and narrow belief closes our options and ability to have empathy with others."

Theodore Zeldin[1]

"Everything involves parting as eventually everything departs."

Bede Griffiths[2]

Friday 30th January

I wake early after an excellent sleep with my mind on the matter of going to 'The Land'. The Jayyous land, the other side of the Separation Barrier has become know to us as 'The Land'. I have seen much of The Land from the high position of the Baladiya; however, some is hidden behind a ridge. The desire to visit 'The Land' concerns me a little as we are here to accompany, and that includes accompanying the 60% in the village who do not have 'permissions' to go to 'Their Land'. There is a case for accompaniment of those who are most affected by the situation, even if this is a hidden act of accompaniment. This situation is compounded by the discussion of my colleagues' visits to 'The Land' in front of those who are unable to go to 'Their Land'.

I am glad that my concern about this issue becomes better formed before I make a last minute effort to find a 'friend' (a farmer with a permit) to work with for the day and so contrive an excuse to go through the Gate. Yes, I would, especially as a geographer, have liked to see 'The Land', but in the circumstances it would seem inappropriate and insensitive not to support those most affected by not having permits. Act on conscience and hold to your own principles. Be clear what is the purpose of one's work and think about how people perceive and interpret one's words and actions.

There is no South Gate today being Friday but by 06.30 there is no sound of Rex getting up, so I quickly dress and leave a note to say I have gone the North Gate as he has over slept. He does not see the note and arrives at the North Gate about 15 minutes after me. This session confirms how different our style of accompaniment has become. *Have I had it wrong all this time?* He says he has another terrible story from his interviewing last night. I am not sure I can cope with yet another story; it is as if we do not have our own stories to cope with.

There is a clear sky and the sun is already hot, so I decide to spend the day on the ridge to the east of Jayyous, overlooking the valley that comes down from Kafr Sir. I find a nice place in the sun, but soon retreat to the shade of a rock. I write and draw, eat a banana or two and do some thinking.

A Quiet Place

It is a very long time since I have been in such a very quiet place. The olive trees, a bee, some children in the distance with just the high notes being heard. A donkey is led by a man, accompanied by his wife along the track below without a sound being carried to me.

Even when the muezzin in Kafr Sir calls the faithful to midday prayers it hardly seems an interruption. There is bird song and the occasional flutter into flight, the puff of breeze. All is quiet. The mouths of the caves are speechless, but most of all the stones keep their silent vigil, undisturbed by politics or bulldozers. This is indeed a wonderfully quiet place. What a joy it is to have discovered the other face of Jayyous. I can see why the Palestinians call their land 'paradise' - the land called 'paradise' or the land called 'promised'.

Picture 28. Almond trees near the Quiet Place

Picture 29. The Dry Valley to the north-east of Jayyous

How well do I know these people? I know a small number of Palestinians reasonably well in a day-to-day way at the Gate. I know a few at a deeper level through conversations at the house and during meetings, I recognise rather more in the village, on the bus to Qalandia and even around the Jaffa Gate in Jerusalem. I do not know enough about the Israelis. The few I have had conversations with, mostly from the peace groups, have been delightful. I found it very difficult to initiate conversations with my travelling companions when I went to Israel. I have a problem with the concept of Zionism and Christian Zionism. The only Christian Zionist I have met here was an American, who spent time shouting at me near the Wailing Wall in Jerusalem, telling me what to tell people when I returned home, comments laced with the need to prepare for the second coming and the Day of Judgement. I suspect she had not seen what I had seen in the West Bank and, even if she had, would have supported the Israeli actions there. Her certainty over the historic claim to the land, the right to build settlements, and the right of Israelis to impoverish their neighbour was part of the arrogance that suggests they have all the answers, the case being presented in such a way as to suggest the Arabs are sub-human and can just be pushed aside. Even in this potential paradise for all, it appears that those who were historically bullied (and very much worse) have become the new bully.

As human beings, we need to attend to matters of conscience. To me this is the principle that we should attempt to respect 'that of God in every person', be they Jew, Muslim, Christian, or any other human being, and that this may be interpreted and expressed through such things as respect for human rights. This position clearly promotes in me a difficulty about the concept of the land of Israel as the 'God-given land'. This seems to stand contrary to respecting 'that of God in every person', as it is exclusive and judgemental. To me the second coming is a spiritual rather than a geographical concept. Do we select a path of peace, fellowship and compassion or a path of self, a path of religious certainty and acquisition, in an attempt to protect ourselves from the brutalities of the world? I am grateful to have had the time to reflect on these paradoxes while doing something to exercise my conscience. Perhaps we need the environment of tension to be able to find the 'inner space' of interest, research, reflection, personal development and creativity, indeed to become fully aware of one's conscience.

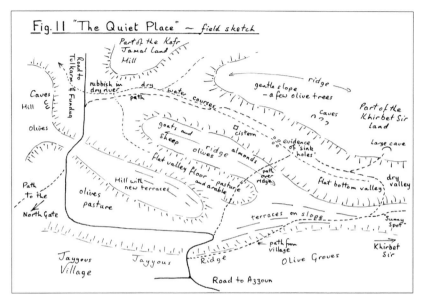

Fig. 11 "The Quiet Place" – field sketch

Charles returns from his visit to Tel Aviv and his attempt to visit Gaza. He carries a request for a possible article for the Palestine-Israel Journal, having sat next to the editor at a British Embassy function.

Saturday 31st January

I go to the North Gate where there is a new team of soldiers. People go through without trouble. The DIY cab tractor driver tells me, "... the soldiers have changed and they are not so bad... older... more reasonable". As the last people go through, they wait for a flock of sheep coming down the lane, followed by another farmer. The shepherd is not allowed through, as his animals need to have a veterinary certificates to enter Israel.

With the sheep still on the apron, the soldier calls me up to the Gate. As we start to converse I notice his gun is pointing at my foot and ask if he minds if I move. He says nothing will happen, but is surprised when I tell him that the gun is cocked ready to fire. I tell him he is the first soldier in two and a half months of my observations who has waited for people coming down the track.

A flock of goats turns up and mixes with the sheep. They are not allowed through for the same reason, no veterinary certificates. I ask the soldier if the sheep will need to have photographs on their permits to enter what is clearly now seen as Israel. As expected, I get no reply. He is not comfortable with all these animals round him, despite being an agricultural graduate of the University of California.

Nadeem comes down the lane with his donkey cart and the soldiers call him through the sheep. I say, "This is Nadeem. He goes through everyday", knowing full well that he does not have a permission. He shows all his paperwork: his ID, his wife's permission, her ID (although she is not here today) and is moving on to his document about paying taxes to get his deed when the soldier says "OK!" and he goes through yet again. I ask the soldiers if they want me to close the inner gate. They say, "that's OK, you can leave it". I say, "No you can't because the inner gate being open is an excuse not to open the main Gate." I tell them about the morning I was first here, and the Gate was open and the soldiers would not allow any farmer through. I tell them about my records of the Gate being open at the wrong times. I am assured "...these are not the orders. The Gate must be opened if people are waiting." I say, "There is a difference between orders and reality".

Do these soldiers realise we have been watching the operation of the Gates over the last ten weeks?

They ask, "Have you complained?" I say, "Yes!" Resisting the temptation to list all the problems of the last twelve weeks, I tell them about the request for a rope on the inner gate and the difficulty both the Jaish and the farmers have in closing it.

Picture 30. The Shepherd with his sheep. A shepherd takes his sheep away from the Gate after being refused passage to his grazing land beyond the fence.

They start to close the Gate. As I walk away, two more fellows are coming down the lane. I turn to be told, "We'll let them through". Are they being nice as a new policy? Have things really changed? Are the farmers being softened up for some new crackdown? As I walk up the lane, the herdsmen are sorting the sheep from the goats. I wonder how many of these animals will survive the Eid holiday, when the streets will run with the blood of sheep.

Charles has picked up that the young soldiers are going to be taken off the Gates. They even ask, "What do the people of Jayyous think?" which I answer with the question, "Why do we always get told, when we say to soldiers we are going to Jayyous, that it is a very dangerous place. These are lovely people, but they don't like your fence, anymore than you would like it if I built a fence in your garden." Charles supports the view that this conscript army is poorly trained, poorly supervised, and there is too much of the 'do-it-yourself' army about them. Perhaps things will be better if older, more experienced soldiers are on the Gates.

Charles and I go to Qalqilya to visit the checkpoint, which does not seem to operate, at the southern end of the wall. The dual-carriageway road just ends at the eight metre high concrete wall, with a watchtower. To one side there is a collection of gates for road and pedestrian traffic, but no sign of them having been opened recently. The other side of the gates is the 55 Road west to Israel and east to the Settlements in the West Bank. A little distance beyond the road are other sections of Separation Barrier around Habla.

It is very busy as we wander round in the holiday weekend crowds. We walk through the market, with butchers and bread shops doing a roaring trade, as well as many stalls with toys and clothes. We find a cafe to have some lunch before taking a bus back through the checkpoint to Azzoun and taxi to Jayyous. The higher view from the bus gives the first opportunity to see Jayyous from the south with the Separation Barrier cutting across the land by the South Gate and into the zigzag around the valleys to the south east of the village. (See Picture 4 on page 30.)

Sunday 1st February

A strange day in that I do not get up until nearly 08.00. We discuss the situation with regard to Polly making a decision about the future of EAs in Jayyous. It is decided that I should, yet again, phone her to establish the latest situation. I leave a message on both her phone and Robert's phone. It is Sunday morning and we suspect they are both at church. Polly rings back two hours later to repeat that there is nobody to follow us and that she will confirm when she has spoken to Abdul-Latif and Sharif Omar. This she does a little later. Therefore, we have two clear days before departure to Jerusalem to say good-bye to people and to catch up with the final jobs.

It all seems rather strange and Sam and Rex are angry, again.

There is talk about how this reflects on our work and the situation in Jayyous. Jayyous is clearly a much more stable place than it was 6 months ago. Less shooting, less IDF in the village, a rhythm of Gate opening, if not satisfactory, that is much better than it was last summer, when the Gates were closed for several weeks at a time. The ending of the placement in Jayyous does not relate to the work we have done in the 12 weeks (more like 10 weeks when the call-backs are allowed for) we have been here. This judgement about the need to continue EAs work in Jayyous must be seen in relation to the needs of other placements and the resources available. I am sad that support will not continue for the village leaders. Personally, I just feel very tired and I am glad that the Eid holiday coincides with our departure, taking the focus away from us and reducing the amount of Gate Watching.

I briefly consider volunteering to stay for another three months, but realise this would not be sensible. Stopping accompaniment is difficult. If accompaniment is converted into friendship or reliance, there is always going to be an issue of how it ends. Accompaniment is time specific. We come, we stay and we go. I hoped that we would eventually be replaced by people who can easily fill the space, who could go on offering accompaniment. If the relationship has moved to friendship it is much more difficult for replacement to take place. The accompanier is like a colleague. Colleagues are always replaceable, but friendships cannot be transferred in the same sort of way. Friendship also infers a degree of, at best, interdependency or, at worst, dependency.

As I have taken a more observational approach to my role as an accompanier, all that I have done could be done by others or by those living in Jayyous themselves. My lack of demand for interdependence, let alone dependency, allows me to leave at least some degree of self-reliance, or, ideally, enhanced self-reliance. I feel these are important factors in the nature of accompaniment. I suspect my position on this relates to, and develops from, my years of experience of working with children. Teachers should always work alongside students. It is less wise for a range of reasons to become a friend. These include the desire to develop self-reliance, for students to be able to move on, and to maintain the same degree of respect for all the children. These are matters of right, access, justice and development.

There is also the problem of an exit strategy. I am not aware if this has been discussed within the Accompaniment Programme. We have decided to leave for Jerusalem on Wednesday on the basis that if there is to be no replacement it is best to go without a fuss. This is a functional solution and it does not allow for the social activity required for the more friendship-based departure.

As suggested above (page 216) if we had had more time, the possibility of the farmers carrying on recording could have been discussed. This would not only continue to provide the Mayor and Palestine Environmental Non-Governmental Organisation Network, PENGON, with information, but it would also have provided an opportunity to develop the self-esteem of those doing this work. These are small but positive things the community could continue for itself. It would be even better if the village could help with the cost of telephoning HaMoked, the Israeli human rights support group in Jerusalem, as many of the farmers phones can only receive calls, having no money to make them. This would allow the farmers to contact the Israeli District Co-ordination Office (the DCO) and to sort out some of the problems for themselves. As it happens, more time has been spent getting a confirmed decision than on developing such a plan. The Eid holiday prevented contact with the people in Jayyous we wished to help. Time ran out.

Considerably more work needs to be done in developing exit strategies from this type of work. Indeed the individual accompaniers' exit strategies need to be thought about much earlier in the programme. The question "How do I get out?" needs to be there in the mind of the accompanier as much as the question, "How do I get in?" This applies equally at the programme level to the management of locations as the situation in Palestine/Israel develops and changes. There needs to be a bringing together of the programme philosophy and practicalities of on-the-ground management to provide a better experience for both the accompaniers and the accompanied when a location is closed.

After a gap of several months, Accompaniers returned to Jayyous later in 2004.

Monday 2nd February

Things are running down smoothly. There is little to do today. I make a final report to the Mayor, do some cooking and the triage of 'to pack', 'to be left here' and 'to be left in Jerusalem'. I make a final parcel of things to post home from Jerusalem, there being no effective postal service in the West Bank.

Tuesday 3rd February

Most of the day is spent packing and tidying the house. We all go for an evening meal in Azzoun as the Jayyous kitchen has been closed after a final cleaning by Charles.

We are back by 19.30 as we are expecting Abdul-Latif and Sharif Omar at 20.00. The first of the party to arrive is Abu Fareed and his brother Nawfal. There is also a man whose daughter had her leg broken by a Humvee at the Tulkarm checkpoint when returning to Jayyous from Eid shopping a couple of days ago. They also tell of a man returning from hospital through this checkpoint after an operation who was hit in the site of his surgery by the back of a gun. There is talk of land, the 'stones', justice, peace and dreams. There is a final exchange of ideas, wishes, expectations, hopes, fears, support, thanks, concerns; and the scream of Israeli jeeps passing the house, followed by gun fire and thunder cracks.

"Are they giving you a send off?" asks one of the Palestinians, "or is it just the end of the holiday?"

There are promises to keep in touch and big bear hugs all round and lots of hand shaking. There is an expression of

247

hope that the lack of 'internationals' in Jayyous will not be seen as a victory by the Israelis, or that the 'internationals' are in retreat as the Gates are no longer observed. With some sadness and much regret, I turn in for the last night in this place. My sleep is broken for the last time by my 'pet' mosquito. As I doze, the words I planned for our leaving party come to mind. They will never be said, as we have no party, and it would have been too pompous to introduce them to the conversation with the small gathering we had this evening:

> *When I first came to Jayyous I found, like you, I had lost my freedom. I was at the South Gate and a single farmer was waiting on the other side of the fence. The Jaish did not come to open the Gate. It was only when the farmer waved to me and walked away from the Gate that I was free to leave. I feel the same now. The new team has arrived so I am free to go. However, because of my experience here part of me will never be free until you have the freedom to come and go as you please. Thank you for your wonderful hospitality. Thank you also for your friendship, which I will pass on to all those people willing to listen.*

Wednesday 4th February

We leave Jayyous at 10.00. Charles and I take a light lunch on the cafe terrace near the Jaffa Gate. We visit the office of the Israel-Palestine Journal and I discuss writing an article on the work we have been doing in Jayyous.[3]

Thursday 5th February

The day is filled with endless meetings.

Friday 6th February

09.00 A liturgy of thanksgiving for the life and ministry of John Aves, Priest, at the Cathedral Church of St George the

Martyr, Jerusalem.

10.00 Debriefing and feedback session. I say too much.

18.00 A final meal together for the whole team. I don't say enough.

Saturday 7th February

02.00 Taxi to the Tel Aviv Airport

04.30 We start the process of getting through check-in, which includes an hour and a half of questioning and searches.

11.15 My brother meets me at Heathrow and drives me to Paddington Station.

12.00 I leave Paddington for Exeter and home; so begins the long process of returning to normal, *whatever normal is.*

Journal End piece - Letting Go

Monday 9th February

UNRWA issue a report about Jayyous on their website. The statement includes the following. On February 9, 2004 the Israeli Defence Force issue new opening times for the Gates in the Separation Barrier around Jayyous.[4] These times are

07.00 - 08.30

12.30 - 13.30

17.00 - 18.30

These new times took into consideration the petition filed by the Association for Civil Rights in Israel (ACRI) on behalf of a number of villages including Falamyeh and Jayyous. It seems strange that I will not be there to check that these new times are being adhered to.

At least these new times will settle any confusion about the inconsistencies in the official opening times that may be apparent in the Journal record.

Chapter 24
No Checkpoints

Yesterday is already a dream, and
Tomorrow is only a vision, but today well
Lived, makes every yesterday a dream of
Happiness, and every tomorrow a vision of
hope...

Days of experience become years of wisdom.
                            Dajani Management[1]

On reflection, accompaniment was often tedious and unglamorous work, requiring a certain amount of endurance. There was a need to accept and be tolerant of one's situation, staying there to work it through, nurturing each moment. There was a temptation to go elsewhere looking for more exciting and stimulating experiences to relieve the monotony.[2] It required patience to fulfil the objectives and to make full use of the three months available. I was glad I did not cut the experience short, as I had thought of doing at one point in mid-December. My accompaniment was grounded in the day-to-day, a piece of grounded research based on a 'lived' experience.

It is hard to see anything done by an individual in the context of the occupation as having any real impact on the situation. It was a great honour to have the opportunity to bring together the work of a range of 'internationals' in Jayyous and provide evidence of the violation of human rights and international humanitarian law. There was little opportunity to prove my nonviolent approach in the nonviolent, non-confrontational atmosphere of Jayyous, but just by being there one was able to support day-to-day acts of nonviolent resistance alongside local Muslim Palestinians and Israeli Peace Activists when they came to visit. We also offered protection through nonviolent presence.

"Each teacher shall think for himself, and work out for himself such methods of teaching as will use his powers to best advantage and be suited to the particular needs and conditions of the school."[3] This concept of a teacher, which stands close to my own professional stance, equally applies to Ecumenical Accompaniment. I selected observation as my method, observation being the method that suited me and my ability and personality. It allowed me a degree of emotional detachment, while, paradoxically, leading to the development of a greater attachment to this practical approach and the regular contact it required with the farmers and the Bedouin family. As a method, it seemed well suited to the needs and conditions found in Jayyous. Central to this method was the process of reflection, indeed of critical reflection, upon one's activities and on how some meaning could be made of them. As with so much learning and research, time was spent trying to find the right question, the right focus. Initially, some of this seemed to be wasted time, or time that allowed a quick and superficial experience to be gained that seemed enough to come home and talk about. However, the opportunity offered by the second and third months took both knowledge and understanding to a deeper level. Because the reality of the situation in Israel-Palestine is so complex, I was 'reduced' to the observation of the detail in Jayyous. I suspect some of my colleagues thought I was 'reducing' my experience too much. The outcome was evidence that became applicable to the whole issue of the Separation Barrier, an example of the 'case study' illuminating the whole. As Jung says, "One does not become enlightened by imagining figures of light, but by making the darkness conscious."[4] He also adds that, "this procedure, however, is disagreeable and therefore not popular."

The Observer works in a process of continually switching between seeing differences and resemblances, of discrimination and correlation, of looking at the individual case and seeing the whole. Edward Robinson says, "It is on our ability to [listen] see, and to [listen] see with an attentive imagination, that the emergence of any new insights must depend."[5] Robinson goes on to say, "The act of observation involves choice and rejection." There were things we collectively chose to record in the Gate Logs, the quantitative and objective basis for the evidence. More difficult is the acceptance or rejection, the selection of the observed evidence. Objectivity has a high status in research. However, I doubt if it was achieved in my work in Jayyous. My hope was to record observations that would convey 'a perspective' of, and, at times, 'the perspective' of the Palestinians I worked with. I also hope it provides evidence, for people unable to go to Palestine, of a different story to that often heard: a story of desolation and of hope, of power and oppression, of illegality and recourse to international law.

I would not go as far as Harold Pinter in his Nobel acceptance speech[6] in which he says that for politicians, "…to maintain power, it is essential that people remain in ignorance, that they live in ignorance of the truth. What surrounds us, therefore, is a vast *tapestry of lies*." (My emphasis.) If such it be, I hope I have poked a finger through this tapestry of lies, to illuminate a very small part of the other people's story: the story of the dispossessed and the oppressed. This would be a contribution to a new *tapestry of understanding*, offering a new dimension to the situation, based on the idea that our enemy is the person whose story we have not heard. Only by considering the never-ending range of reflections of others was it possible to see this world of occupation and its sapping of human dignity.

The approach to this work could have been through the traditional missionary zeal, of certainty, of having answers. However, I came from outside with no real comprehension of what it was like to live under a military occupation, let alone live under one for forty years. As Paulo Freire says, in his classic work the Pedagogy of the Oppressed[7], "Who are better prepared than the oppressed to understand the terrible significance of an oppressed society? Who suffer the effects of oppression more than the oppressed? Who better understands the necessity of liberty?" We could easily substitute 'occupied' for the 'oppressed' in the above. I found these occupied people to be oppressed at one level: their economy is in tatters, their freedom is restricted, their resources of land, water and trees have been stolen and there was, and is still, an oppressor.

Despite all this, I found their humanity had not been lost, indeed, it had been affirmed by the desire for justice, freedom and their wish for peace.

It was a privilege to work for and with these dignified people and to receive more than we gave. It was an honour to be taught how to live by people who are spiritually rich, if socially, economically and environmentally oppressed.

My experience suggested another similarity with teaching in that accompaniers are seldom able to follow things through to a conclusion. As Elise Boulding suggests of peace workers, "We are always acting out of the present but we never get feedback about the effectiveness of what we have done", which is very like teaching.[8] What was the long term impact of being in Jayyous: being at the Gate, talking to people in Jerusalem, talking to people on my return, most of whom were sympathetic but also included members of a Reform Synagogue, and several groups of Christian Zionists who attended my meetings?

The one piece of feedback which did come my way, was in July 2004, when I heard that the International Court of Justice's adjudication was that the "Security Wall", the Separation Barrier, was illegal. It was good to feel that we had provided several stitches in the *tapestry of evidence* provided by the Palestinians in setting out their case, as opposed to the tapestry of lies suggested by Pinter above. However, as Sharif Omar commented, "The U.S. will doubtlessly use the veto in the Security Council to block the will of the Court, as it has done countless times before when measures were introduced to protect the rights of the Palestinian People." His comments also added the positive rider that, "The Court's decision will encourage Palestinians in our nonviolent resistance to this Apartheid Wall, and to all other aspects of Israel's illegal occupation."[9]

Sadly, this was indeed the case. The advisory decision of the Court was not taken as a basis for new work towards peace.[10] However, we do not know where the seed of an idea might be sown. Writing in The Independent newspaper in March 2005, on the second anniversary of the invasion of Iraq, the late Robin Cook, the former British Foreign Secretary who resigned over the war, made the following remark, "We would have made more progress against terrorism if we had brought peace to Palestine rather than war to Iraq."[11] On his appointment as Foreign Secretary in 1997, Cook had set out by saying he wanted to introduce an ethical dimension to British foreign policy.   While this did not lead to an immediate, perceptible change, it did make a rather neat and telling comment on the nature of British foreign policy in the past. A policy littered with interventions and manipulations in other people's lands, often with anything but peaceful outcomes. To name just two: firstly Suez, which included the manipulation of Israeli involvement, and secondly, the removal of the Chagos Islanders to make way for a U.S. military base in the Indian Ocean, an event described as "A very sad and by no means creditable episode in British History."[12]

How different modern British foreign policy could have been. How different public opinion seemed to be.   Nearly one hundred years ago, people marched in the streets to accompany the soldiers to war; to the war that would end all wars between 1914 and 1918. More recently, people marched through the streets of London to protest at the coming war in Iraq. These demonstrations, on the 15th February 2003, were of a size that had never previously been seen before a war. Between one and two million people marched in London, and the number would have been more if the halt, sick and lame, who wished to be there, had been able to join the throng. There were similar demonstrations in cities around the world. It was suggested that those of us who marched must justify our doubts about the war, that we did not know the reasons for the war, while the Government continued its shamefully contrived and spurious justification of the coming invasion.

It is clear in my mind that this march and the invasion of Iraq were preconditions in my responding to the request for people to go to Palestine. A flexible lifestyle allowed me to transform my "armchair pacifism" into action. It permitted the close engagement with what I had always seen as the root of the problem in the Middle East. It justified my demand for peace with action, rather than simply hope. It is in the here and now that we need to engage.

One of the most uncomfortable realisations on returning to my 'normal life' (as if life will ever be normal again) was the regression towards one's old modus operandi, losing the sense of emotional equanimity that had been found in Palestine.

The title of this chapter, No Checkpoints, indicates how the experience stayed with me, both in the short and long term. On leaving the main A30 Road from Exeter to go into Okehampton a few weeks after coming home, suddenly the words "no checkpoints" came to mind. This, now meaningless phrase, had been code for a good journey in the West Bank. However, each time I think of Palestine it is in effect a checkpoint, making me review what is happening there and how we live our lives here.

Chapter 25
On Peace and Justice

'We should put out a clarion call to the government of the people of Israel, to the Palestinian people, and say: "Peace is possible, peace based on justice is possible. We will do all we can to assist you to achieve this peace... and you will be able to live amicably together as sisters and brothers".

Desmond Tutu[1]

Justice claimed by one people at the expense of another is not justice.

Sabeel[2]

Integrity – Justice – Peace – Integrity

The Occupation of Palestine, the West Bank and Gaza is a very different occupation. When Germany occupied France (and Belgium, the Netherlands, Luxembourg, Denmark and Norway and most of Eastern Europe), the concept of resistance, 'The French Resistance', was supported by those fighting the Nazi Regime and given cultural credence after 1945. They were the French Resistance, not the French freedom fighters, nor the French terrorists. The people of Tibet and Chechniya are not condemned by the 'western world' for their resistance to China and Russia. In Palestine, Halper suggests the occupier is cast in the role of the weak party, the victim that must protect itself from the terrorist, the freedom fighter or the resistance.[3] I say this as a fact, not as an indication of support for terrorist or freedom fighters. As clearly stated above I do not support a violent solution to this issue by either side.

There is however a problem even with nonviolent resistance to the crushing military occupation. On the 'seventh day' of the

Six-Day War, 12 June 1967, Israel, "…enthusiastically chose to become a colonial society, ignoring international treaties, expropriating lands, transferring settlers from Israel to the occupied territories, engaging in theft and finding justification for all these activities. The oppressive regime exists to this day. This is a harsh reality that is causing us to lose the moral base of our existence as a free, just society and to jeopardise Israel's long-range survival."[4] These are not my words but the words of Michael Ben-Yair, the Attorney General of Israel from 1993-1996.

Israel persistently refuses to comply with the conditions of the Fourth Geneva Convention, which cover the conduct of an occupying power.[5] For example Article 49 forbids the deportation and any 'forcible transfer' of population, which would include such common practices as revoking Jerusalem Identity Cards held by Palestinians, or banning Palestinians from returning from work, study or travel abroad;[6] not to mention the demolition of houses for planning or security reasons.[7] The Convention also stipulates, "The Occupying Power shall not… transfer… its own civilian population into territories it occupies."[8] Israel clearly breaches this in both ways, restricting the Arab population of East Jerusalem while surrounding the Arab city with its own illegal settlements, to which it encourages its own population to move, attracted by various incentives. Add to this scene the building of the eight metres high Separation Wall (Separation Barrier) around the residential areas and one can only wonder as to which community is in the ghetto. To this must be added the irony that much of the 4th Geneva Convention was established as a response to the transfer of populations, especially in East Europe, during the 1939-45 War. History repeats itself, but with the methods of control in new hands.

At the time the Fourth Geneva Convention was being created, Israel was trying to establish its statehood. Shlaim says, "The moral case for a Jewish State in Palestine was widely accepted from the beginning (dating back to the Balfour Declaration); after the Holocaust it became unassailable."[9] With this in mind, the various Israeli armed factions, the Haganah, the national Military Organisation or Irgun and the Fighters for the Freedom of Israel, also known as the Stern Gang, inflicted considerable problems and casualties on the British Forces during the final year of the Mandate between November 1945 and July 1946. Today we would call these people terrorists. While these attacks possibly hastened the end of the British Mandate, Britain had been left in a very bad economic state at the end of the 1939-45 War. It was heavily in debt to the Americans, a bill for 'war services' being presented shortly after the election of the 1945 Labour (socialist) government. This meant that the new Government had to make economies in its overseas commitments to release much needed funds to cover its major social reform programme, principally the creation of the National Health Service and the implementation of the 1944 Education Act.

The breaches of international law are not recognised by Israel as it says it is not occupying Palestine, but that Palestine was captured in 1967 and therefore the Geneva Convention does not apply. This does not seem to match conditions on the ground. If Palestine was a fully democratic and borderless part of a fully integrated State of Israel, stretching from the Mediterranean to the Jordan, peopled by Jew and Arab together, with one legal system, equality of rights, movement and access to water, all the things that make a modern, democratic country, it might be possible to say it is one state. Israel has in reality set up a system of apartheid as in South Africa or even, and a very much more uncomfortable concept, a system of "Ghettoisation",[10] especially in the densely populated areas around Jerusalem and the other Palestinian towns.

It is time I returned to the suggestion, made four paragraphs above, that there is a problem with nonviolent resistance to the Israeli military occupation. One of the foundations of nonviolent resistance is that it is not only a moral right but also that it is supported by international law. This sets out what is acceptable in the conduct of a modern, democratic and civilised state in its relationships with other states and by implication its behaviour within its own borders. By saying

Israel has captured Palestine and that it is therefore not occupied, the Israelis have erected a barrier between the Palestinians and international law. The proud, modern democracy of Israel has disenfranchised its neighbour, which it says, along with much of the international community (the U.S., the U.K. and the E.U.) must become a democracy. Palestine has elections both at a local scale and 'across' the West Bank and Gaza. (I can only say 'across', as to say elections were held nationally is not exactly the case as Palestine is not a nation.) These elections are seen as valid by international observers. However it cannot become a true democracy without international recognition as a state, which would allow full recourse to international law. Because Palestine is not a state it does not have a seat in any international forum, and when access to international law is achieved through the International Court of Justice, its adjudications are ignored.[11] (In early 2007 as many as a third of the members of the Palestinian Legislative Council were arrested by the Israelis and imprisoned without charge.)

In addition, a democracy cannot operate without a functioning economy. As has been shown above it is impossible to have a fully functioning economy under the restrictions of the occupation. As is the way of capitalist economies, they are always looking for new markets. The West Bank has become a captive market for Israeli goods as the Palestinian economy collapses. This means the aid money paid by the international community to support the refugees and to support the Palestinian economy is re-cycled into the oppressor's economy as Palestinians become more reliant on Israeli goods. The need for external support for the Palestinian economy was very obvious when the international community cut off aid after the election of the Hamas Government in 2006.

Justice is a pre-condition for peace. Integrity is a pre-condition for justice and therefore for peace. Peace develops integrity. The question seems to be how can we develop integrity without peace. To build integrity there needs to be respect, equality and dignity for all peoples and cultures, by all peoples and cultures. Justice claimed by one people at the expense of another is not justice.

The only way forward in this situation is for the parties to work through a truth and reconciliation process as has happened in South Africa. The commitment to violence by some on both sides, be it 'terrorist' or 'state' violence, the failure to recognise human rights of all individuals, the failure to nurture the communities of the other by settlement building or consigning people to refugee camps would need to be exposed in such a process. If the failure to observe international law were to be aired and the transgressions healed, there might be the basis of a reconciliation.

However, it must be recognised that the positions are probably even more entrenched than in South Africa. There is probably more prejudice and interference from outside here than in South Africa; so, this would be a very demanding process. It can happen. It took nearly forty years to bring peace in Northern Ireland since the start of the most recent 'troubles' in 1969, and to start to resolve 300 years, or more, of 'colonial' power, prejudice and bigotry. It will still take several more generations to achieve a fully integrated society in the Province. As with all processes of peacemaking or reconciliation, there must be something in the outcome for both sides. While these situations are all different, it is remarkable that the international community seems to have an inability to transfer concepts of peace-making from one situation to another. Each one is dealt with pragmatically rather than from any sense of underlying principle.

This may be difficult to achieve as each of the sides, especially the Israeli Zionists, do not wish to see any Palestinians in the area of Eretz (Greater) Israel, a view based on the 'land without people for the people without land' simplicity. Some of the orthodox religious Jews would like to live in the Holy Land, side-by-side with the Palestinians, with no Israel and no Palestine. It is hard to see how a reconciliation could be produced to accommodate all the differences in this land. As the strategies of fighting the enemy or the terrorist with violence is counterproductive, leaving yawning chasms between the various elements of the conflict, perhaps there is a crying need for a new approach.

Prevention of conflict can work. It is by nature multi-faceted, flexible and different in every case. It may be concisely described under four main headings; firstly, the early warning of situations where rights are being abused, secondly the promotion of democracy, human rights and nonviolence by local groups and non-governmental organisations (NGOs), thirdly the use of information technology, especially E-mail, when other means of communication are unavailable or controlled, and fourthly the introduction of funding of various forms of peace monitoring. The second of these worked well in Kosovo when the Organisation for Security and Co-operation in Europe deployed 1300 monitors. There is good evidence to show that wherever their orange 'Land Rovers' went violence stopped. The monitors were withdrawn before the NATO bombing started and in the intervening period a wave of killing and eviction took place. The fourth idea has been used in South Africa, with monitors being present at events where violence might flare up.[12]

Essentially this idea amounts to an unglamorous, slow and possibly dangerous process of unravelling hatred. Governments are closely related to power, power is maintained by short-term strategies; armies are quick (well at least that is the theory and sometimes the case as in the Six-Day War). The short-term strategies, based on politicians watching out for the next election, distort the long-term processes of peacemaking. As I have suggested this type of work is slow and plodding. It is also massively under funded. If ten percent of the money put into armies and weapons went into peace work, what a difference it would make. Perhaps there should be a Ministry of Peace in every democracy; indeed it should be part of the definition of a democracy, based on the concept that the modern world does not have 'spare people',[13] surfs and slaves, who can be the cannon fodder for the powerful.

Such an approach might arrest potential conflicts in what Curle refers to, in his Swarthmore Lecture "True Justice", as the Stage of Quiescence. He suggests in these early stages of conflict people are adversely affected by situations they hardly understand and certainly do not grasp fully, or which have implications they do not realise. Conditions at this stage leave the victim powerless, disenfranchised, and potentially aggressive, seeing no way to change the situation. At this stage the situation might be susceptible to resolution before it moves onto the second Stage of revolution, where violence is used to change the situation.[14]

Interestingly, Curle uses his experience in teaching and the work of Danilo Dolci with the Mafia ridden society in Sicilian Society and Paulo Freire, both mentioned above (p146 and 253 respectively above), to illustrate the change in strategy required in the resolution of conflict at an early stage. Let us follow the Dolci explanation. When a teacher is frightening and domineering, the children are so concerned to keep their good grace, they pay little attention to each other. The power resides with the teacher, which forms this sort of pattern.

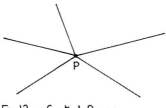

Fig 12a Central Power

If the teacher relinquishes power and ceases to be the focal point of the structure, the relationships can be transformed to bring about this pattern.

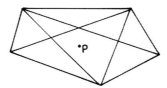

Fig 12b Changed Power

The power of the teacher, the Mafia as in Dolci's case, the enemy or the superpower is by-passed in this pattern. The activity of learning, co-operating over projects or bringing about peace comes from the community. These co-operative activities, Freire suggests, allow the communities to understand their oppression.

As the Israel-Palestine conflict is not a conflict between equals (Curle Third Stage) a great deal of balancing work needs to be done. The number of people committed to the second structure from Israel would initially be small, but this would grow as people saw the effectiveness of the process. This is such a complex situation it would require a more complex pattern than is suggested here. This is where the imagination comes in to play, where human beings see a problem more difficult than any before and they find the energy, desire, and skills needed to resolve the problem. The prize is great. The benefits are great. Are we up to the challenge?

In "When the Rain Returns", prepared by an International Quaker Working Party on Israel and Palestine, it is suggested that the Quaker perspective on the Israel - Palestine conflict is deeply rooted in four key concepts.[15] These are:

"1) All persons are of equal humanity and are entitled, as individuals, to human rights.

2) The rights of all people who have a direct stake in the situation should be respected and each of these direct stakeholders given an equal voice in the process of determining the outcome to this conflict.

3) Only mutual respect can lead to long-term security; no human community can assure its own security by imposing a state of insecurity on others.

4) Violence always leads to more violence; creative nonviolent ways do exist that allow the parties to this conflict to work together to bring about a fair, stable, and hope-filled outcome."

Perhaps we will only resolve the Palestine-Israeli problem when religions become a domain of true justice. Until this happens, religions will preach peace but support the waging of war at the same time.[16]   We also cannot develop true security or peace without learning to distinguish between the criminal methods of fundamentalist ideologies, be they Christian, Muslim or Jewish, and the grievances that drive people to committing provocative, desperate and horrific acts. We cannot move from terrorism and war to security and peace without understanding the root of the terrorist grievance.[17]

The last word in this chapter goes to Paul West talking after the Quaker Meeting in Ramallah (above) when he said of the Quaker Testimonies of equality, simplicity, integrity, peace, environment, "the most important is integrity."[18]   This is fundamental in resolving the Israeli-Palestinian conflict and the search for a resolution is as much a search for people with the integrity to be able to conduct the process. Palestine needs a Mandela, or a Tutu. Mr Bush or Mr Blair simply will not do.

Chapter 26
A Lost Vision

"A nation is a group of people united by a mistaken view about the past and a hatred of their neighbours."

Ernest Renan[1]

"A new type of thinking is essential if mankind is to survive and move to higher levels."

Albert Einstein[2]

"A land without people for a people without land." This statement was used by many Zionists in their demands for a Jewish State and, once Israel had been established, by politicians like Golda Mier.[3] However, it needs to be set against the text of the Balfour Declaration of 1917. This says, ".... it being clearly understood that nothing shall be done which may prejudice the civil and religious rights of existing non-Jewish communities in Palestine...."[4] With the human need to be exclusive, and the desire to have a Jewish democracy, there was no place for what would be a majority of Arabs in the new State of Israel. As a result, we see the great movement of Arab refugees in 1947-48 and the complete disregard for this inconvenient part of the Balfour Declaration, as the Jewish State was created in Palestine. Pappe says that today this movement would be called ethnic cleansing.[5]

The State of Israel was created out of the aftermath of genocide. It may be suggested there are a number of stages in the progression towards genocide. Stage one may be seen as the demand for space, exclusivity and purity. Stage two supports this with propaganda, promoting fear and hatred. This may be followed by the stripping of rights from the target population in the easy environment of the prejudice that has been created. This provides a foundation for stage three, the dispossession or removal of people from their land. The final stage is the genocide itself, the putting to death of the people who are 'in the way' of some plan, to which they are seen as 'inconvenient'.

It is of interest to note the 1914-18 war led to the killing, the genocide, of about 1.5 million Armenians by Turkey, killings documented in the Museum in the Armenian Quarter (the smallest quarter) of the Old City of Jerusalem. In addition, some 300,000 Armenians fleeing the genocide were added to about 3.5 million dispossessed and displaced persons in 1918 in a swathe from Russia and Germany in the north to Turkey and Armenia in the south. This was the prelude to the genocide of 6 million Jews, and others, under the Nazi regimes up to 1945.[6]

In this series of stages Palestine has perhaps reached stage three in the preconditions, the dispossession of the Palestinian people well beyond the original, internationally agreed plan for creation of the State of Israel, firstly by the extension of its boundaries and then by the occupation that has allowed the construction of Israeli settlements in the West Bank. It is easy to see how this stage relates to the historical situations in North America, Australia and New Zealand, where indigenous people were violently pushed to one side, losing their land and cultural roots.[7] These situations became the silent genocides of history.

While the 'safe guard' of the Balfour Declaration (above) was disregarded, the main clause states, "His Majesty's Government view with favour the establishment in Palestine of a national home for the Jewish people, and will use their best endeavours to facilitate the achievement of this object."[8] This indicates the propensity for colonial and military powers to think that they can give away what is not theirs to offer. Britain had just taken Palestine from the Turks as part of a 'side show' of the 1914-18 war.[9] Indeed, throughout the colonial period indigenous people have faced intractable enemies that were convinced that they had the right to steal the land and destroy the inhabitants as peoples and cultures, and in fact, that it was a right and proper thing to do.[10]

This attitude has its foundation in the most base of human traits: the desire to say that one group of people is better than another; that one group of people hold some truth, knowledge or history that makes them superior to another; that one group has the power or technology to control another; that discrimination and racism is a valid solution to the differences between people; and that ignorance of the other person's position is acceptable. In the age of the Declaration of Human Rights, and its associated Conventions, such attitudes must be condemned. The only way forward in this crowded world is for all people to have recourse to the same standard and application of justice through international law, wherever or whoever they may be.

The new State of Israel, with its religious and socialist aspirations, might have led to a new form of nation, but it followed the old route. It was a state, so it behaved like a state. It took offensive actions and expanded its territory in the face of threats from its neighbours, thus capturing and controlling part of the designated international territory of Jerusalem. It could be suggested Israel followed this path to gain control of Jerusalem, which would have been impossible if it had appealed to the International Community for protection from the attacks of its neighbours. This was a great prize of war for the new nation and part of the concept that nations establish themselves through war, the need for war being part of establishing a state's national identity.[11] The opportunity to stand back and think of a different way forward, a different way to create nationhood, does not seem to be part of the lexicon of political responses made by this young nation. It is possible to build states on a different basis; for example, Costa Rica does not have an army.

The thought of a different way forward was missing after the second attack on and catastrophic destruction of the World Trade Center in 2001. The thought was also not present after the earlier, and almost forgotten, bombing of the same buildings in February 1993, when ironically one of the popular media 'sound bites' was, "It felt like an airplane hit the building."[12] This incident might have raised questions like,

"Why have these people done this?" and started actions that could have prevented the second attack by reducing tension in the Middle East. The historical analysis that one catastrophic event leads to another, originating from the philosophy of Hegel and Marx, may illuminate this situation. That the 1914-18 War would provide the context for the Balfour Declaration, the foundation for the Holocaust and so much of the present Middle-East situation could not be seen in 1917. But what could be seen was a history of European wars, and those fought elsewhere (often as proxy for European wars), that had not settled, and often exacerbated, international disputes, wars which had the relentless habit of getting more deadly and repetitious.

Later British influence seemed to be one of partition and division rather than integration. India and Pakistan split, with horrendous implications of death and displacement as populations, estimated to be as high as 30 million people, moved between the new states. Years of building an integrated society of Hindus and Muslims, started in Mogul times, was lost over night at Independence. This attitude did not bode well for creating a new Palestine with an integrated Jewish and Muslim population, when partition and separation seemed to be easier for the politicians of the day.

If only the young United Nations in 1948 had been able to influence its new creation and gain support from member nations to keep Israel within the internationally agreed boundaries while also protecting her from attack by her neighbours. If only the international status of Jerusalem had been maintained as in the original plan as an Internationally administered 'Corpus Separatum':[13] if only the United Nations headquarters had been established there, in a neutral city with free access to the three great religions and universal access for all in pursuit of international agreement and understanding. If only humankind could be better at foresight and dreams of peace than at hindsight, or better at peace than creating structures to be maintained by war.

All the above ideas for Jerusalem could still come about, but it will be next to impossible with forcefully established power structures and the facts on the ground that 'fence' in hopes of peace and stifle creative and imaginative solutions.

It seems that the vision for a new Israel has become lost in the militarism of the occupation. This was a vision of peace after the horrors of war and persecution. The vision of peace for the Palestinians has also been lost in the failure of peace agreement after peace agreement and the lack of recognition of Palestine's existence or needs. This wonderful land, the home of the monotheistic religions, continues to exist amidst the strife of conflicting visions of the future.

The occupation of Palestine is at the core of the conflict in the Middle East; indeed, it is at the core of the supposed confrontation of Christianity and Islam. To end the occupation may be the first step in bringing peace to the whole area. Perhaps, therefore it is the role of all those who stand for peace to continue to bring this occupation into the light, and so end "the silence" of the years of suffering of the Palestinian people, and indeed all the people of the Middle East.

Coda

Reflections written by John Aves

January 2004

The Revd Canon Dr John Aves, the priest in charge of St Giles Norwich, and Ecumenical Accompanier from November 2003, died in Bethlehem on the 25th January 2004 at the age of 52. John had a heart attack while he was walking on Star Street on Sunday afternoon. At his funeral requiem in Norwich on the 6th of February, his wife, Anne, read out this piece written by John a few days before he died. It is reproduced here in his memory.

Within a few days of my arrival in Israel and Palestine this last November, I saw Israeli teenagers, the same age as my sons, in jeans and sweaters walking the streets with rifles slung across their backs. They were off-duty conscript soldiers. All school leavers, except ultra-Orthodox Jews, must do three years of military service. Males are also required to do reserve duty until the age of 45 (Arab citizens of Israel are usually exempted from military service).

Chillingly, returning to Bethlehem one night at 6p.m., I saw the same young soldiers drinking coffee at the checkpoint and across the road in the cold night air. They were detaining 40 young Palestinian men, their faces against the wall, hands held up. They would be kept there all night, their crime illegally entering Jerusalem that day seeking work and returning home that night to Bethlehem. The site of Christ's birth now has an unemployment rate of 70% due to the roadblocks and the dearth of tourists. Stopping people from going to Jerusalem from Bethlehem is like stopping people from the [close by] towns of Wymondham or Aylsham visiting or working in Norwich.

I came here with little background knowledge, a vague awareness of a British presence once through the Mandate, horrific stories of Jewish people fleeing the Holocaust to find a

271

new home, stories of the Kibbutz movement of young Jews coming to build a socialist utopia, memories of the 1967 and 1973 wars when brave Israel seemed to defeat the might of the Arab world, and lately the unremitting stories of Palestinian terrorism and suicide bombers.

Three months after having spent some time with the Israeli peace movement and now living here in the Ibdaa Cultural Center* at the Dheisheh Refugee Camp on the edge of Bethlehem, my initial knowledge has been corrected. The new State of Israel in 1948 was founded, at least in part, on the deliberate expulsion of many of the indigenous population. Some of these people and their offspring remain in camps like this, in many cases only a 40-minute drive away from their original land, after more then 50 years. Whilst Israel proudly proclaims the law of return and automatic citizenship to all Jews throughout the world and is frantically encouraging more Jewish immigration from Russia, it denies this right to the Palestinians it expelled, ignoring repeated United Nations resolutions.

In 1948, with one third of the population, Israel took control of 78% of the Mandate Palestine. Since the 1967 war, backed with all the military hardware of the United States, it has retained control of the remainder and, against all international law, it has colonised this area with settlements of 383,000 people. In negotiating a peace, Israel has sought to retain much of the land where settlers have been placed, giving the Palestinians a kind of a state in separated cantons. This 'state' would be economically unviable, guarded, encircled by walls and checkpoints and divided by major Israeli roads. All this seems to be in the process of construction. Under any other circumstance we would be using the language of rampant old-fashioned colonialism and ethnic cleansing to describe what's happening to the Palestinian population, hence the sometimes violent resistance movement you see on your television screens. However, our perception of what is going on has been dulled by our reluctance to criticise because of Western guilt about the Holocaust and, more recently, by simplistic literal readings of the Old Testament applied to the present situation by Christian Zionists. The latter believe that God gave the land only to the Jewish people and, worse still, justify the expulsion and transference of the existing population. This expulsion includes the Christian Arab population and yes, our brother and sister Anglicans.

Do I come back with much hope? The answer is yes. Why? Because (and I would need longer to explain), I see the story of Christ here not only in the Holy places and the Bible, but also in countless stories of courage and dignity. As we prepare to follow the way of the cross and resurrection in Lent and Easter we learn again that death-dealing cannot ever have the last word. For besides recognising that colonising powers always end in defeat, I see tremendous God-given hope in the centre where I help. This centre is run by some of the many Palestinians who, whilst acknowledging that a few of their neighbours choose the way of suicide bombing, are also placing their hopes in educating their children, in dance groups, in self-confidence and language skills and computer technology to carry on the long-term political struggle with dignity and grace.

John Aves, Ecumenical Accompanier, Bethlehem.

*Ibdaa, means to create something out of nothing.

Anne Aves and the Diocese of Norwich have given permission to use this reflection here. Permission has also been given to reproduce this by WCC/EAPPI/QPSW.

Notes and references

Notes

1 Arraf, S. Institute for Palestinian Studies - www.palestine-studies.org

2 Pappe, I. The Ethnic Cleansing of Palestine. Oxford: Oneworld, 2006.

Introduction

1 Curle, A. True Justice – Swarthmore Lecture 1981. London: Quaker Home Service, 1981, p1.

2 Kurlansky, M. Nonviolence – The History of a Dangerous Idea. London: Jonathan Cape, 2006, p76. Kurlansky outlines the way opposition to wars reduces once they have started.

3 For the purpose of this work the structure, the fence, will be referred to as the Separation Barrier, which best describes its function and impact in Jayyous. Where the structure is a wall, the word wall will be used.

4 The views expressed in this book are those of the author and not those of EAPPI or WCC.

5 Verifiable in that I have seen pictures in a known context or have reports from two independent sources.

6 Boulding, E. in Quaker Faith and Practice 22.34, London: Yearly Meeting of the Religious Society of Friends, 1989.

7 'You' is taken in this comment to mean all 'internationals' rather than just EAs. The Palestinians refer to all visitors working in the situation as 'internationals'. This includes members of the International Solidarity Movement, charity workers like those from Save the Children, those who come to pick olives, and many others.

8 Switzerland has Cantons; they are normally considered benign, so here we have a corrupted word. Part of a B'Tselem's map of the West Bank is shown on the back cover of this book.

9 The International Court of Justice (ICJ) was established in 1945, by the United Nations Charter. Its main functions are to settle legal disputes submitted to it by member states and to give advisory opinions on legal questions submitted to it by duly authorised international agencies. The number of decisions made by the ICJ has been relatively small, but since the 1980s there has been an

increasing willingness to use the court, especially by developing countries. Since 1986, the United States only accepts the court's jurisdiction on a case-by-case basis.

10 Apartheid - an Afrikaans word meaning apartness or segregation. The policy of Apartheid was introduced into South Africa in 1948. It demanded the territorial separation of people of different colour and established nominally autonomous African 'homelands' or Bantustans. A pre-end of Apartheid comment says, "These [Bantustans] are not economically viable and could require considerable financial support if they were to become genuinely independent states." The Fontana Dictionary of Modern Thought, Eds Bullock, A. et al, London: Fontana, 1977.

11 The terms 1914-18 War and 1939-45 War are used in preference to the more popular 'World War One and Two', which may suggest they were only two wars in the twentieth century, and detracts from the pain and suffering of all the other wars that have occurred.

12 Dauenhauer, B. quoted in, Muers, R. Keeping God's Silence. Oxford: Blackwell, 2004, p5.

Chapter 1

1 Galliabias are the long, nightshirt-like, robes worn by Palestinians, indeed many in the Arab world. Traditionally the female garment is decorated with embroidery, while the male equivalent comes in grey, brown or less practical white. While many Palestinians now wear western dress, a significant number still wear traditional costume, especially in rural areas.

2 Shlaim, A, quoted in, Facts on the Ground. London: Christian Aid, 2004.

3 UNRWA, the United Nations Relief and Works Agency for Palestinian Refugees in the Near East is a relief and human development agency providing education, healthcare, social services and emergency aid to over 4.4 million refugees living in the Gaza Strip, the West Bank, Jordan, Lebanon and the Syrian Arab Republic. UNRWA is by far the largest UN operation in the Middle East, with over 28,000 staff, almost all of them refugees themselves, working directly to benefit their communities as teachers, doctors, nurses or social workers. It is through UNRWA that the international community picks up the cost of Israel's

displacement of the Arab population.

4 Israeli settlers, numbering nearly 400,000, are now twice the number at the start of the Oslo Peace process (see 5). Many of them, especially around Jerusalem, are in the West Bank for economic reasons, considering themselves as residents of 'normal' neighbourhoods which happen to be beyond the 1967 border. These are not the ideological settlers of the West Bank hills and towns. (Halper, J. Obstacles to Peace, Jerusalem ICAHD, 2003, p3-4.)

5 Oslo Accords, signed in 1993, provided a mutual recognition between the Palestinian Liberation Organisation and Israel, with some Palestinian self-rule in the West Bank and Gaza. By 2000, the area of Palestinian control was about 40%, not the 90% expected. Despite the peace deal, there was no agreement on issues of territory, borders, and Jewish settlements, the status of Jerusalem or the Palestinian Refugees. Israeli incursions since 1993 have made the Accords meaningless. (CAAT, Arming the Occupation - Israel and the Arms Trade, London: Campaign Against the Arms Trade, 2003, p4.)

6 Note mid-2007: This scene has been completely changed by the construction of a section of 12 metre high concrete Separation Barrier down the middle of the dual carriageway to the south of the checkpoint towards Ram.

7 Ateek, Rev. Dr. N. Suicide Bombers - What is theologically and morally wrong with suicide bombings? Sabeel Documents, No1, Jerusalem: Sabeel, 2003.

8 Rock, A. The Status Quo in the Holy Places. Jerusalem: Franciscan Printing Press, 1989.

Chapter 2

1 Intifada (or Intifadah) is Arabic for 'a shaking off', used to describe an uprising among the Palestinians. The first intifada was from 1987-1993. The second intifada, known as the Al Aqsa Intifada, was provoked by Ariel Sharon's year 2000 visit to the Al Haram al Sherif, in Jerusalem.

2 The Oslo Accords divided the Palestinian areas into three zones: Area A (17%), disconnected areas in the West Bank with full control by the Palestinian Authority (P. A.), Area B (24%), under P. A. control but with Israeli security control and Area C (59%)

under full Israeli occupation.

3 The Danish Government seems to support Medical Students working abroad as part of their medical education, providing both experience for the student and an element in Denmark's overseas aid programme.

4 HaMoked is an Israeli organisation, the "Center for the Defence of the Individual", based in Jerusalem. It contacts the Israeli Defence Force (IDF) via the District Co-ordinating Office (DCO) on behalf of the farmers and gate watchers, asking for the Gates to be opened.

Chapter 3

1 This matter seems to be an example of the poor budgetary control exercised by the European Union (EU). The EU puts money into projects like this irrigation scheme and does not monitor what happens to it. There is little point in the EU supporting Palestinian development if it allows Israel to destroy the investment without any compensation. Is this a form of aid corruption with the benefit of the funding not being realised by the intended recipients?

2 Palme, O. Common Security – A Programme for Disarmament. London: Pan Books, 1982, p71.

3 One of the ageing pumps seen in the outskirts of Qalqilya was carrying the name of its manufacturer, Ransoms of Lincoln, suggesting it was installed under the British Mandate. It was lovingly cared for in all its oily glory by an ageing Palestinian pump master. I wonder what they do for spare parts?

4 Source: Institute for Palestinian Studies, Washington DC, in, Fact on the Ground. London: Christian Aid, 2004.

5 Article 33 of the Fourth Geneva Convention, which states, "Pillage is prohibited", would obtain to the extensive use of West Bank water resources.

6 Halper, J. Obstacles to Peace. Jerusalem: ICAHD, 2003, p3.

7 I refer to 'countries' although Palestine is not recognised as a country in the international arena. It does not have many of the characteristics that define a country, fixed borders around a territory with a single authority, its own (unimpeded) police force, its own currency, postal services and so on. It does however have a flag and a President. Since 2006 it also has a

democratically elected, if internationally unrecognised, government.

8 Always the internationalist, my father tried to maintain links with Germany. He was unable to re-establish contact after 1945. He assumed his friend and his family had been killed, or that they had become part of the huge movement of refugees and others on the move in Europe in 1945-46.

9 This is a little known story of an architect who helped many people leave Czechoslovakia, despite lack of support from the British Government. When his professional interest took him to Eastern Europe in 1949, he disappeared. He was held in Poland for six years unable to contact his family. This amazing story is told in, Field, H. and Field, K. Trapped in the Cold War. Stanford: Stanford, 1999.

10 Haffner, S. Defying Hilter, London: Orion Press, 2003.

11 Having left Germany Helmut and his family were interned in Britain during much of the 1939-45 period.

12 While children, "infants to under 17 years" were allowed entry, via "The Kinder Transports" as long as they had a £50 guarantee towards the cost of their eventual re-migration, adults were still restricted. A similar scheme in the U.S. failed to get past the Congressional committee stage. Hermann Field's private letters (9 above), refer to the British Foreign Office having to be persuaded to issue visas for those he was helping to leave the Sudetenland, the occupied part of Czechoslovakia, in 1939.

13 Masalha, N. A Land without a People. London: Faber and Faber, 1997.

14 To me, the sad part of the history of 1956 is that Britain was chasing the dying days of empire in the shameful military operation in Suez, including conspiring with Israel to initiate the attack, rather than signing up to a European future.

15 The original letter containing the Balfour Declaration may be seen at www.imagesonline.bl.uk, the website of the British Library.

16 Hobsbawn, E. Age of Extremes. London: Michael Joseph, 1994, p32.

Chapter 4

1 Dr Barghouti was a candidate for the presidency of the Palestinian

National Authority in 2005, finishing a distant second to
Mahmoud Abbas. In 2006, he became the Information Minister in
the newly elected Palestinian Government. He is often seen on
U.K. television as a Palestinian Spokesperson.

2 Under the Blair administration, the British Foreign Office seems to
have become weakened by the rejection of advice offered to the
Prime Minster and a possible loss of confidence in its roll.

3 Loring, P. Spiritual Discernment. Wallingford, PA: Pendle Hill
Publications, 1992.

4 A joint report by CPT, EAPPI, QPSW, and UCP, "Palestinian
Students talk about University Life under Occupation". Summer
2002.

5 In this he predicted the situation in 2006, when in free a election
approved by international observers, Hamas gained a majority.
The response of the rest of the world was to withdraw financial
support for the new government. So much for western support
for democracy, which might be better defined as having the
freedom to elect a government liked by the US, as has often been
seen in South America.

6 Shlaim, A, The Iron Wall - Israel and the Arab World. London:
Penguin, 2001, p19.

7 Welcoming the stranger in the land is a tenet of both Judaism and
Islam.

8 Triangulation is a research method where one piece of evidence is
collated with another to confirm its validity, the triangle being the
two pieces of evidence and the researcher.

Chapter 5

1 Words are so important in this situation. 'Settlement' is inevitably
linked with Israeli as in 'Israeli Settlement'. To use the word
'solution' has horrific historic baggage when linked to the word
final, so is best not used. With settlement and solution
unavailable, we have to pursue an agreement or accord.

2 Irgun was the National Military Organisation, which violently
directed its operations against the British, from the 1930s through
to 1948 and the ending of the Mandate.

3 Shlaim, A, The Iron Wall - Israel and the Arab World. London:
Penguin, 2001, p33 and p55.

4 Carter, J. Palestine Peace not Apartheid. New York: Simon and
   Schuster, 2006, p74.
5 Desert Island Discs is a long running radio programme in the U.K.,
   where guests select the eight records they would take to a desert
   island.

Chapter 6

1 Curle, A. True Justice – Swarthmore Lecture 1981. London: Quaker
   Home Service, 1981, p2.
2 There is more information on various EAPPI websites at these
   addresses www.eappi.org, or www.oikourmene.org, or
   www.wcc-coe.org
3 There is information on the wider work of UNOCHA on their
   website address www.ochaonline.un.org
4 For more on the Israeli house demolition policy see the ICHAD
   website www.ichad.org
5 There are details of the Palestinian campaign against the
   Separation Barrier and other issues on the PENGON website at
   www.pengon.org
6 Grass, G. Peeling the Onion. London: Harvill Secker, 2007, p196.
7 RSPCA, the Royal Society for the Prevention of Cruelty to Animals
   in the UK. On my return, I contacted the Donkey Sanctuary in
   Devon about the condition of the donkeys I had photographed in
   Palestine.
8 "…our stones": our culture, our way of being, our connection with
   the land.
9 Loring, P. Spiritual Discernment. Wallingford, PA: Pendle Hill
   Publications, 1992.
10 Hopper, M. The wonder has gone out of them - Changing
   Classroom Practice in the teaching of Adult Students. University
   of Exeter: Unpublished Master Dissertation, 1998.

Chapter 7

1 *Gänseliesel* (*Goose girl*) Gottingen,
   http://en.wikipedia.org/wiki/Gänseliesel
2 These Jerusalem based 'clerics' refer to the Separation Barrier as the
   Wall, as its 8 metre high concrete sections are the most familiar to

them in and around Jerusalem and Bethlehem.

3 How often is this the topic of songs on UK children's television?

4 PENGON, Stop the Wall in Palestine - Fact, Testimonies, Analysis and Call to Action. Jerusalem: Pengon, 2003.

5 The 'Stop Caterpillar' boycott is closely related to the work of Rachel Corrie's parents after their daughter was killed by a Caterpillar machine. See www.catdestroyhomes.org In May 2005, The Church of England's Ethical Investment Group decided not to withdraw its £197,000 investment in Caterpillar. Also, see www.waronwant.org/caterpillar

6 UNESCO website www.unesco.org

7 This is the official explanation for Dr Kelly's demise.

8 If Cecil Rhodes had completed his dream of a railway across Africa from Cairo to the Cape it would have been possible to travel by train from London to Cape Town with ferries across the English Channel, the Bosporus and Lake Van in Turkey, and to experience quite a few changes of train and track gauge.

9 UIC - Union Internationale Chemin du Fer, the international organisation, originally established to develop standards of track and rolling stock to allow through-running of trains across Europe.

10 www.jewishvirtuallibrary.org/jsource/US-Israel/foreign_aid

11 Quigley, J. The Case for Palestine - An International Law Perspective. London: Duke University Press, 2005, p220.

12 Graham Watson, U.K. Member of the European Parliament, at a public meeting in Exeter, 9th February 2007.

13 The old, steeply graded and twisting railway to Jerusalem was not re-open until 2006.

Chapter 8

1 Rigoberta Menchu Tum, Nobel Peace Laureate, in an Open Letter to President Bush, September, 2001

2 Mordecai Vanunu was 'arrested' or, as it was outside Israeli jurisdictions, 'kidnapped' by Mossad, the Israeli security services, in Rome on Sept. 30, 1986.

Chapter 9

1 My detailed accounts are committed to my Journal at the rate of about eight hundred words a day.

2 Hardy, T. The Return of the Native. London: Macmillan, 1878.

3 Chai - tea, normally made with milk in the kettle. It should not be confused with the Hebrew chai, which means living.

4 Waugh, E. Brideshead Revisited. London: Penguin Classics, 1945.

Chapter 10

1 Fourth Geneva Convention, the final paragraph of Article 49 states, "The Occupying Power shall not deport or transfer parts of it own civilian population into the territory it occupies." See www.unhchr.ch

Also Lein, Y Land Grab - Israel's Settlement Policy in the West Bank. Jerusalem: B'Tselem., 2002, p38.

2 Fox, G. quoted in Quaker Faith and Practice 19.32. London: Britain Yearly Meeting, 1995. From a letter sent when Fox was in prison in Launceston in Cornwall.

3 Quaker Peace and Social Witness, The Quaker Testimonies. London: Quaker Books, 2003.

4 As I write this in 2007 I realise this simple, if unusual manoeuvre, is no longer possible as there is now an eight metre high wall down the middle of this road, separating Israeli and Palestinian traffic and housing areas.

5 On one occasion, I caused some upset as I used the word settlement in conversation with a Palestinian in its geographical sense, a place; village, town or city; a settlement with a small 's'. In Palestine the word is only associated with Settlements, i.e. Israeli Settlements, with a big 'S'.

6 Figures from the State of Israel, Central Bureau of Statistics, in Facts on the Ground. London: Christian Aid, 2004.

7 This is a 2007 figure from 'Peace Now'.

8 Halper, J, Obstacles to Peace. Jerusalem: ICAHD, 2003, p4.

Chapter 11

1 Quoted in, Hopkins, M. The Contemporary Way of the Cross.

Internet: Moving Stories, 2005.

2 'Chip' is a word used for fruit and vegetable trays/boxes made from wood in the UK up to the early 1960s.

3 This figure of 120,000 employed in Israel would support a dependent population of up to one million, when considering the large family size in Palestine. Therefore, some 40% of the West Bank population have been affected by these restrictions. These workers were similar in status to the Bantus brought in to support the white South African economy before the end of Apartheid. Israel is replacing them with non-Jewish workers from such places as Thailand and the Philippines.

4 Dolci, D. On Nonviolent Revolution. In Wink, W. edit. Peace is the Way. New York: Orbis Books, 2000, p224.

Chapter 12

1 Leopold, A. A Sand County Almanac. London: Oxford University Press, 1949.

2 Sacks, J. Thought for the Day BBC Radio Four, 11th April, 2006.

3 The concept of environmental degradation is covered in Diamond, J. Collapse - How Societies Choose to Fail or Survive. London: Allen Lane, 2005.

4 "Resistance Birth Rate" is my own term for a birth rate inflated by the desire to have a larger birth rate than your neighbour in a conflict situation. Historically birth rate has been used to provide security, the most significant examples being in France post 1918 and in the former USSR post 1945.

5 Hopper, M. Geography and Security: citizenship denied? Teaching Geography 30, 3, 2005.

6 Basem, R. The Geography of Occupation. Jerusalem: Al Quds University. www.alquds.edu/press/articles/geography.php

Chapter 13

1 Tutu, D. No Future without Forgiveness. London: Ebury Press, 1999.

2 Ibid p35 and52

Chapter 14

1 Quoted in the address at the funeral of a former colleague's mother.

2 Sacks, J. Thought for the Day, BBC Radio 4, 29th December, 2006.

3 The final agreement in Northern Ireland was as much about the level of water changes, which caused a refocusing of the issues in the election for the Northern Ireland Assembly, as it was about 'The Troubles'.

4 Tutu, D. BBC Radio 4, date not recorded.

Chapter 15

1 Zaru, J. Quoted by Purnell, D. in, The Friend, 27th February 2004.

2 Barghouti, M. "I Saw Ramallah", New York, Anchor Books, 2003.

3 Gilbert and Sullivan "… tossed about in a Steamer from Harwich" Act 1, HMS Pinafore.

4 The Church of the Beatitudes. On the top of a hill, this Catholic chapel designed by architect Antonio Barluzzi, was built in 1939 by the Franciscan Sisters with the support of the Italian fascist, Mussolini.

5 Forman, R. Meister Eckhart - Mystic as Theologian. Shaftesbury: Element, 1991, p82.

6 Kelly, T. Reality of the Spiritual World and The Gathered Meeting. London: Quaker Home Service, 1944.

7 Also in, Fisher, L. The Life of Mahatma Gandhi. London: Granada, 1982, p196.

8 cited in "FM3-24: American Master Plan for Iraq", reported by Robert Fisk, The Independent 11th April 2007.

Chapter 16

1 Heideggar, M. Time and Being, in On Time and Being, translated by J. Stanbargh New York: Harper Row, 1972. Cited by Hopper, A. Dying Values: A study of professional Knowledge and Values in Health Care Practice. Unpublished doctoral dissertation: University of Exeter, 2000.

2 Our mobile phone calls are routed via Israeli 'Orange' masts that also provides phone connections for the settlements. This poses a

moral dilemma that we have to work with. The alternative coverage by 'Palnet' did not seem to be good in Jayyous.

3 Muers, R. Keeping God's Silence. Oxford: Blackwell, 2004, p144.

Chapter 17

1 Schiller, F. Ode to Joy.

Chapter 18

1 Zeldin, T. BBC Radio Three: Belief. 2nd April 2007.

2 Qumisiyeh, M. Sharing the Land of Canaan. London: Pluto, 2004, p15.

Chapter 19

1 Archbishop Desmond Tutu, BBC Radio 4, Today Programme, 27th June 2007.

2 A group of EAs planned to visit the 'Tent of Nations', which is situated to the southwest of Bethlehem, surrounded by the Israeli settlements of Neve Daniel, Beitar Ilit among others. This project has the goal of facilitating positive encounters between the young people of various cultures, allowing them to make positive contributions to their future through respectful coexistence. The land where the 'Tent of Nations' has been established, was purchased in 1924 and has remained in the same family ever since, until a portion of it was declared to be Israeli state property, a matter that is the focus of a continuing Israeli court case. The track to the land is blocked by piles of rocks placed by Israeli settlers.

For further information, www.tentofnations.org

3 The maps and guidebooks do not agree, giving heights for abal al-Ma rif (Mount Scopus) the highest point at the northern end of the Mount of Olives, in the range of 782m to 903m.

4 Blue Guide, Israel and the Palestinian Territories. Black Norton, 2002.

5 See Viveca Hazboun, A Psychotherapeutic View of Violence. Jerusalem: Palestine-Israel Journal, 10, 4, 2003, p24.

6 See Eyad Hallaq, An Epidemic of Violence. Jerusalem: Palestine-

Israel Journal, 10, 4, 2003, p37.

7 Figures from UNRWA.

8 A joint report by CPT, EAPPI, QPSW, and UCP, Palestinian Students Talk About University Life Under Occupation. Summer 2002. No publisher information provided.

9 B'Tselem, Civilians Under Siege, Jerusalem: B'Tselem, 2001.

10 Fourth Geneva Convention, Article 50.

11 Further details at <nswas.net>

12 http://www.unicef.org/specialsession/wffc/

13 Shlaim, A. The Iron Wall - Israel and the Arab World. London: Penguin, 2000, p 33.

14 Ra'ad, B. The Vision for Cultural Tourism and National Heritage in Palestine. Website of Al-Quds University, Jerusalem. www.alquds.edu

Chapter 20

1 Tagore, R. Quoted in Resurgence, c2002.

2 Ta'ayush www.taayush.org

3 Women in Black www.womeninblack.org.uk

4 Women to Women for Peace www.coalitionofwomen.org

5 Bat Sholam www.batshalom.org

6 New Profile www.newprofile.org

7 Machsom Watch www.machsomwatch.org

8 Rabbis for Human Rights www.rhr.israel.net

9 Balslev, E. et al, Security or Segregation. Geneva: World Council of Churches, 2003, p5.

10 HaMoked - Center for the Defence of the Individual www.hamoked.org.il

11 B'Tselem - The Israeli Information Center for Human Rights in the Occupied Territories. www.btselem.org

12 ICHAD Israeli Campaign Against House Demolition www.icahd.org

Chapter 21

1 Tutu, D. BBC Today Programme 27th June, 2007.

Chapter 22

1 United Nations Resolution 242 November 1967. If the conditions of this resolution for the withdrawal of Israeli armed forces and the acknowledgement of territorial sovereignty and integrity by all parties, and the preconditions for peace had been observed, the history of the last forty years might have been very different. The lack of implementation of this resolution has done much to delay peace in the Middle East and to reduce the impact of the UN.

2 In a later hearing the Israeli High Court rules in favour of the Palestinians in the matter of the location of a length of Separation Barrier Wall to the north of Jerusalem.

3 Barghouti, M. "I Saw Ramallah", New York, Anchor Books, 2003.

Chapter 23

1 Zeldin, T. BBC Radio Three Beliefs 2nd April, 2007.

2 Griffiths, B. Quoted in Resurgence - date not known.

3 Hopper, M. Working with the Barrier - the Separation of Jayyous. Jerusalem: Palestine-Israel Journal, 11, 1, 2004.

4 UNRWA Website
www.un.org/unrwa/emergency/barrier/profiles/jayous

Chapter 24

1 Mr Dajani's welcome notice in the foyer of the New Imperial Hotel, Jerusalem.

2 Nouwen, H. Seeds of Hope. New York: Doubleday, 1989.

3 An historical quote from 1905, in a lecture, Education, Education, Education, given to the Exeter Society for Curriculum Studies by Colin Richards, 30th June 2007.

4 Jung, C. Collected Works. London: Routledge and Kegan Paul, 1969, p265-6.

5 Robinson, E. Tolerating the Paradoxical - A Scientific Approach to Religious Experience. Oxford: The Religious Experience Research Unit, Manchester College, 1978. Sadly, Edward is loosing his sight, so I hope he will not object to my editing his original from 'listen' to 'see'.

6 Pinter, H. The Nobel Acceptance Lecture; Art, Truth and Politics.

BBC News, 8th December 2005.

7 Freire, P. Pedagogy of the Oppressed. London: Penguin, 1972.

8 Boulding, E. Envisioning the Peaceable Kingdom. In, Wink, W. edit. Peace is the Way. New York: Orbis Books, 2000, p133.

9 electronicintifada.net/v2article2922 The electronic intifada is a good way of keeping up with what is going on in Palestine.

10 It would not be seen as politically 'sensible' for a President (George W. Bush) and the Republican Party, that relies on the American Christian (and Christian Zionist) vote to follow the Court's ruling and criticise the Israeli Government and its breaches of International Law.

11 Cook, R, in, The Independent, London, 8th August 2005.

12 Quoted from Sir Sydney Kentridge QC the barrister for the Chagos Islanders, describing the forced removal from their 'paradise'. The Chagos Islands: 'A Sordid Tale' BBC News, Friday 3rd November, 2000.

Chapter 25

1 Tutu, D. Quoted in "One land many voices - Strands of Christian thought about who lives in the Holy Land", London, Christian Aid. Undated.

2 Sabeel, Principles for a Just Peace in Palestine - Israeli. Jerusalem: Sabeel, 2000, p1.

3 Halper, J. Obstacles to Peace. Jerusalem: ICAHD, 2003, p2.

4 Ben-Yair, M. Ha'aretz (An Israeli newspaper), 3rd March, 2002, Quoted by Halper, J. Obstacles to Peace. Jerusalem: ICAHD 2003, p1.

5 UN Website.

6 Halper, J. Ibid, p81.

7 ICAHD Website.

8 Halper, J. Ibid, p81, also B'Tselem, 2002 "Land Grab" p38

9 Shlaim, A. The Iron Wall - Israel and the Arab World. London: Penguin, 2000, p23.

10 Halper, J. Ibid, p74.

11 The 2004 ruling on the Separation Barrier by the International Court of Justice. www.icj-cij.org

12 Elworthy, S. Give Peace a Bank. Resurgence. 199 p20, 2000.

(Scilla Elworthy is director of the Oxford Research Group, which investigates alternatives to military power.)

13 Williams, R., BBC Radio Three, Interval Talk, Tuesday 28th August, 2007.

14 Curle, A. Swarthmore Lecture - True Justice. London: Quaker Home Service, 1981.

15 International Quaker Working Party, When the Rain Returns. Philadelphia: American Friends Service Committee, 2004.

16 Agrivesh, S and Thampu, Rev. V. 2002 "Preaching Peace, Waging War" Resurgence No.213, p1.

17 Capra, F. True Security. Resurgence, 211, p9, 2002.

18 Quaker Peace and Social Witness, The Quaker Testimonies. London: Quaker Books, 2003

Chapter 26

1 Renan, E, Quoted by Shlaim, A. The Iron Wall. London: Penguin, 2000.

2 Einstein, A. Quoted by Kurlansky, M. Nonviolence - The History of a Dangerous Idea. London: Jonathan Cape, 2006.

3 Prime Minister of Israel from March1969 to June 1974.

4 Balfour Declaration. A copy of the original letter from Balfour to Rothschild is to be found on the British Museum Website. The full text is quoted on p52 above.

5 Pappe, I. Ethnic Cleansing of Palestine. Oxford: Oneworld, 2006. An interesting work by a brave and principled Israeli historian who clearly sets out the basis of the creation of the Israeli State.

6 Hobsbawn, E. Age of Extremes. London: Michael Joseph, 1994, p50-51.

7 Jacobs, W. Dispossessing the American Indian. Oklahoma: University of Oklahoma Press, 1985.

8 Balfour, Ibid.

9 Allenby's reference to Lawrence's work in Palestine.

10 Kurlansky, M. Nonviolence - The History of a Dangerous Idea. London: Jonathan Cape, 2006, p65.

11 Kurlansky, Ibid p13.

12 BBC News at bbc.co.uk On This Day 26th February, 1993 "It felt like an airplane hit the building." Bruce Pomper, eyewitness.

13 In the Partition Plan under United Nations Resolution 181, Jerusalem had the status of an internationally administered 'Corpus Separatum'.

Glossary

Baladiya - The Municipality or Town Hall, both the administrative centre and a public meeting place.

Checkpoint - There are checkpoints between the West Bank and Israel. There are fixed checkpoints within the West Bank and there are "flying checkpoints" which can be set up anywhere. The fixed checkpoints have gates, turnstiles and queuing areas set out with railings. A flying checkpoint may be a jeep and four soldiers, partly blocking a road. Palestinians need the correct papers to pass a checkpoint. They are often kept waiting for many hours. The atmosphere at checkpoints is one of tension, tension for the Palestinians about whether they will be let through and how long they will have to wait, and tension for the Israeli soldiers about being attacked. The ever-present guns, often cocked and ready to fire, are at times used to direct people through the checkpoint.

Closure - There are two types of closure, general and internal. The term general closure, refers to the closing of the 'borders' around the West Bank, which restricts movement into East Jerusalem, Israel and through Israel to Gaza. Internal closure is the restriction of movement within the West Bank, mostly around towns like Nablus.

Collective Punishment - This policy is explained as a deterrent. It is supposed to reduce Palestinian support for attacks on Israeli security personnel, as the whole community is punished, usually by limiting or completely stopping movement. The imposition of curfews not only has an economic impact but also denies access to health and education services. Article 33 of the Fourth Geneva Convention states, " No protected person may be punished for an offence he or she has not personally committed." Collective punishment may also be directed at families, where one member has come to the attention of the occupying power.

Curfew - This is the prohibition of movement, sometimes for long periods, with only short breaks to allow people to fetch basic requirements.

Gate or Bowaba - A gate in the Separation Barrier, which is only opened at restricted times to allow access to Palestinian land in the seam zone, between the Green Line and the Separation Barrier.

Green Line - The de facto border between the Palestinian West Bank and Israeli from 1949 to 67, recognised by the United Nations as the border.

Identity Card or Howada - A personal identity card that must be carried by all Palestinians.

Al Nakba or The Catastrophe - The Palestinians' term for the impact of the Israeli War of Independence 1947-48, when 419 villages were destroyed and 400,000 Palestinians became refugees. As the actions of Israeli troops involved more than 30 documented massacres, it could be described as ethnic cleansing.

Permit or Tasreeh - This is the permission needed by Palestinians to pass through a Gate in the Separation Barrier to their land.

Seam Zone - The area between the Green Line and the Separation Barrier.

Separation Barrier or Jada - The fence and wall that is being built around the West Bank to contain the Palestinian population within a much reduced area than before 1967.

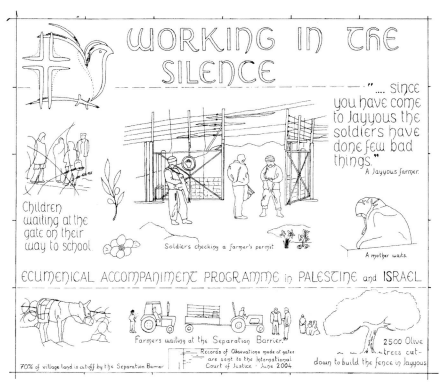

WORKING IN THE SILENCE

".... since you have come to Jayyous the soldiers have done few bad things."
A Jayyous farmer.

Children waiting at the gate on their way to school.

Soldiers checking a farmer's permit

A mother waits.

ECUMENICAL ACCOMPANIMENT PROGRAMME in PALESTINE and ISRAEL

Farmers waiting at the Separation Barrier.

Records of Observations made at gates are sent to the International Court of Justice - June 2004

2500 Olive trees cut down to build the fence in Jayyous

70% of village land is cut off by the Separation Barrier

© Maurice Hopper 2006

This is the design for an embroidery panel based on the author's accompaniment work in Jayyous in the style of the Quaker Tapestry. The Quaker Tapestry, that depicts the story of Quakerism, is to found in Kendal in the English Lake District.

The Challenge of Peace

How about you?

When I told my friends and former colleagues of my plans to go to Israel / Palestine these were some of the responses.

Oh good! They need people like you. G. C-G.

We need things like this to test ourselves. L. E.

The students need to know that someone is doing something like this. It's all round College! A. H.

I can see you doing this work. A. R.

These are things we have to do. E. Y.

This is more important than chair-making. D. L.

If you would like to find out more about going to Palestine / Israel to accompany those calling for peace, contact the World Council of Churches website, www.eappi.org and click on National Co-ordinators.